# ANIMATING
## SHORT STORIES

# ANIMATING
# SHORT STORIES

## Narrative Techniques and Visual Design

CHERYL BRIGGS

BLOOMSBURY ACADEMIC

LONDON · NEW YORK · OXFORD · NEW DELHI · SYDNEY

BLOOMSBURY ACADEMIC
Bloomsbury Publishing Inc
50 Bedford Square, London, WC1B 3DP, UK
1385 Broadway, New York, NY 10018, USA

BLOOMSBURY, BLOOMSBURY ACADEMIC and the Diana
logo are trademarks of Bloomsbury Publishing Plc

First published in Great Britain 2020

Cover design: Louise Dugdale
Cover image © UCF 2017 Character Animation Cohort Dreamweaver team,
Character Design by Kelly Herbut and Katherine Ryschkewitsch, Model by Erika Johnson

A catalogue record for this book is available from the British Library.

A catalog record for this book is available from the Library of Congress.

ISBN: HB:    978-1-3501-0392-4
       PB:    978-1-4725-7015-4
       ePDF:  978-1-4725-7016-1
       eBook: 978-1-3500-3151-7

Typeset by Lachina Creative, Inc.
Printed and bound in India

To find out more about our authors and books visit
www.bloomsbury.com and sign up for our newsletters.

# Contents

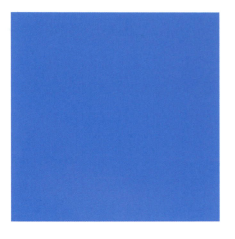

# Acknowledgments

I want to thank the following people for their help during the long process of book writing.

God, for His continued guidance and for giving me the ability to live my life with strength and grace.

My acquisitions editors at Bloomsbury, Katie Gallof, James Piper, and Georgia Kennedy. Their encouragement and confidence saw me through this entire journey and through every obstacle I encountered. I will be forever thankful for their support!

My husband Robert, who has been so supportive and understanding, as well as amazed when I pause every movie we watch to mark the end of Act I, where the Hero is forced to take on the problem (which always falls in the 20–25 minute mark) and the midpoint, the lowest point for the hero and farthest from achieving his goal (which always falls in the middle of the movie).

My children, Joshua, Taylor, Nathanael, and Ian, who give me a reason to wake up every morning and never give up.

My friends and family. Too many to list here, but those I especially consider near and dear to my heart who are always checking in on me and being there for me are Eugene and Marlene, George, Vickie, Letha, Byron and Terry, Stephen and Nancy, Mike and Christy, Elizabeth and Roy, Darlene and Bob, June and Bill, Denise and Bob, Nancy and Hal, Lucilla and Mark, Jeanna, Penny, Tracie, Tom, Randy and Ann, Dana, Dave and Lauren, Heidi and Steve, and Susan and Ben.

A special thanks to my former students: Greg Hulet, for answering my questions about camera lenses from the industry perspective, and Heather Knott, for always being there to bounce ideas off of and to vent to, and verify that I am, in fact, not going crazy.

Thank you to the faculty, staff, and administration of the School of Visual Arts and Design and the College of Arts and Humanities at the University of Central Florida, for their constant support and questions of "How's the book going?" Extra special thanks to my colleagues and mentors, Dr. Rudy Mc Daniel, Phil Peters, Dr. M.C. Santana, and Dr. Stella Sung.

An extra special thanks to the BFA and BA students of the Character Animation and Visual Language degree programs at the University of Central Florida. Their hard work is utilized to illustrate the many concepts covered in this book. Each student team is listed following this section.

A very special thanks to my two colleagues JoAnne Adams and Darlene Hadrika, who are my work sisters. As one of our students pointed out, the three of us are the fairy godmothers of animation at UCF. Together we act not only as faculty advisors but take turns as faculty directors/producers on these films. I have learned so much from them over the past ten years.

## Atlas' Revenge (UCF Digital Media Cohort of 2009)

MFA Student Director: Brad Lewter
Faculty Advisors: Jim Story, Darlene Hadrika, Jo Anne Adams, Phil Peters, Max Croft
Creighton Ashton
Kenneth Bell
Paul Blackford
Bruce Boman
Richard Carlton
Joshua Dugan
Lauren Fattal
Gregory Hall
Zachary Hansen
Douglas Hardy
Nicholas Hoefly
William Jones
Shannon Kroll
Heather LaFave
Kendall Litaker
Kyle Luo
Robert Lutz
Brice Miret
Daniela Morad
Michael Navarro
Kenneth Peter
Michael Sanders
Kevin Sternschein
Nathan Szerdy
Khuong Tran

## Shadow Play
### (UCF Digital Media Cohort of 2010)

Faculty Director: Jo Anne Adams
MFA Student Director: Chelsea Guthrie
Faculty Advisors: Darlene Hadrika, Phil Peters,
Cheryl Cabrera, Max Croft, Jim Story
Viviane Assaad
Michael Bakerman
Alexandra Baldwin
Stephanie Cangemi
Andrew Catron
Elissa Cordero-Hansen
Ryan Cummins
Elizabeth Dawson
Nathan Dawson
Jacqueline Fenton
Kimberly Henry
Priscilla Landerer
Matthew Macar
Kevin Mahaney
Barak Moshe
Krista Nicholson (Staggs)
Mary Rugg
Peter Staffa
Jamie Stone
Christopher Vasquez
Stephen Vaughan
Katie Weddle

## Squeaky Business
### (UCF SVAD Character Animation Cohort of 2011)

Faculty Director: Cheryl Cabrera
Faculty Advisors: Darlene Hadrika, Jo Anne
Adams, Phil Peters, Terrell Theen
Vincent Angerosa
Silvia Arana
Travis Barton
Amanda Beaver
Cody Brunty
Sara Engelhardt
David Gian-Cursio
Hannah Moon
Levi Parker
Javier Perez-Cardarelli
Caitlin Pollard (Rodriguez)
Joseph Rosa
Ashley Trawick
Colby Whitman
Stephen Wong
Seto van Boxtel

## Mustache Mayhem
### (UCF SVAD Character Animation Cohort of 2011)

Faculty Director: Cheryl Cabrera (Briggs)
Faculty Advisors: Darlene Hadrika, Jo Anne
Adams, Phil Peters, Terrell Theen
Sebastian Amunategui
Carl Boger
Ryan Bregenzer
Christopher Brown
Jessica Damerst
Taylor Flanagan
Justin Green
Samuel Hecht
Gregory Hulet
Daniel Jones
Scott Knapp
Heather Knott
Kyle Martin
Reece Mayer
Aaron Morse
Zachary Murray
Eric Schoellnast
Bryan Vensen

## Box Forts
### (UCF SVAD Character Animation Cohort of 2012)

Faculty Director: Darlene Hadrika
Faculty Advisors: Jo Anne Adams, Cheryl
Cabrera, Phil Peters, Stella Sung, Terrell Theen
Student Director: Anthony Fariello
Hugo Brandt
Ryan Eubanks
Anthony Fariello
Matthew Justice
Michael Kemp
Bridget Kieffer
Jessica Lang
Shanel McCall (Sosa)
David Piedrahita
Derek Reese
Daniel Stone
William Watkins
Eric Werlin
Charles Yribarren

## Flower Story
### (UCF SVAD Character Animation Cohort of 2012)

Faculty Director: Darlene Hadrika
Faculty Advisors: Jo Anne Adams, Cheryl Cabrera, Phil Peters, Stella Sung, Terrell Theen
Student Director: Adam Tazi
Sean Buck
Robert Campbell
Daniel Culliver
Ashley (Demattos) Barnes
Lauryn Duerr
Charles Fernandez
Joshua Garriss
William Groff
Jacob Hemphill
Philip Negroski
Juan Rivera
Adam Tazi

## Ember
### (UCF SVAD Character Animation Cohort of 2013)

Faculty Director: Jo Anne Adams
Faculty Advisors: Cheryl Cabrera, Darlene Hadrika, Phil Peters, Stella Sung
Student Director: Trey Buongiorno
Alissa Babineau
Kelsey Binninger
Heather Bojerski
Trey Buongiorno
Michael Contardo
Austin Diehl
Dominic Gonzalez
Kyle Hutto
Steven King
Deanndra Meno
Andrew Pace
Mariya Pierce (Martinez)
Alex Silverboard
Chelsea Stewart (Fariello)
Damian Thorn-Hauswirth
Shanice Ward

## Gaiaspora
### (UCF SVAD Character Animation Cohort of 2013)

Faculty Director: Jo Anne Adams
Faculty Advisors: Cheryl Cabrera, Darlene Hadrika, Phil Peters
Student Director: Matthew Mann
Andrew Ahern
Amir Alequin
Nicholas Arbeiter
Aaron Bley
Amanda Bell
David Castillo
Emily Gallagher
Angelo Gazzia
Jason Gralnick
Melissa Jimenez
Sara Johnson
Matthew Mann
Sarah Reinstein
Benjamin Rhoades
Matthew Trudell

## Celestial
### (UCF SVAD Character Animation Cohort of 2014)

Faculty Director: Darlene Hadrika
Faculty Advisors: Jo Anne Adams, Cheryl Cabrera, Phil Peters, Stella Sung, Terrell Theen
Student Directors: Ashley Morrow and Philip Wigner
Zachary Bombka
Joshua Janousky
Lindsey Jones
Daniel Lukas
Jacqueline Malvin
Ashley Morrow
Ida Phillips
Christopher Sanchez
Adrienne Seufert
David Silva
Ward Silverman
Philip Wigner
Samuel Zilberstein

## Yours, Mime, and Ours (UCF SVAD Character Animation Cohort of 2014)

Faculty Director: Darlene Hadrika
Faculty Advisors: Jo Anne Adams, Cheryl Cabrera, Phil Peters, Stella Sung, Terrell Theen
Student Director: Teresa Falcone
James Bridges
Clinnie Brinson
James Chambless
Joshua Cooper
Jacquelyn Dalton
John Doromal
Juan Escobar
Teresa Falcone
Maral Khatcherian
Brian Sawyer
Sherika (Williams) Shields

## Enchanted Ink (UCF SVAD Character Animation Cohort of 2015)

Faculty Director: Jo Anne Adams
Faculty Advisors: Cheryl Cabrera, Darlene Hadrika, Phil Peters, Stella Sung, Terrell Theen
Student Directors: Lauren Hart and Brandon Scarry
Keshia Dublin
Laura Feltgen
Katherine Freeman
Michelle Gallagher
Lauren Hart
Ashley Lawrynowicz
Robin Marcoe
Samantha Mohr
Brandon Scarry
Michael Shulterbrondt
Christine Tu

## Snacktime (UCF SVAD Character Animation Cohort of 2015)

Faculty Director: Jo Anne Adams
Faculty Advisors: Cheryl Cabrera, Darlene Hadrika, Phil Peters, Stella Sung, Terrell Theen
Student Directors: Lacey Hasson and Mattew Sveum
Francis Caldarazo
Celia Calderon
Dana Dunson
Lacey Hasson
Elena Jacobson
Dalissa Javier
Christina Leung
Ann Liang
Cayla Massarelli
Jessica Minoso
Michelle Nemeth
David Parker
Brian Phinn
James Rivera
Lawrence Susenburger
Matthew Sveum
Charlie Tong

## Farmer Glorp (UCF SVAD Character Animation Cohort of 2016)

Faculty Director: Darlene Hadrika
Faculty Advisors: Jo Anne Adams, Cheryl Cabrera, Phil Peters, Stella Sung
Student Directors: Bryan Colvin and Timothy Keebler
Yanjun Chen
Kevin Cheng
Bryan Colvin
Anthony Del Re
Angela Hernandez-Carlson
Timothy Keebler
Megan Koch
Kathleen McGovern
Ryan Newman
Melissa Shutts
Bailey Steggerda
Kaitlyn Thomas

## Moth Effect
### (UCF SVAD Character Animation Cohort of 2016)

Faculty Director: Darlene Hadrika
Faculty Advisors: Jo Anne Adams, Cheryl Cabrera, Phil Peters, Stella Sung
Student Directors:
Leah Augustine
Jacqueline Baldoquin
Anthony Ballinas
Dana Barnes
Samantha Bennett
Daniel Garcia
Lindsay Green
Ana Guerra
William Perez-Valines
Nicolas Ruiz
Zakiya Nicole Stubbs
Haley Vallandingham

## Cuddle Fish
### (UCF SVAD Character Animation Cohort of 2017)

Faculty Director: Cheryl Briggs
Faculty Advisors: Jo Anne Adams, Darlene Hadrika, Phil Peters, Stella Sung
Jared Bittner
Shanique Brown
Tyler Burns
Brianna Jaeger
Jenin Mohammed
Rachel Nainstein
Alexis Planer
Marchand Venter
Thomas Vinas
Connor Waugh

## Dreamweaver
### (UCF SVAD Character Animation Cohort of 2017)

Faculty Director: Cheryl Briggs
Faculty Advisors: Jo Anne Adams, Darlene Hadrika, Phil Peters, Stella Sung
Seun Ademoye
Grace Cusimano
Kendal Drewke
Kelly Herbut
Erika Johnson
Kelvin Nguyen
Katherine Ryschkewitsch
Erich Schulz
Samantha Sokolis
Jessica Wrubel

## Ukelayla
### (UCF SVAD Character Animation Cohort of 2018)

Alina Alikhanyan
Xenia Benitez
Carol Eastwood
Tal Minks
Haleigh Mooney
Daniela Muiño
Adriana Reiley
Daniela Reiley
Emma Schmitz
Kelly Taylor
Tabitha Thomas
Kim Tong
Christine Yim
Tony Yon

# Introduction

Our Heroine has only one lifelong dream that has sustained her through the most harrowing experiences encountered thus far in her journey through life: her desire to create award-winning animated short films. Realizing that she has no idea where to begin, she searches for the path that will bring her the knowledge needed to succeed in her goal.

On her journey she browses through the volumes in the library and bookstore. Overwhelmed with the multitude of different books available, a copy of this book presents itself, as if there was an invisible mentor giving her just the tool she needed. She looks through the chapters and realizes she has been searching for exactly this book as the perfect guide and overview of the process.

Full of excitement and anticipation for what is to finally be realized, she sits down at her computer and pulls out her sketchbook, beginning the process of solidifying her ideas on her journey to animating short stories.

The first chapter launches our Heroine into the foundations of animation genres and an understanding of story structure. She learns the different approaches to storytelling and realizes that there truly is a formula, or at least the overview of a recipe, that will help shape and define the stories she wants to tell.

The second chapter guides the Heroine in finding an idea. While she already knows (or thinks she knows) the subject for her story, this chapter helps her consider the different ingredients of a story. She writes everything down in an idea journal, sketching characters and jotting down thoughts that could not only be part of the story she is developing, but additional concepts that could be developed later.

Chapter Three introduces the obstacles that our Heroine might encounter on her journey to creating her animated short story. This chapter gives her a moment of reflection, along with the suggestion of different tools to overcome the challenges that she is sure to face.

Chapter Four presents the techniques of developing an idea into a fully fleshed story worthy of the time it takes to create as an animated film.

Chapter Five explains how to write a script, giving her just enough information and resources to complete her first draft of a spec script. She finds the companion website to be very helpful, with resources that supplement this book, such as a script template.

Chapter Six illustrates the cinematic techniques used in other films and helps our Heroine begin to imagine her story through a camera lens.

Chapter Seven begins the development of choosing an artistic look and style while explaining the concepts of screen design and the storyboarding process.

Chapter Eight describes the animatic and introduces the editing techniques she must consider to start bringing her storyboards to life through movement and sound.

Chapter Nine energizes our Heroine, giving her the next steps of feedback, revisions, and planning.

Chapter Ten provides a case study as an overall example of everything covered in the preceding chapters.

Our Heroine, satisfied with her journey, completes the chapters, resulting in the items needed to plunge into production with her best story to tell and the understanding that it will continue to evolve until completion.

Now it is time for your story to be told . . .

# The Narrative Short

All humans tell stories. In every culture and every time period, we tell stories for many reasons. We tell stories to teach. We tell stories to entertain. We tell stories to connect with each other. Stories inspire us, enlighten us, scare us, make us cry, and make us laugh. But what makes a good story? And how do we make a good short story? Once we have a good short story, how do we translate that story from the written or verbal word into a visual experience that can be animated? These are the questions that inspired this book and the answers I have found will be explored within its contents.

Before we begin to understand how to develop a great story for the animated short film, we should first understand the different genres of animation and theories of storytelling. By building a strong foundation of knowledge, one can then build a structure that leads to great storytelling through animation.

Figure 1.1
Story.

# Genres of Animation

There are many different genres of animation. This book focuses on the narrative genre. However, this next part of the chapter will briefly explore the most commonly seen genres so that there is a clear understanding of the differences. There can be mixtures, and also variations. The main genres are listed as follows.

## Narrative

A narrative tells a story as a series of connected events. This genre is the focus of this book and will be covered thoroughly in the pages and chapters that follow.

## Documentary

A documentary documents real life. Usually created in live action, the documentary can successfully, and sometimes more effectively, be created using animation. A perfect example of this is Nick Park's *Creature Comforts*, where the voices of each character were obtained mostly from interviews of residents in an old folk's home. The animation created put the stories in the context of zoo animals.

Figure 1.3
Still image from Nick Park's *Creature Comforts* (1989).

**Figure 1.2**
Still image from the narrative short film *Celestial* (2014). Courtesy of the University of Central Florida Character Animation Specialization.

**Figure 1.4**
Still image from Marcos Carrasco's *"HERE"* (2014).

**Figure 1.5**
**Steven Woloshen, animator.** All rights owned and used with permission of Steven Woloshen.

**Figure 1.6**
Still image from *Playtime* (2010), an experimental animation by Steven Woloshen. All rights owned and used with permission of Steven Woloshen.

## Political

A political animation is used to bring light to current or historical political events. Also known as an animated political cartoon, political animation has evolved from the editorial cartoon. While humor and satire is usually used to convey a message, political animations can also be more serious or dark and disturbing. An impactful example would be *"HERE"* by the Venezuelan animator and filmmaker Marcos Carrasco:

> "Ten years from now, twenty years from now, you will see: oil will bring us Ruin . . . Oil is the Devil's excrement." Juan Pablo Pérez Alfonso (Venezuelan diplomat, politician, and lawyer primarily responsible for the inception and Creation of OPEC). Based on this apocalyptic quote by Juan Pablo Pérez Alfonso, *"HERE"* is a surrealistic portrait of war for oil.[1]

## Experimental

With its beginnings in experimental film that began in Germany in the early 1920s, experimental animation (also known as abstract animation) is usually characterized by the absence of the linear narrative and an exploration of animation as a fine art, using techniques such as painting or scratching on film, rapid editing, and abstract visuals. Experimental animations explore the visual expression of poetic interpretations as well as visual representations of sound. Experimental animation relies heavily on the elements and principles of design as well as cinematic techniques to create an emotional experience for the audience.

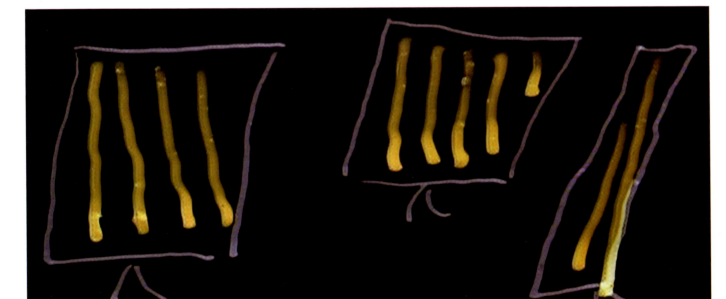

**Figure 1.7**
Still image from "Goodbye Blue Sky" in Pink Floyd's *The Wall* (1982).

## Music Videos

Animation can be utilized in music videos for part or the entire length of a song and is created for promotional or artistic reasons. Many music videos are a mixture of live action and animation, but there are fully animated music videos as well. Some great examples of animated music videos include Peter Gabriel's *Sledgehammer*, Aha's *Take On Me*, Tool's *Sober*, The Black Eyed Peas' *XOXOXO*, or any of the Gorillaz' music videos. In addition, there have been fully animated songs that are part of movies, such as "Goodbye Blue Sky" in Pink Floyd's *The Wall*, animated by Gerald Scarfe.

## Commercials

Commercials are advertisements used to sell products or make announcements. Animation has been used in this capacity since the early 1940s and is still used widely today in the same manner. Some popular commercial campaigns include Coca-Cola's Polar Bears, Poppin' Fresh Pillsbury Doughboy, the California Raisins, Mars' M&Ms, and DeLijn's Take the Bus.

**Figure 1.8**
Hal Miles, animator for Poppin' Fresh, the Pillsbury Doughboy. All rights owned and used with permission of Hal Miles.

## Video Art Animation

Video art animation is a derivative of video art and relies on animation which can be combined with audio to create an experience. Many of these works are interactive.

There are two variations of video art:

1.  Single-channel, which is projected onto a screen or played on a television.
2.  Installation, which involves the creation of an environment inside a gallery or other venue and may include multiple display screens or be combined with other traditional artistic media such as painting or sculpture.

A contemporary example of an animation installation is *Forms*, by visual artists Memo Akten and Quayola. Using animation, *Forms* brings the motion of athletes into abstract visualization for the viewer.

*Forms* is an ongoing collaboration between visuals artists Memo Akten and Quayola, a series of studies on human motion, and its reverberations through space and time. It is inspired by the works of Eadweard Muybridge, Harold Edgerton, Étienne-Jules Marey as well as similarly inspired modernist cubist

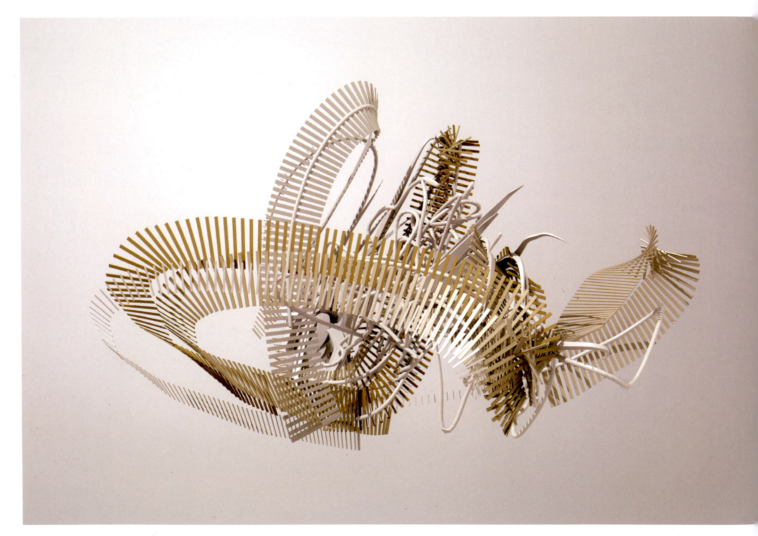

**Figure 1.9**
Still image from Memo Akten's installation *Forms* (2012).

works such as Marcel Duchamp's "Nude Descending a Staircase No. 2." Rather than focusing on observable trajectories, it explores techniques of extrapolation to sculpt abstract forms, visualizing unseen relationships – power, balance, grace and conflict – between the body and its surroundings.

The video installation was commissioned by and exhibited at the National Media Museum's '"In The Blink of an Eye" Exhibition, 9th March–2nd September, 2012, alongside classic images by photographers such as Harold Edgerton, Eadweard Muybridge, Roger Fenton, Richard Billingham and Oscar Rejlander as well as historic items of equipment, films and interactive displays.[2]

## Projection Mapping

Projection mapping (also known as video mapping and spatial augmented reality) creates an optical illusion in a real environment with video projected directly onto two-dimensional or three-dimensional objects and is usually combined with audio to create an audio-visual narrative. Once the animated content is created, specialized software is used to digitally reproduce the objects and environment so that the visuals can be spatially mapped onto them. The digital animation is then projected onto the objects during the event to create optical illusions and depth as well as add animation to static objects. These objects can range from a simple box to a football field, or the complicated architecture of a building. Current projection mapping is an update of the technique first developed using 16 mm film projection to create the "animated" singing busts in the graveyard of the Haunted Mansion ride, first seen when the ride opened at Disneyland in 1969. Today, projection mapping has also been used in a variety of venues, including theme-park attractions, half-time shows of sporting events, as well as film and theatrical stages to create animated virtual sets.

**Figure 1.10**
Virtual set created with projection mapping. *Red Silk Thread*, an opera by Stella Sung (2014). Ninjaneer Studios (located in the Orlando, Florida area) created virtual sets with subtle animations using projection mapping to give the illusion of depth and the feeling of a living environment on the stage. Image used with permission of Ninjaneer Studios and Dr. Stella Sung, 2014.

# Creating the Narrative

As stated earlier in this chapter, the narrative tells a story as a series of connected events. While the word "narrative" is often used synonymously with the word "story," a "narrative" is actually the retelling of the story while a "story" is the account of events that have occurred. During a narrative, the perspective or point of view shapes the story by whomever is telling it. For example, almost everyone has heard the tale of Sleeping Beauty, which is told from the point of view of those that knew the royal family. In 2014, the movie *Maleficent* offered another perspective of these events, complete with the backstory, which explained the motivation of the troubled fairy. From *Maleficent's* point of view, the story events take on a completely different narrative.

## How to Tell a Story

We have been taught, since childhood, that every good story has a beginning, middle, and end. The question of how to tell a captivating story is an age-old problem that many have tried to answer. With animation, however, just having a great story to tell isn't enough, because the additional task of telling the story visually adds another level of complexity. My goal in answering the question of "How do I tell a story?" is to present these different ideas and allow you to choose which approach works best for the story that you want to tell.

## Different Types of Story Structure

Let us first take a look at the different theories of dramatic story structure. I am a strong proponent of constructing a sturdy foundation from which to build upon. Because of this, we will look at the different types of story structure and how it has evolved over time. A quick search at any online bookstore will yield many books dedicated to this topic. In this chapter, we will be looking at those that form the foundation, which others build upon, as well as a few variations. This section may seem a bit boring and redundant, but it is important to understand the evolution of the theory of dramatic story structure when trying to craft your own.

It is important to note the difference between a comedy and a tragedy in dramatic structure refers to the outcome of the story and how it is resolved. A comedy usually ends in a celebration after everyone has a true recognition of the events that have occurred, learns from it, forgives and forgets, and either returns to normalcy or to a better situation than the beginning. There is an emphasis of everyone involved reintegrating and recommitting to a future of happiness and harmony. A tragedy, by definition, is one where the conflict is only resolved with the death of the hero. This death does not signify the end of the story, as there is usually a reflection of lessons learned and the significance of the life of the fallen hero.

Pretty much every Hollywood movie or animated movie is a dramatic comedy, which end as a celebration of a future filled with joy and hope. In contrast, the dramatic tragedy ends with a focused recollection of the past.

I have chosen the following writings based on the evolution of story and have divided them into four sections: Three-Act Structure, Five-Act Structure, the Hero's Journey, and Short Story Structure. The table below lists them in chronological order. They will be discussed, however, by section in the next part of this chapter.

| 330 BC | Aristotle *Poetics* | Three-Act Structure |
|---|---|---|
| 19 BC | Horace *Ars Poetica* | Five-Act Structure |
| 1709 | Nicholas Rowe *The Works of Mr. William Shakespear; Revis'd and Corrected* | Five-Act Structure |
| 1846 | Edgar Allen Poe *The Philosophy of Composition* | Short Story Structure |
| 1863 | Gustav Freytag *The Technique of the Drama* | Five-Act Structure |
| 1949 | Joseph Campbell *The Hero with a Thousand Faces* | Three-Act Structure/Hero's Journey |
| 1979 | Syd Field *Screenplay* | Three-Act Structure |
| 1992 | Christopher Vogler *The Writer's Journey: Mythic Structure for Storytellers and Screenwriters* | Three-Act Structure/Hero's Journey |
| 1994 | Algis Budrys *Writing to the Point* | Short Story Structure |

## Three-Act Structure

The Greek philosopher Aristotle recognized that all human beings tell stories the same way. When Aristotle wrote *Poetics* around 330 BC, he outlined the first theory of story structure, which we know today as Three-Act Structure, and focused on the dramatic tragedy: dramatic (meaning that the story is performed instead of narrated) and tragedy (a story that arouses emotions of pity and fear, and by the end it achieves a catharsis of these emotions).

Here are the key points of Aristotle's theory:

1. Every tragedy can be divided into six component parts, ranked in order from most important to least important:
   a. Mythos (usually translated as plot, but really means how the elements come together to form a comprehensible and cohesive whole that delivers a message)
   b. Character (desires, reactions, motivations)
   c. Thought
   d. Diction (expression of thoughts through speech)
   e. Melody (the rhythm of the dialogue and action)
   f. Spectacle (set and costumes)

2. The elements of plot are:
   a. Completeness: A clear beginning, middle, and end (Prologue, Episode, Exode)
   b. Magnitude: A length that can easily be embraced by memory
   c. Unity: A common theme or idea in which all of the action centers around
   d. Determinate structure: Sequence of events that are intertwined and necessary
   e. Universality: The character speaks or acts as most humans would
   f. "according to the law of probability or necessity"

3. Plot is the most important part of the tragedy and must follow a plausible or essential sequence of events from beginning to end. In addition, the following components can also be included:
   a. Astonishment: The ability for a tragedy to elicit pity and fear from the audience as a result of the events of the plot come as a surprise, and when it occurs between family or friends
   b. Reversal: The change in the main action of the story from bad to good or good to bad; usually occurs at the climax of the story and is known also as the turning point, which drives the story towards conclusion and brings the story full circle

c.  Recognition: A revelation that occurs when the character passes from ignorance to knowledge and usually causes the reversal to follow

d.  Suffering: Often the result of a reversal or recognition, suffering is an action that is painful or destructive, and relied on by all tragedies to elicit pity and fear from the audience

4.  There are four types of plots: simple, ethical, pathetic, and complex

a.  Simple plots do not contain reversal and recognition

b.  Ethical plots are motivated by a moral purpose

c.  Pathetic plots are motivated by passion

d.  Complex plots rely entirely on recognition and reversal of the action at the point of climax

5.  The best plots contain reversal and recognition and produce emotions of fear and pity in the audience. In addition, a good plot consists of the following four elements:

a.  It must focus around one single issue

b.  The hero must go from fortune to misfortune

c.  The misfortune must occur from an error in judgment otherwise known as the "tragic flaw"

d.  The hero must be average or better than the average person

6.  Pity and fear are best when the tragic act occurs between family or friends and one of the following occurs:

a.  Conscious action with the knowledge of the people involved

b.  An action done ignorantly, and the tie of family and friends discovered afterwards

c.  The act is not done, because the hero realizes that he can't go through with it (least dramatic choice)

d.  The act is stopped before it does harm after the true identities of the characters are revealed (most effective choice)

7.  The hero must embody certain characteristics:

a.  The hero must be good, with good moral purpose

b.  The qualities of the hero must be appropriate to the character

c.  The hero must be "true to life"

d.  The hero must be consistent in his actions and behaviors

8.  Writers (poets) should do the following when writing the plot:

a.  Visualize the action as vividly as possible as if it is playing out on stage in front of you

b.  Act out the events as they are written in order to express them more vividly

c.  Create an outline of the overall plot and fill in the details later

d.  Write the plot with *desis* ("tying") and *lusis* ("untying"); in other words, all plot threads from the beginning of the action (inciting moment) are woven together (complication) until the turning point (climax), when these plot threads begin to unravel. Here, the hero's fortunes must turn from good to bad (tragedy) or bad to good (comedy). The end of this unraveling leads to the end of his transformation (denouement).

e.  Include all important parts of the plot

f.  Write only one plot, not an entire epic structure

g.  The chorus should be treated like an actor, and the choral songs should be an integral part of the story

Many storytellers who came after Aristotle refined the Three-Act Structure by identifying the fundamental elements and purposes of each act and how they drive the narrative forward. Syd Field was a screenwriter and teacher who made the Three-Act Structure the foundation of his classes. His book *Screenplay* breaks the feature-length film into the three acts as follows:

1.  The Setup: Act I (approximately the first quarter of the movie) establishes the following:

a.  Exposition: The writer sets up the story by introducing the characters and some of their interrelationships within a time and place. It also establishes:

    i.   The main character: This character has a goal and his/her actions drive the story.

    ii.  The dramatic premise: What the story is about.

    iii. The dramatic situation: What circumstances surround the action.

b.  Inciting Incident: Occurs approximately halfway through the first act and sets the plot in motion.

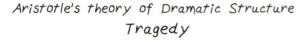

## Aristotle's Theory of Dramatic Structure
### Tragedy

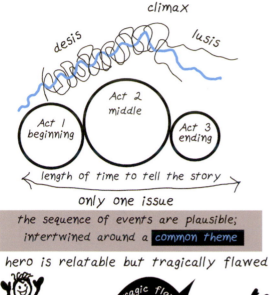

**Figure 1.11**
Aristotle's theory of dramatic structure.

c. Midpoint: Approximately halfway through the film, the midpoint is the lowest point for the character. Here he seems farthest from achieving his goal.

d. The Second "Plot Point": The second plot point occurs at the end of Act II, is another reversal, and drives the story into Act III.

3. The Resolution: Act III (approximately the last quarter of the movie) establishes the following:

a. Climax (Second Culmination): The plot reaches its maximum tension and the main character confronts his greatest obstacle at an extreme height of physical or emotional action. The problem is resolved by either achieving the goal, changing the goal, or not reaching the goal.

b. Denouement: A state of peace and balance returns at the end of the film.

The average length of a feature film is 90–100 minutes. Therefore, Act I is approximately 20–25 minutes in length, while Act II is 40–50 minutes and Act III is another 20–25 minutes.

Using the image below, you can analyze any feature film made in Hollywood and identify this structure: exposition, inciting incident, plot points, obstacles, first and second culmination, climax, and denouement.

**Figure 1.12**
Three-act structure as defined by Syd Field.

c. The First "Plot Point": Field established that there were only two plot points and each separated the three acts. Each plot point was a reversal (using Aristotle's terminology), pushing the plot toward a new direction and leading to the next act. The first occurs at the end of Act I and is the moment when the hero is forced to take on the problem.

2. The Confrontation: Act II (approximately the next two quarters of the movie) establishes the following:

a. Obstacles: The main character encounters a series of obstacles that keeps him from achieving his goal. Each failure forces the character to change his approach and brings on another obstacle.

b. First Culmination: Right before the midpoint, the character seems to be close to achieving his goal, but something happens and everything falls apart, which then leads to the midpoint.

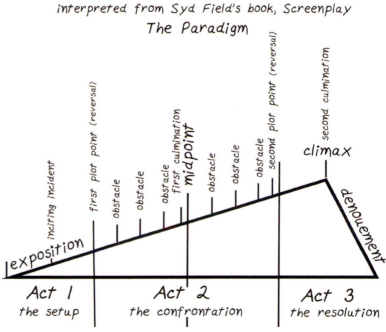

## Five-Act Structure

The Roman poet Horace wrote *Ars Poetica* somewhere around 18 BC. In this 541-line poem written in Latin, which takes the form of a letter of advice, Horace states in one line that a play should have five acts. Horace is considered to be the most influential Roman critic, even though his ideas rely heavily on those written by Aristotle in *Poetics*. His main points are as follows:

1.  There should be five acts (Horace does not clarify the structure of the acts).
2.  Plot should be borrowed from familiar material, but if not then the theme should be consistent throughout the work.
3.  The chain of events should also be consistent.
4.  The middle should harmonize with the beginning, and the end with the middle.
5.  Anything horrific in nature should not be shown, but rather, reported and left to the imagination of the audience.
6.  No more than three characters should speak in a scene.
7.  The chorus should be treated as an actor and an integral part of the plot.

William Shakespeare is known to have written all of his plays in Elizabethan Five-Act Play Structure; however, he did not divide the plays into acts and scenes. The playwright Nicholas Rowe was the first to do so when he published *The Works of Mr. William Shakespear; Revis'd and Corrected* in 1709. What is known today as Shakespeare's Five-Act Structure is as follows:

1.  Introduction or Exposition: Act I: During the first act, the time and place are established, the characters are introduced, and the story background is presented. Towards the end of the first act, the conflict is initiated.
2.  Complication or Rising Action: Act II: During the second act, the hero encounters a series of obstacles and events that become more and more complicated as tension mounts and momentum builds.
3.  Climax or Crisis: Act III: During the third act, the building conflict reaches its peak, known also as the turning point or point of no return.
4.  Falling Action: Act IV: Here, all plot twists are revealed and momentum slows as the story is coming to an end.
5.  Conclusion or Denouement: Act V: The conflict is resolved through either triumph (transfiguration) or failure (catastrophe) of the hero, and lessons are learned.

The German playwright and novelist Gustav Freytag wrote *The Technique of the Drama (Die Technik des Dramas)* in 1863, after identifying recurring patterns in the plots of stories. In this book, he described a system for dramatic structure based on the Five-Act Structure mentioned by Horace, which was further developed through the Renaissance. This book is really worth the read, and because it is a classic, you can download a PDF of it online.[3]

Later named Freytag's Pyramid, this pyramidal structure analyzes and defines the dramatic art as being divided into the following five parts:[4]

1.  Introduction: Part I: The introduction is the exposition to the story that:
    a.  Establishes the location and time period
    b.  Introduces the main characters
        i.   Protagonist: Hero or heroine who has an objective
        ii.  Antagonist: Villain
    c.  Creates the mood and atmosphere
    d.  Initiates the basic conflict with an exciting event that propels the story to move forward and signals the beginning of the main conflict

**Figure 1.13** Freytag's pyramid.

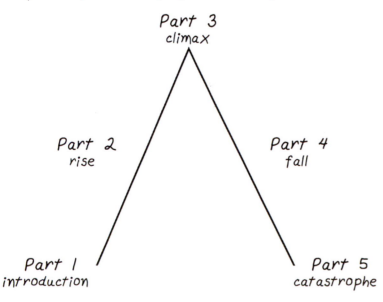

Five-Act Structure and Freytag's Pyramid
as explained by Gustav Freytag in The Technique of the Drama

Part 3
climax

Part 2
rise

Part 4
fall

Part 1
introduction

Part 5
catastrophe

2. Rise: Part II: The rising action creates growing tension and further complicates the basic conflict in the story by:
   a. Introducing a series of obstacles which prevent the protagonist from achieving his or her objective
   b. Including a series of secondary conflicts which come from the antagonist or other enemies
3. Climax: Part III: The climax is the turning point and moment of greatest tension in a story. It is the most exciting event that the rising action builds up to and leads to the falling action. During the climax, the protagonist will face his obstacle and the outcome will either be:
   a. Success (comedy) leading to a happy ending
   b. Failure (tragedy) leading to a disastrous ending
4. Fall: Part IV: Events during the falling action begin to resolve the conflict, which has ended with the climax, and the story now is headed towards ending.
5. Catastrophe: Part V: The catastrophe, also known as the denouement, conclusion, or resolution, is when the catharsis occurs. This involves an event or series of events that lead to the resolution of all conflicts, allowing the tension to relax or unfold. The characters return to normalcy, which then leads to a celebration (comedy) or a retrospection (tragedy).

### The Monomyth and the Hero's Journey

In 1949, the American mythologist, writer, and lecturer Joseph Campbell published *The Hero with a Thousand Faces*, in which he discusses his theory of a fundamental story structure that is shared by every myth that has transcended time. After studying these myths, Campbell found a pattern present in them that involved certain stages during the structure of the story. Nothing he says is new, but instead, he builds upon the three-act structure that had been established by Aristotle and all of those who followed. Campbell identified this pattern that is present in every story ever told and identified this story as the "Monomyth" or "Hero Myth,"

because he determined that there is only one story that has been retold with variation. This book has had a major impact on storytelling and movie-making, and is known to many as the most influential book of the 20th century. If the tools outlined within to compose a story are used, the resulting story will appeal to everyone since it will deal with universal themes and universal concepts. Some of the most popular movies to follow the Monomyth pattern are *Harry Potter*, *The Lord of the Rings*, *The Matrix*, *Star Wars*, and *The Lion King*. Analyzing these stories using the 17 stages listed below clearly shows this structure.

Campbell was a student of the Swiss psychologist Carl Jung, and Campbell based his book on the "archetypes" that Jung identified in his theory of the human psyche. These archetypes are repeating characters that are found in the global collective unconsciousness and represent personality patterns of human nature. The different character archetypes will be explored in Chapter 2 of this book.

Campbell calls his structure "The Adventure of the Hero," and divides his structure into three sections:

1. Departure or Separation
2. Initiation
3. Return

Again, we can look at these three sections as the three acts established by Aristotle, or in other words, the beginning, middle, and end. Campbell summarizes these three sections of the Monomyth in a single sentence of the prologue when he states:

> A hero ventures forth from the world of common day into a region of supernatural wonder: fabulous forces are there encountered and a decisive victory is won: the hero comes back from this mysterious adventure with the power to bestow boons on his fellow man.

Each section of the journey is divided into a series of stages. Not all of the stages are present in every story. The 17 possible stages of the Hero's Journey is diagrammed on page 245 of his book and is summarized as follows:

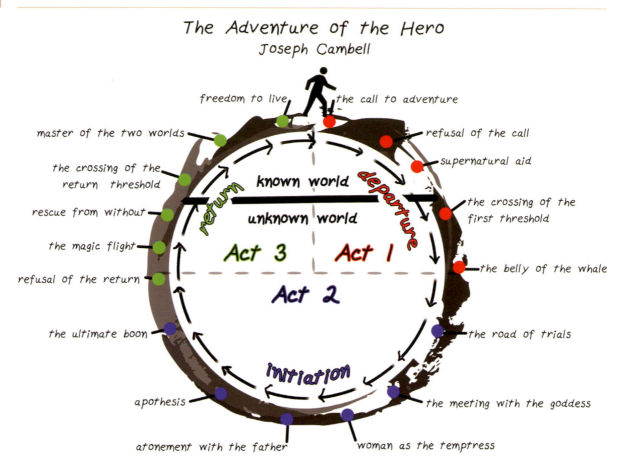

Figure 1.14
The adventure of the hero as defined by Joseph Campbell.

Act I: Departure or Separation
(from the known world)

1.   The Call to Adventure: Our Hero/Heroine is presented with an adventure by a Herald/Harbinger to undertake, a problem to solve, or a challenge to accept, which requires that he/she leave the world in which he/she resides and enter into the unknown.

2.   Refusal of the Call: Motivated by fear of the unknown, feelings of inadequacy, or responsibilities in their known world, our hero finds reasons to refuse the Call to Adventure and stay in his current environment and situation.

3.   Supernatural Aid: Once the Hero accepts the Call, he/she will meet a Mentor or guide who usually gives the Hero advice as well as a supernatural item that will help them at some point during their journey.

4.   The Crossing of the First Threshold: This is the point where the Hero/Heroine will actually cross into the unknown world and into the start of the adventure.

5.   The Belly of the Whale: At the point of entry into the new world, the Hero/Heroine must undergo a metamorphosis. The Hero/Heroine must face death, either figuratively or literally, in order to be reborn before he or she continues on the journey.

Act II: Initiation (to the unknown world)

6.   The Road of Trials: The Hero/Heroine encounters a series of trials and usually fails one or more of these tests or tasks, which customarily occur in threes.

7.   The Meeting with the Goddess: The Goddess is a symbol of the Guardian of Knowledge, which the Hero/Heroine encounters. The Hero/Heroine will either be freed by the newfound enlightenment or die as a result of it. This can also refer to the Hero/Heroine experiencing unconditional love.

8. Woman as the Temptress: This milestone can be combined with the Meeting with the Goddess, as both are symbolic of facing mortality and the darkness within. At this point, the Hero/Heroine will be tempted to abandon or stray from the quest.

9. Atonement with the Father: The center point of the journey when the Hero/Heroine must confront whatever holds the utmost power in his or her life. In many stories, it is the Father or a father figure, but it can be anyone or anything that holds this power.

10. Apotheosis: The Hero/Heroine will recognize the divine within, allowing him/her to accomplish the impossible because the hero becomes godlike.

11. The Ultimate Boon: The Hero/Heroine achieves the goal of the quest and acquires whatever object, knowledge, power, or ability that he/she will bring back and share with the known world.

Act III: Return (to the known world)

12. Refusal of the Return: After the Hero/Heroine succeeds, he/she may not want to return to the known world or may be prevented from doing so.

13. The Magic Flight: The Hero/Heroine may have to escape or finish off the opponent in an additional battle in order to return home to the known world. This battle may also be an internal struggle within the Hero/Heroine.

14. Rescue from Without: The Hero/Heroine may require guides or rescuers to help him or her return home, especially if the Hero/Heroine has been injured.

15. The Crossing of the Return Threshold: Upon returning to the known world, the Hero/Heroine must retain and share the newly found wisdom with the rest of the known world.

16. Master of the Two Worlds: The Hero/Heroine achieves balance within themselves by releasing their fears. The unknown world is no longer unknown. There is balance between the spiritual and material worlds.

17. Freedom to Live: The Hero/Heroine is energized by the journey and embraces the present, without fear of the future or death.

Campbell's Monomyth structure has been modernized and modified many times. However,

Campbell's foundation exists throughout each modification, and his foundation built upon those who came before. Because of this, the Monomyth structure is widely used as the standard in story structure.

In 1992, Christopher Vogler published *The Writer's Journey: Mythic Structure for Storytellers and Screenwriters*, which reduced the 17 stages to 12, adding, combining, and renaming some of the stages as follows:

1. The Ordinary World
2. The Call to Adventure
3. Refusal of the Call
4. Meeting with the Mentor
5. Crossing the First Threshold
6. Tests, Allies, and Enemies
7. Approach to the Innermost Cave
8. The Ordeal
9. Reward
10. The Road Back
11. The Resurrection
12. Return with the Elixir

In *The Writer's Journey*, Vogler takes the theory and stages of *The Hero with a Thousand Faces* and turns them into a practical guidebook for those who want to tell stories for the screen. Now in its third edition, Vogler makes the ideas of Carl G. Jung and Joseph Campbell more relevant through the use of contemporary films, and his book is a must read for potential filmmakers.

## Story Structure for the Short as Compared to a Feature

The models of story structure we have studied so far are easy to apply to feature-length films, but are really difficult to apply to short films. The preceding story structure models show us the big picture and how to map out a complete story. They show us all of the ingredients that most stories contain, which change a series of events into a compelling tale; but for a short film, it is really hard to fit everything in.

If we look at successful animated short narrative films or stories, we will notice that they, too, can be analyzed according to Three-Act Structure, Five-Act Structure, or the Hero's Journey, but the structure has been simplified. Not all stages are present. Even Campbell realized that not every stage of the 17-stage Monomyth would be present in every story. With the short film, however, you can get away with having a very simplified structure as long as you mention, combine, or imply other stages. This is one area where creativity as a storyteller comes into play.

Most theories for short narrative story structures are based on the simplified structures of Three-Act Structure, Five-Act Structure, or the Hero's Journey. The two that follow are the ones we will be focusing on in this book. It is important to note, however, that there are many variations out there.

## The Unity of Effect

Edgar Allan Poe is considered to be the father of the modern short story because he was the first to establish the essential elements of what he referred to as the "short prose narrative," "the prose tale," and the "brief tale." According to Poe's theory, which was referred to as "the unity of effect" or "the single principle," a "tale proper" could be achieved with precise mathematical calculation, planning, and close attention to detail. In a published article from 1846 entitled *The Philosophy of Composition*,[5] Poe explained the formulaic steps he used to write his poem *The Raven*. In doing so, he states, "no one point in its composition is referrible [sic] either to accident or intuition—that the work proceeded, step by step, to its completion with the precision and rigid consequence of a mathematical problem." He established that the following formula for poetry could also be applied to prose:

1. Establish the length. Keep the story short.
2. Determine the impression (theme) to be conveyed and keep this in mind throughout.
3. Consider your audience; make the story universally appealing.
4. Establish the tone.
5. Brainstorm ideas for characters and topics that illustrate your theme and tone.
6. Choose one protagonist and one antagonist.
7. Start at the end; establish the climax first.
8. Carefully plan the plot with great care, make every incident that happens and the tone at every point advance the objective of the storyline.
9. Make sure to build the tension leading up to the climax. The climax is the highest point of tension.
10. Be original. Even though originality is elusive, it should be pursued.
11. Focus on a single clear event, an "insulated incident."
12. Keep your location limited to a single area.
13. Use your setting elements to enhance the story.
14. Use every element to enhance the story.
15. Use contrast as a means to emphasize plot points to make a stronger impression.
16. The denouement should happen rapidly and directly.
17. Use some amount of complexity and suggestiveness to add richness.

These steps can be considered as Poe's "How to Write a Short Story" method. Poe seems to have developed his concept off a simplified Three-Act Structure, where the beginning and ending have been streamlined and the crux of the story happens during the middle.

## Seven Parts of a Short Story

In 1994, Algis Budrys, a Lithuanian-American science fiction writer and critic, established his Seven-Point Structure for the short story in his book, *Writing to the Point*. Like Poe, Budrys' structure is based on the Three-Act Structure:

1. A character or characters
2. in a situation
3. with a problem or a goal
4. makes two to three attempts to solve the problem or achieve the goal but
5. does not succeed and usually makes the problem worse.
6. A final attempt occurs at the climax of the story, and the main character or characters either succeed, by achieving the goal/solving the problem, *or* absolutely fails (Victory or Death).
7. In the denouement (Affirmation), the result of the final attempt is confirmed as final.

The great thing about the short story for the animated film is that the audience is more accepting of an ending where the hero is not successful. Unlike a feature-length film, the audience has not invested so much time empathizing with the hero and rooting for their success.

## Components of a Good Story

As we can see, there are many ways to tell stories, but what defines the good ones from the mediocre? It is evident now, after we have studied story structure, that there are many similarities that are shared in the Three-Act, Five-Act, and Hero's Journey. In order to simplify our understanding, I have listed the five common elements of these structures, breaking them into elements that must be present in all successful stories:

Element 1: Beginning; also known as Set-Up, Prologue, Exposition, or Departure. This is where the setting, time, and characters are established.

Element 2: Inciting Moment; also known as Exciting Event, Initiation of Conflict, Reversal, or Belly of the Whale, and occurs at the end of the story beginning and launches us into the middle of the story. This is the event where something happens to propel the main character into his quest.

Element 3: Middle; also known as Episode, Rising Action, Conflict, Complication, Obstacles, Desis, Tying of Events, Road of Trials, Quest, and Attempt (to solve a problem or achieve a goal). This is where a series of events challenge the main character, progressively intensifying, until the Climax occurs.

Element 4: Climax; also known as Reversal, Crisis, or Turning Point, and occurs at the end of the story middle and launches us into the end of the story. This is the event that is the highest point of tension in the story.

Element 5: End; also known as Exode, Lusis, Untying of Events, Falling Action, Denouement, Resolution, or Return. This is where the story is resolved.

We will be exploring other elements throughout this book that make a good story better, but these five elements are the foundation for you to build upon. In addition to these elements, there are four common principles that are also shared in the Three-Act, Five-Act, and Hero's Journey.

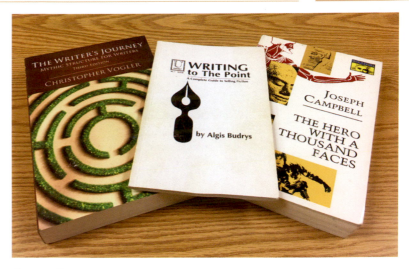

**Figure 1.15**
**Suggested reading.** There are many different theories on story structure.

Principle 1: Premise; also known as situation, idea, foundation, or basis. This is what the story is about. It is usually a question or series of questions, which the story explores. The Premise is also known as the hook. It grabs the audience's attention and pulls them into the story. It usually happens within the first 5–10 minutes of a feature film. A good hook catches the audience's attention and holds it, leading them into the story. It can occur before the true beginning, or exposition, of the story.

Principle 2: Theme; also known as message, unity, or lesson. Something the audience will learn as a result of the story. There can be multiple themes in a story. The theme ties the story together and provides meaning.

Principle 3: Length; also known as magnitude. No matter how long or short, everything within the story should be there for a purpose and only that which is necessary should be included.

Principle 4: Universality; also known as simplicity. A good story works for any audience. The story should be told in a way that is easy to understand and appeals to an intended audience with clear language and believability. The audience should not need to spend time interpreting and dissecting what is occurring. The lesson should be easy to understand and memorable. The characters are appealing and have an emotional arc (they learn something over time and may change because of it), which in turn, appeals to the audience's emotions through humor, sadness, joy, anger, frustration, etc.

You can apply these elements and principles when analyzing any of your favorite animated short narratives to understand what makes one stand above the others, or apply them to a short story idea that you are considering developing into an animation.

For a simplified example, the basic elements of a good story can be understood by reading a simple nursery rhyme:

Little Miss Muffet (protagonist) character
Sat on a tuffet (location)
Eating her curds and whey (goal)
Along came a spider (antagonist)
Who sat down beside her (conflict)
And frightened Miss Muffet away (climax and resolution)

Whenever a topic needs to be understood, the best place to start is with studying the masters. I learned this concept when studying art at university. When learning to draw, we studied the masters, learned their medium and re-created their marks. When learning pastels, we studied Degas. When learning value and light, we studied Rembrandt. Afterwards, we applied their techniques to our own works, slowly developing our own style and voice.

So here is where we will begin applying what we have learned thus far. The analysis of works by Disney and Pixar, two masters of the animation medium in both long and short form, will allow us to identify the elements and principles present that are crucial to a good story. Let us approach this by analyzing a short narrative. Start off by watching the film several times. The first viewing is for pure entertainment purposes. Then, watch it a second time, taking

notes on what stands out to you the most. You may want to watch several more times to really get a grasp of everything that is coming across, and to try to pick up on subtleties that enrich the story with detail. I suggest watching one of the following short films, which happen to be some of my favorites: *Presto*, *Partly Cloudy*, *Day & Night*, or *Paperman*. You can usually find these on the Internet, purchase them for streaming on Amazon, or download them on iTunes.

For an example, I will analyze Pixar's *Partly Cloudy* using a cross between Budrys/Poe. This short film has had mixed reviews, but I think it is a great example to discuss the elements and principles of story that have been identified. The first time I saw *Partly Cloudy* was when it was screened before the feature-length animation *Up*. I remember liking the short for both the visual style and story. For me, the story had that "aww" factor that warms my heart in a short period of time. I decided to use it as an example of great storytelling within an animated short for one of my classes. Watching the short for a second time, I took notes, summarizing the story as it unfolded.

**Figure 1.16**
**Exposition.** Still image from Pixar's *Partly Cloudy*.

1.  The story opens as storks are delivering cute and cuddly babies, both humans and animals. We follow them up into the sky as they are reunited with the clouds whose job it is to make the babies and ready them for delivery. (Element: Exposition; Timecode: 00:00–00:44)

**Figure 1.17**
**The hook.** Still image from Pixar's *Partly Cloudy*.

2.    The hook of the story is revealed. This idea, that clouds make the babies, is the premise of the story. (Element: Exposition; Timecode: 00:45–01:30)

**Figure 1.18**
**Introduction to Hero Protagonist, supporting protagonist, and problem.** Still image from Pixar's *Partly Cloudy*.

3.    Our attention is brought to focus on a lonely gray cloud whose specialization is the creation of baby animals that are cute but dangerous to be around. He wants his creations to be delivered. His delivery stork flies into and lands on the cloud, appearing a bit worn but eager for his next assignment, a baby alligator, who straightaway latches onto the stork's head. The gray cloud takes the baby alligator, bundles it, and gives it to the stork who then flies away to make the delivery. (Element: Introduction to Hero Protagonist, Supporting Protagonist, and Problem; Timecode: 01:31–02:23, 52 seconds)

**Figure 1.19**
**First attempt, problem worsens.** Still image from Pixar's *Partly Cloudy*.

4.    After the stork returns, slightly damaged and a little hesitant, he is immediately attacked by his next delivery, a baby ram. His attention is grabbed by the cuteness of a puppy that a nearby cloud has created. The gray cloud notices the distraction and becomes concerned. The stork, embarrassed by his apparent act of disloyalty, takes the next bundle of joy and flies away while being battered by the baby ram. (Element: First attempt, problem worsens, contrast is used to create emphasis for the conflict and foreshadow; Timecode: 02:23–03:06, 43 seconds)

**Figure 1.20**
**Second attempt, problem worsens.** Still image from Pixar's *Partly Cloudy*.

5.    Again the stork returns, but this time with a blackened eye and much more hesitant. The gray cloud presents the stork with a ball of cloud matter, which the stork quickly tries to hold with his wings, only to have the ball of smoke turn into a prickly baby porcupine, leaving quills imbedded in his poor wings. Still, he manages to take the bundle of joy off to his new parents. (Element: Second attempt, problem worsens; Timecode: 03:07–03:33, 26 seconds)

**Figure 1.21**
Third attempt, problem worsens, climax begins. Still image from Pixar's *Partly Cloudy*.

**Figure 1.23**
Climax. Still image from Pixar's *Partly Cloudy*.

6.  The stork returns once again, this time wearing a headdress of quills and a hesitant smile, startling the gray cloud who looks concerned and tries to help the stork remove them and a big hug. When presented with the next shape of cloud matter, which appears to become a baby shark, the stork shrieks and flies away. (Element: Third attempt, problem worsens, Climax begins; Timecode: 03:34–04:06, 32 seconds)

8.  The stork returns with a bundle of joy, and opens it to reveal a football helmet and shoulder pads, which he eagerly and quickly adorns to keep him safe from the next dangerous delivery. (Element: Climax; Timecode: 04:38–04:58, 20 seconds)

**Figure 1.22**
Climax. Still image from Pixar's *Partly Cloudy*.

**Figure 1.24**
Final Attempt and Affirmation. Still image from Pixar's *Partly Cloudy*.

7.  Angered and saddened by his abandonment, the gray cloud creates a thunderstorm that exemplifies his emotional state. (Element: Climax; Timecode: 04:07–04:37, 20 seconds)

9.  The gray cloud is delighted and relieved, hugs the stork and then presents him with his next delivery, an electric eel that then shocks the stork. The gray cloud continues to hug the stork because he realizes that the eel keeps shocking the stork and hurting him as we pull out from the scene. (Element: Final Attempt and Affirmation; Timecode: 04:59–05:13, 14 seconds)

10. Credits (Timecode: 05:13–05:49, 36 seconds)
    Premise: If storks deliver babies, where do the storks get the babies? What if clouds made them? Who is responsible for the dangerous animal babies?
    Theme: Things aren't always what they seem.
    Length: 05:49 (including credits)
    Universality: Visually and emotionally appealing, no language barrier.

I first started really understanding this storytelling device when I was writing with Bob Peterson on "Finding Nemo." And we would call this the unifying theory of two plus two. Make the audience put things together. Don't give them four, give them two plus two. The elements you provide and the order you place them in is crucial to whether you succeed or fail at engaging the audience. Editors and screenwriters have known this all along. It's the invisible application that holds our attention to story. I don't mean to make it sound like this is an actual exact science, it's not. That's what's so special about stories, they're not a widget, they aren't exact. Stories are inevitable, if they're good, but they're not predictable.

Andrew Stanton[6]

## Emotional Structure

Story structure is represented visually by charting the intensity of the plot over time on a graph. Freytag's pyramid was probably the first attempt at visualizing the emotional structure of the story. When writing a story, we can begin a rough layout of the story structure using a graph where the vertical axis (y) indicates the intensity level of the story and the horizontal axis (x) indicates the time length of the story. Taking what we have learned from Syd Field and Edgar Allen Poe, we can mathematically formulate when and for how long certain plot points should occur in order to keep the audience engaged and the momentum building throughout the film. Using the graphing technique during writing helps us visualize how the story emotionally impacts the audience over time.

(EX) Exposition
(IM) Inciting Moment
(CO) Conflict
(CL) Climax
(RE) Resolution

An emotion graph can also be made for each character in the story. The horizontal axis of the graph indicates the time length of the story, and each shot (from your shot list) is listed. The vertical axis of the graph indicates the emotional intensity scale. The 0 indicates a

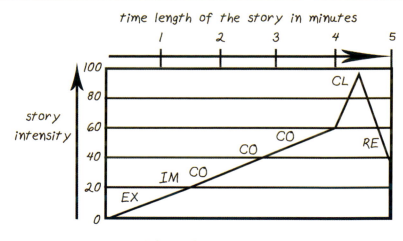

A list of each shot description

lack of emotion and 100 indicates the maximum emotional tension. Each character's emotions are represented on the graph to show the dynamic between them.

Whether a story follows the Three-Act, Five-Act, Hero's Journey, or some variation thereof, we have established that every story has a beginning (exposition), middle (conflict building to climax), and end (denouement), no matter how short or long it is. Using story structure as our guide to plot points, we can analyze the emotional structure of any story or film. Abbreviations help us in placing these elements on the graph so that we can see where the plot points occur, as in the example by Pixar, *Partly Cloudy*.

It is important to remember that every story should be built around the design and foundation of the emotional structure. Since the emotional structure looks at the high and low points of the story, we can visually determine if the intensity is increasing over time. This is essential to do as the story develops, since the writer wants to purposely build the tension of the plot so that the most impact occurs at the climax. The hardest part of storytelling is the middle, and emotional structure helps ensure that tension is building progressively to keep the audience engaged and interested.

As the story unfolds, the audience should be able to intuitively connect emotions of one scene to another. The action that is occurring is entertaining to the audience, but not what makes a good story. The emotional transformation of the hero is what illustrates the story's theme, which is the true purpose for the story. Audiences

**Figure 1.25**
The story structure graph.

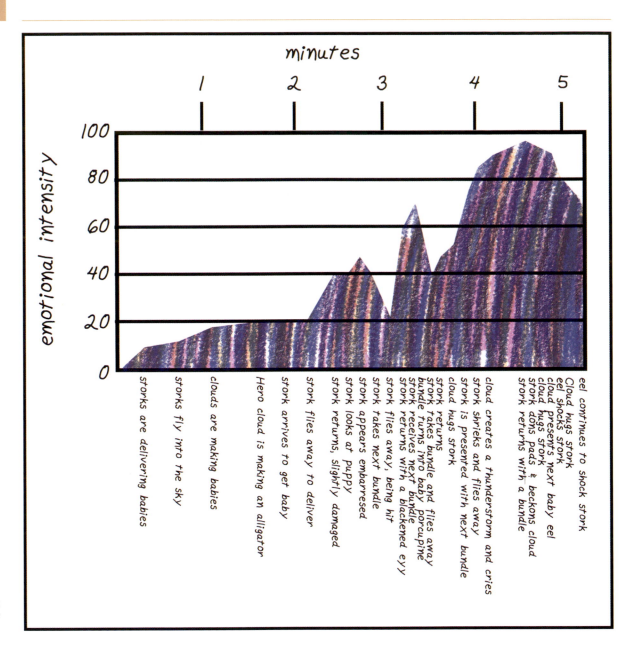

**Figure 1.26**
An emotional structure graph of Pixar's *Partly Cloudy*.

are looking for an emotional connection to the hero/heroine and his or her journey. When the character arcs (learning and growing as a result of their struggle) the audience connects because there is a universal desire to succeed by overcoming our flaws and becoming better human beings as a result of our experiences.

## Visual Structure

Visual structure parallels the emotional structure of the story. As visual storytellers, we must take the written story and use the elements

and principles of art and design to create visual intensity that parallels the emotional intensity of the story structure.

In 2001, Bruce Block, an American film producer and visual consultant, published *The Visual Story*, in which he explains how to apply film theory in order to create the ultimate visual story for the screen. Block borrows and combines some of the elements and principles of art and design into his theory of how visual components are used on the screen. The components he establishes are the following:

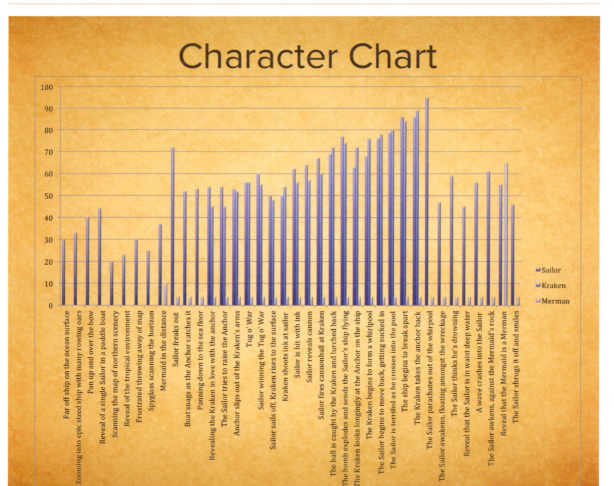

**Figure 1.27**
Emotional
structure graphs
of *Cuddle Fish*
(2015). Courtesy
of the University
of Central Florida
Character
Animation
Specialization.

1. Contrast and Affinity: Here Block uses these words as synonyms for Different and Similar.[7] Block states that understanding and applying Contrast and Affinity is the foundation of visual structure. The greater the contrast, or differences in visual components, then the higher the visual and emotional intensity of tension. Affinity or similarity of visual components results in a lower emotional impact. This component is applied to all of the following components as a way of creating visual and emotional tension.

2. Space: Block considers the physical space in front of the camera (three-dimensional) as well as the space on the screen (two-dimensional). In addition, the final screen size must be considered depending on what you are designing your end output to be displayed upon; this could be as small as a cell phone screen or as large as IMAX. The following affect space and how it is perceived: perspective, size and scale, object movement within the space, camera movement, atmospheric perspective (which he calls textural diffusion and aerial diffusion), shape changes, depth enhanced by tonal and color separation, vertical position of the objects or subjects, overlap of objects or subjects, focus (depth of field), stereoscopic, deep space, flat space, limited space, and ambiguous space.

3. Line and Shape: Block explains that both actual and implied line and shape need to be considered. Lines are powerful in directing the viewer's eye on the screen, establishing orientation, as well as dividing the space for emphasis. The quality of line (referred to as straight or curved) has pre-existing emotional

associations and can be used effectively to elicit emotion from the audience or imply suggested meanings. Shapes come in three basic categories: circle, square, and triangle. Shapes also have pre-existing emotional associations.

4.  Tone: Block refers to tone as the range of brightness of objects as compared to the gray scale. Tone is powerful because the brightest areas of the screen attract the most visual attention, especially if there is contrast. He establishes three ways of controlling tone: art direction, lighting, and camera/lens adjustments.

5.  Color: Block gives a really good foundation of color theory, how we see color, and how color interacts with other colors. He also talks about color schemes, a brief introduction to the color script, and how to control color in film production.[8]

6.  Movement: Block discusses movement as it relates to objects, the camera, and the audience's point of attention.[9] Movement of an object creates the audience's point of attention, but it can also be created by contrast in tone or color as well as vanishing points using perspective. He also discusses the Continuum of Movement, which refers to the audience's point of attention as it occurs within a shot and from shot to shot throughout the length of the film. In addition to movement, brightness, saturated color, and visual contrast, the audience's point of attention is focused on a dominant character's eyes in any shot. By controlling the position of the audience's eye movement, the visual intensity can be increased by darting the eye around the screen. Keeping the eye movement in the same area or slowly moving it across the screen creates affinity and less tension.

7.  Rhythm: Block establishes that we perceive rhythm by hearing it, seeing it, or feeling it. He defines rhythm by using a metronome and divides it into alternation (a moment of sound followed by a moment of silence), repetition (repeating the alternation creates a rhythm), and tempo (the speed of the silence between the sounds of the alternation, or how long the silence lasts between the sounds).[10] Block states that there are two ways to create visual rhythm: editorial repetition (creating a beat at every cut or edit) or pictorial repetition (repeating the same shot). The editorial tempo can remain constant, speed up, or slow down. Intensity is increased with faster cutting tempos.

These visual components will be explored further in Chapter 7. The ability to understand and control these components results in the ability to portray emotions and deliver the meaning of the story to the audience.

When graphing these components, the horizontal axis (x) indicates the time length of the story, but the vertical axis (y) changes based on the component and the visual choice. The bottom usually represents the affinity, that is, what is most consistent throughout (or the starting point). The top usually represents the contrast. Some examples bottom and top of the (y) axis are listed as follows:

Visual structure should remain simple. Many of the visual components can remain constant, using visual component changes sparingly. An overly complicated visual structure can make it difficult for an audience to follow.

| Component | Bottom of y-axis | Top of y-axis |
|---|---|---|
| Space | Flat<br>Recognizable<br>Open | Deep<br>Ambiguous Closed |
| Line | Quality: Straight<br>Intensity Direction: Horizontal | Quality: curved<br>Intensity Direction: Vertical |
| Shape | 2D<br>Circle/Square/Triangle | 3D<br>Circle/Square/Triangle |
| Tone | Brightness<br>Affinity<br>Coincidence | Darkness<br>Contrast<br>Noncoincidence |
| Color | Warm<br>Desaturated<br>Hue<br>Hue | Cool<br>Saturated<br>Different Hue<br>Complementary Hue |
| Movement (camera) | Object: Fast Camera 2D | Object: Slow Camera 3D |
| Rhythm (editorial) | Slow<br>Regular<br>Continuous | Fast<br>Irregular<br>Fragmented |

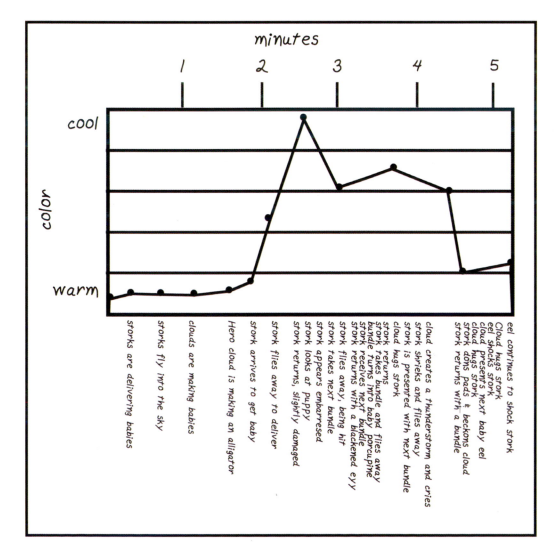

Figure 1.28
An example of a color visual structure graph for Pixar's *Partly Cloudy*.

## How to Tell a Story Visually

Using emotional and visual structure graphs to analyze the story is the first step in translating the words from the paper into visuals on the screen. As Aristotle suggested in *Poetics*, a writer must visualize the action as vividly as possible as if it is playing out on stage in front of you. Whether you write the story you will develop or not, the next step should be visualizing the story in your mind's eye.

Be creative and unique in your decisions. Blend familiarity with the unexpected. Use variation to keep things interesting. Chapter 7 will explore these concepts in more depth through art direction and style. There is a fine balance to making the visuals work, but if they do, they can transport us to another place and time. The best visual stories are like the best written stories: solid, compact, intuitive, evocative, and effective.

It is not enough to make things look visually appealing. Every visual decision should be connected directly to the story and used to deliberately drive the story forward. Visual storytelling improves the universality of the story. The number one rule of telling a story visually is SHOW, DON'T TELL! Don't rely on dialogue or narration. Telling a story without dialogue or narration makes that story international, but it doesn't make it universal. It is a great challenge to convey a story visually.

## Every Decision and Inclusion Must Drive the Story Forward

Remember, at the end of production the visual story must make sense to the audience. This does not mean that every single detail of the story must be spelled out or shown to the audience. Audiences are smart. They can make connections from implications; just make sure that the visual clues you give them are brought to their attention and are clear. Explaining too much or providing too much information can stall your story and loosen the tension. Edit to ensure that all that remains is necessary and essential to telling the story. Beware: Unclear or little information makes the story pretty but meaningless.

In an article Edgar Allen Poe wrote:

> In the whole composition there should be no word written, of which the tendency, direct or indirect, is not to the one pre-established design. And by such means,

with such care and skill, a picture is at length painted which leaves in the mind of him who contemplates it with a kindred art, a sense of the fullest satisfaction. The idea of the tale has been presented unblemished, because undisturbed; and this is an end unattainable by the novel.[11]

Take anything out that is not important. The true test is this: If something is removed, does the story change? If something is removed and your story or hero is not affected, then remove it or find a reason to keep it.

The five elements of the story structure that have been identified in this chapter are the foundation for driving the story forward: revealing the necessary information in the exposition, the inciting moment, the conflicts, the climax, and even the resolution. Each scene moves the story forward. Each element must be relevant. There must be a cause-and-effect relationship between each element. Ask yourself, "And so?"[12] to test the relevance of information as you develop your story. Ask "What is the point of this being included? What is its purpose? How does this information further the story?" Each scene should trigger the next one.

Your audience is eager to find out if your hero succeeds or fails in his quest. The rising action of the conflicts, which build tension as each task or encounter gets more difficult, feeds into the curiosity of the audience.

Intertwining levels of meaning using visuals and connections between characters and their environment adds another level of purpose. Using different literary devices, such as foreshadowing, symbols, and point of view, can help build these connections. Because of the short format, it is best sticking to linear storytelling, with minimal usage of non-linear devices such as flashbacks.

It is best to write your short story without dialogue. Dialogue can be a crutch because it is an easy way of delivering information to the audience. If you must use dialogue, make sure that it is imperative to driving the story forward and keep it concise.

It is imperative to avoid overly complicated storylines, characters that don't have a purpose, scenes that serve no purpose, gimmicks, and the latest trends. Make sure that the audience can identify with the hero or heroine.

Remember, everything must work together to support the story. After writing a story (or when watching a film), it may be helpful to answer the following questions:

1. Who are the main characters and can I relate to them?
2. What does the main character want?
3. Do the characters and events seem plausible for the world that is created by the storyteller?
4. What is the conflict? How many conflicts are encountered?
5. Is anything funny?
6. Is anything painful?
7. Is anything joyful?
8. Do the conflicts build suspense?
9. At what point do we reach the climax?
10. Does the main character learn something or change before the end?
11. Can I understand what is going on?
12. Is there a reason this should be animated?
13. What is/are the message(s) of the story?

This chapter has focused on the foundational information of the different genres of animations and how stories are told. Now that we have a better understanding of the different parts of story, the next chapter begins the journey of story development and how to cultivate ideas.

## Bibliography and Further Reading

Aristotle. (330 BC). Poetics. (Butcher, S.H., Trans.). Retrieved from http://classics.mit.edu/Aristotle /poetics.html.

Bellantoni, P. (2013). *If it's purple, someone's gonna die: The power of color in visual storytelling*. Burlington, MA: Focal Press, an imprint of the Taylor & Francis Group.

Block, B. A. (2008). The visual story: Creating the visual structure of film, TV and digital media. Amsterdam: Focal Press/Elsevier.

Budrys, A. (1994). Writing to the point: A complete guide to selling fiction. Evanston, IL: Unifont.

Campbell, J. (1972). *The hero with a thousand faces*. Princeton, NJ: Princeton University Press.

Cousineau, P., & Campbell, J. (1990). The hero's journey: The world of Joseph Campbell: Joseph Campbell on his life and work. San Francisco: Harper & Row.

Cron, L. (2012). Wired for story: The writer's guide to using brain science to hook readers from the very first sentence. New York: Ten Speed Press.

Field, S. (2005). *Screenplay: The foundations of screenwriting*. New York: Delta Trade Paperbacks.

Freytag, G. (1894). *Freytag's Technique of the drama: An exposition of dramatic composition and art*. An authorized translation from the 6th German ed. by Elias J. MacEwan. Retrieved from https:// archive.org/details/freytagstechniqu00freyuoft.

Horace. (19 BC). *Ars Poetica*. (Kline, A.S., Trans.). Retrieved from https://www.poetryintranslation.com/PITBR/Latin /HoraceArsPoetica.php.

Poe, E.A. "Review of Twice-Told Tales" [Text-02], *Graham's Magazine*, May 1842, pp. 298–300. Retrieved from https://www.eapoe.org/works/criticsm/gm542hn1.htm.

Poe, E.A. "The Philosophy of Composition" [Text-02], *Graham's Magazine*, vol. XXVIII, no. 4, April 1846, 28:163–167. Retrieved from https://www.eapoe.org /works/essays/philcomp.htm.

Sohn, P. (Director). (2009). *Partly Cloudy* [Video file].

Stanton, A. (2012). The clues to a great story. Retrieved from https://www.ted.com/talks/andrew_stanton_the _clues_to_a_great_story?language= en.

Vogler, C., & Montez, M. (2007). *The writer's journey: Mythic structure for writers*. Studio City: Michael Wiese.

## Notes

1. http://worldfilmpresentation.com/film/here
2. http://www.memo.tv/forms/
3. Freytag, G. (1894). *Freytag's technique of the drama: An exposition of dramatic composition and art*. An authorized translation from the 6th German ed. by Elias J. MacEwan. Retrieved from https:// archive.org/details/freytagstechniqu00freyuoft.
4. Freytag, G. (1894). *Freytag's technique of the drama: An exposition of dramatic composition and art* (p. 115). An authorized translation from the 6th German ed. by Elias J. MacEwan. Retrieved from https://archive.org/details/freytagstechniqu00 freyuoft.
5. Read the *Philosophy of Composition* here: http:// www.eapoe.org/works/essays/philcomp.htm
6. Stanton, A. (2012). The clues to a great story. Retrieved from https://www.ted.com/talks/andrew _stanton_the_clues_to_a_great_story?language=en.
7. When I learned about contrast in art school, it was high contrast and low contrast.
8. What I find interesting is that Block doesn't discuss the emotional impact of color. We will be exploring this in Chapter 7, but there is another book that covers this topic extensively entitled *If It's Purple, Someone's Gonna Die: The Power of Color in Visual Storytelling* by Patti Bellantoni.
9. This is also known as focal point in art.
10. Block doesn't discuss rhythmic patterns until later when he talks about visual editing patterns, but patterns are an important part of rhythm.
11. Edgar Allan Poe, "Review of Twice-Told Tales" [Text-02], *Graham's Magazine*, May 1842, pp. 298–300. Retrieved from https://www.eapoe .org/works/editions/mgm001.htm.
12. Cron, L. (2012). Wired for story: The writer's guide to using brain science to hook readers from the very first sentence. New York: Ten Speed Press.

# 2

## The Story Idea

The way ideas come to fruition varies from person to person and story to story. Many creative people say their ideas come when they are doing other activities and are not even trying to come up with one: walking, cleaning, organizing, trying to fall asleep, doing yoga, reading, looking at artwork, or looking through magazines or books, among others. Everyone has ideas. It is what a person does with the ideas after they have had them that make the difference. Creative people pay attention to the ideas when they come along.

# How to Come Up with Ideas: The Creative Process

There is a great little book by James Webb Young, an American advertising executive, called *A Technique for Producing Ideas*. Within its 36 pages is his five-step formula for anyone who wants to become more creative in advertising or in any creative field. In this book, Young states, "an idea is nothing more nor less than a new combination of old elements." Young establishes the following five steps:

1. Gathering Raw Material: Young establishes that this is a chore, so many creatives try to dodge it and go straight to step four and simply sit around while waiting for inspiration. He suggests using 3×5 index cards to write down one item per card as you go along, and classify them by subject. He also suggests storing other materials in scrapbooks or file folders for easy access. Gather materials for your immediate problem, but also gather materials in an ongoing fashion for enrichment, inspiration, future projects, and general knowledge.

2. Mental Digestive Process—Conscious Processing: Work over the collected materials in your mind. Take time to sift through the materials that you have collected. Try finding two facts and look for their relationship. He compares this to putting together a jigsaw puzzle. As you go through this process, partial ideas come to mind. He suggests recording these also on 3×5 index cards no matter how crazy or incomplete they may be. He says that we may be tempted to give up too soon, but we should continue, looking for a second wind. This step should not be stopped until everything becomes a jumble in the mind with no insight left, what he calls the hopeless stage.

3. Mental Digestive Process—Unconscious Processing: This is the incubating stage. Young stresses the importance of this step of the process. At this point you are to drop the problem completely. Walk away and engage

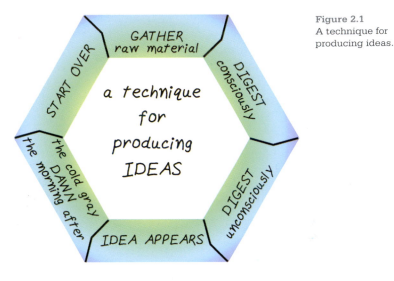

Figure 2.1
A technique for producing ideas.

in an activity that gets your conscious mind off of the process and engages your emotions. Give the problem over to your unconscious mind. Listen to music, read, go to the theater or to the movies, or take a nap.

4. Out of Nowhere the Idea Will Appear: The idea will come to you when you least expect it: while shaving, bathing, half awake in the morning, or suddenly waking you in the middle of the night. This is the birth of the idea, the "Eureka, I have it!" stage.

5. The Cold Gray Dawn of the Morning After: In this stage, you take your idea into the real world. Subject it to criticism, input, and feedback. Allow your idea to expand and change. Be open to possibilities that you may have overlooked. In this stage you shape and develop the idea until it is useful.

The steps that Young has outlined are the foundation for the creative process. Everywhere you look, no matter how they are defined, these steps are present in every creative endeavor and utilized by writers, artists, designers, composers, actors, filmmakers, and every creative professional worldwide.

Here are some synonyms that are commonly used for these steps or stages of the preproduction creative cycle:

1. Preparation: Brainstorm, research, data collection, idea file, idea notebook
2. Elaboration: Development, reflect, review, first draft, answering questions, design, plan, sketch, explore, experiment
3. Incubation: Creative procrastination, break, daydream, reflection
4. Insight: The "a-ha" moment, breakthrough, epiphany
5. Evaluation: Critique, rewrite, revise, refine

Depending on the length of time for your project, you can divide your time proportionally with these five steps. For example, for one eight-hour day turnaround for an idea, you could divide the steps into the following schedule:

1. Preparation: 8–9 am
2. Elaboration: 10 am–12 pm
3. Incubation: 12 pm lunch and 30-minute walk after lunch
4. Insight: 1:30–2pm
5. Evaluation: 2–5pm

This is just one example of how to break up the time. Two eight-hour days could be divided this way:

Day 1:   Preparation: 9 am–12 pm
         Elaboration: 1 pm–5 pm
         Evening: Incubation (sleep on it)

Day 2:   Insight: First thing in the morning
         Evaluation: 9 am–12 pm
         Evaluation: 1 pm–5 pm

If the project allows for longer time, you can repeat this process daily, refining it until one of three things happens: time runs out, money runs out, or you finally come to a solution that you are passionate about.[1]

Figure 2.2
A two-day plan for idea creation.

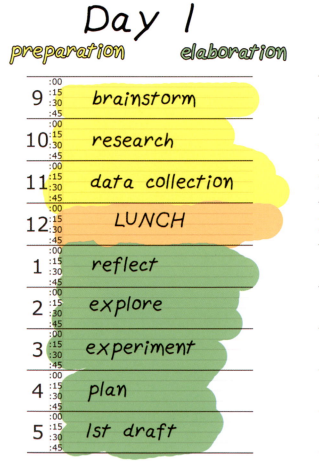
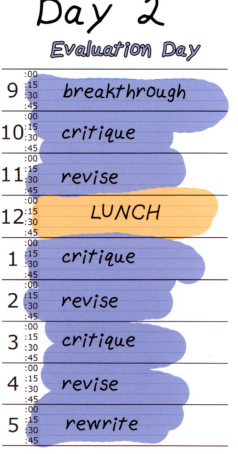

# Brainstorming

When beginning a project, whether the project is writing a short story or any other creative endeavor, the first place to start is with brainstorming. Start with a stack of blank index cards, write one item onto each card, and then sort them into categories. It can be helpful to use different colored cards for the six different categories.

Alternatively, one could use a spreadsheet or digital database. I find that it's much easier and more practical to use index cards since they can be easily sorted and spread out on a table or floor when pulling ideas together. First, brainstorm variations of story principles and elements, before beginning to write the first draft:

1. Genre
2. Theme (lesson or meaning)
3. Characters (protagonist and antagonist)
4. Locations (time and place)
5. Events (topics or problems)
6. Conflicts (or attempts to solve the problem)

Brainstorming can be done as follows:

- Time limit: For each category, set a timer for 15 to 30 minutes and create cards for each item that comes to mind for each category. This works well for those who work well under pressure.
- Number limit: Set a precise number of items for each category, e.g., 25, 50, or 100. This takes the time pressure off and you will know that brainstorming is finished when the number of items is met.

Points to consider:

- Do not stifle possibilities: If a particular element has already been decided, like a character, brainstorm the other elements as related to the decided one, but add options that do not necessarily fit.
- Exhaust all possibilities: Remember that usually the first third of the items may be the worst. Be persistent. The best item may

**Figure 2.3**
**The brainstorm session.** Courtesy of the University of Central Florida Character Animation Specialization.

not appear until the end of the brainstorm session.
- Do not evaluate any item while brainstorming. At this stage, nothing is off limits. Do not be tempted to judge the silliness or blandness of an item. Include everything that comes to mind.
- Stay focused: Do not be tempted to jump into the next stage of the creative process until the time is up or the goal is met.
- Review: Look over the initial brainstorm session items. Identify and gather any additional items that come to mind.
- Allow breaks and have some fun during this process: Walking away from the brainstorming session allows your subconscious mind to take over. Take a walk. Walking is a great way to clear the mind and get some exercise. Fresh air is always helpful for inspiration.

In addition to (or in lieu of) using the 3×5 index cards, you can create a mindmap. Using paper or software like XMind, start by writing the key topic in the center. You can create a mindmap for each element. Branching off the center, use lines to make connections and write new items around the page. Starting with a large sheet of paper can be helpful, as can posting the paper on the wall. If collaborating with others, bubbl.us can be a helpful resource, because it allows for online collaboration when making mindmaps.

**Figure 2.4**
A sample mindmap.

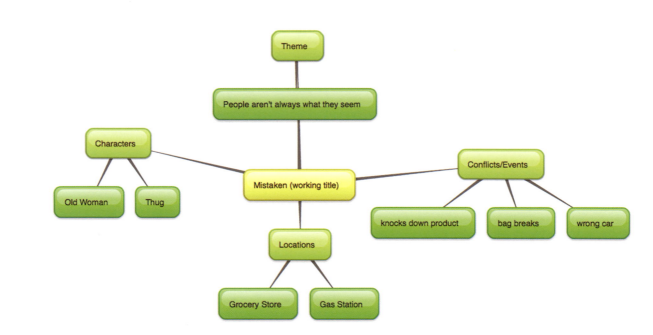

# The Idea Notebook or File

A great way to keep all of your items together is to create an idea notebook or keep an idea file. Here you can jot down sudden thoughts and paste or gather newspaper or magazine clippings, images, drawings, doodles, or other items that you come across that give you inspiration. Having both a digital and physical file can be a great way to go; however, printing the digital images can be helpful when processing items and trying to make connections. It is also great to make the physical items digital by scanning or taking pictures, storing them in the cloud for access at any time. Pinterest.com is also a great place to quickly pin images found on the internet. It all depends on your preference and working style.

The idea notebook or file can be utilized for both a specific project and as an ongoing resource. These are specific activities that should be part of your ongoing collection routine and process:

1. Research: Read short stories and watch short animated films. Start building a daily and weekly research goal. As an ongoing process, challenge yourself to watch one short animated film daily and read one short story a week. Take notes and add them to the file or notebook. Write down items that fit into the categories you have established. Think about how these items can be recombined in a new way. Become familiar with what is current and what has happened in the past in areas that both interest and challenge you. Create a wide collection of resources to draw upon.

2. Dream: Keep a notebook by your bed so that if you have an interesting dream you can write elements or ideas down the moment you wake.

3. Story Starters: Write down scenarios, quotes, pieces of dialogue, or phrases that can be later used as an opening line or starting point for a story. The can be found in books, online, newspapers, magazines, and elsewhere. Try www.thestorystarter.com or a book such as *The Pocket Muse: Ideas and Inspirations for Writing* by Monica Wood.

4. People Watch: Go somewhere public where you can people watch. Observe people coming and going at places such as a grocery store, park, or coffee shop. Bring a sketchbook and jot down ideas about where they are going and what they are buying. Take a camera and discreetly snap shots. Start building stories about them.

5. Browse: Look through magazines, newspapers, and even gift catalogues. Clip, scan, or photograph any interesting or shocking images, items, or stories. Google search images for specific characters, locations, or conflicts.

6. Travel: Whether exploring the nearest town or places all over the world, always be on the lookout for items to include. Photograph people, places, artwork, signage, buildings, houses, and anything of interest.

7. Hobbies: Find a hobby that is interesting or intriguing. Collect images, quotes, and information about the hobby. Play an instrument or game, sail, fish, ride horses, watch birds, collect, sew, paint, taxidermy, and so on. Find something unusual and explore the characters that would be interested in pursuing this hobby.

8. Visit Museums and Galleries: Bring a camera and a sketchbook (or blank index cards) to collect items from artwork. Choose a detail section or the entire piece. Make sure you have permission to photograph the work, or draw a quick sketch.

**Figure 2.5
The idea
notebook.**

9. Collect: Old photographs, postcards, objects, or other materials from anywhere, including thrift or second-hand stores. Again, take photos or sketch ideas if you cannot possess the actual item.

10. Carry: Always carry a pen and a notebook or blank index cards to jot down anything that comes to mind.

For a current project, simply peruse through the files or notebook for items that relate. For the initial project, treat gathering items as a brainstorm session. Set a time limit or number limit for each category and begin collecting.

# Developing Story Around: Genre

Within the narrative, there are many genres, which can significantly influence the story as it develops. However, choosing a genre presents the age-old dilemma of the chicken or the egg. Selecting a genre from the beginning will allow you to craft the story with specifics that directly relate to the genre. Writing a first draft of the story first, however, and then trying that story in several different genres can open other possibilities that have not been considered during the story development. Not all genres are suitable for a short story because of sheer length, but multiple subgenres or certain aspects of these genres are usually combined to form intriguing, stylized, and successful animated shorts. Some genres can be considered subgenres of another as well as its own category. Most animated feature films are a mixture of action, adventure, comedy, family, and fantasy.

Figure 2.6
Genres.

The following, while not an exhaustive list, are common contemporary narrative genres:

| Genre | Characteristics | Examples in Feature and Short Animation |
|---|---|---|
| Action | Fast-paced, high adrenaline, plenty of activity, effects and action | Most animated feature films |
| Adventure | Filled with the unknown and risk, seeks something out of the ordinary and full of danger | *Up* (2009) |
| Children/Family | Subgenres include almost any narrative genre that are considered family friendly (content devoid of nudity, sex, violence, horror, profanity, drug use, etc.) and are directed towards a young audience with a limited level of comprehension | Most Pixar and Disney animated feature films |
| Comedy/ Humor | Meant to make people laugh | Most animated feature films |
| Creative Non-Fiction | A true story told in a way that is captivating and vividly dramatic; the story is not embellished and facts are not made up | |
| Drama | Serious in nature, portraying realistic characters, settings, and events | *The Fox and the Hound* (1981) |
| Epic | Often historical, fantasy, religious, or western, the story covers an enormous span of time and is located in a vast, elaborate setting | *Epic* (2013) |
| Erotica | Situations that involve sexual relationships between the characters and are meant to arouse the audience | *Le Parfum de l'invisible* (1997) |
| Fables | Meant to teach a moral lesson; main characters are represented by animals or inanimate objects which take on human characteristics and abilities | *For the Birds* (2000), *La Luna* (2013) |
| Fan Fiction | Stories that use existing characters, settings, and/or events from a television series, movie, or book (note: this material violates copyright laws but is usually not pursued in court unless a profit is made) | *The Fastest and Funniest LEGO Star Wars Story Ever Told* (2010) |
| Fantasy | Settings in imaginary worlds and characters who possess magical powers; the laws of the created world must be defined and followed, but anything is possible | Most animated feature films |
| Folklore/ Folktale | Originally passed on from one generation to the next by word of mouth, these traditional stories were based on superstition that originated among the common people | *The Book of Life* (2014), *Corpse Bride* (2005) |
| Gothic | A combination of horror and romance, set in locations such as castles; terrifying experiences with very powerful males that rescue females | *Hotel Transylvania* (2002) |
| Historical/ Period | Set in the past or during a particular time period and characterized by imaginative creation of historical events; mixes details of reality with completely created events and/or characters | *The Good Dinosaur* (2015) |
| Horror | Meant to frighten the audience using common fears to create an eerie atmosphere and build suspense | *Monster House* (2006) |
| Inspirational | Meant to inspire the audience to think, feel, or act in a new way | *Up* (2009) |
| Legend | A larger-than-life, historically based story that is regarded as true, but not verifiable; a story based on factual people, places, or events that has been elaborated upon for interest and impact | *Pocahontas* (1995) |

| Genre | Characteristics | Examples in Feature and Short Animation |
|---|---|---|
| Musical | Uses songs and choreographed dance to deliver essential parts of the story | *Lion King* (1994), *Frozen* (2013), *Nightmare Before Christmas* (1993) |
| Mystery | Focuses on investigating and solving a crime, it is imperative that clues are planted along the way to answer questions; the main question is "whodunit?" | |
| Mythology | A story that may or may not be true, linked to the religion of a particular people (Egyptians, Greeks, Romans, Native Americans) that is used to teach morals or explain the world and the experiences of man; characters, settings, and events involve supernatural deities and creatures | *Hercules* (1997) |
| Suspense | The audience is aware of things that the protagonist does not know | *Triplets of Belleville* (2003) |
| Thriller | The protagonist is in danger from the beginning and the audience figures things out as the protagonist does | *Cars 2* (2011) |
| Parables | Meant to teach a moral or spiritual lesson by example; similar to a fable, but uses human characters | *Veggie Tales* (1993) |
| Political | Within the context of a story, makes a statement about a social or political view, supporting or criticizing it | *South Park* (1997–present) |
| Persuasive | Using story to convince the audience to support a certain belief or idea, often used to sell a product | Public service announcements or commercials |
| Religious | Stories found in religious texts or themed around a religious holiday | *The Little Drummer Boy* (1968) |
| Romance/ Romantic Comedy | A love story in which two characters meet and fall in love, full of passion and against all odds; can be combined with any other genre | *Shrek* (2001) |
| Science Fiction | A story created around futuristic science and technologies such as space travel, time travel, extraterrestrial life, or parallel universes; the laws of the created world must be defined and followed, but anything is possible | *Mr. Peabody & Sherman* (2014), *WALL-E* (2008) |
| Silent Film | Stories using mime, gestures, and title cards to express dialogue and narrate story points; only live music and sound effects were performed during the screenings, but contemporary homages use recorded sound as an underlying soundtrack | *Gertie the Dinosaur* (1914) |
| Sport | Stories that focus on a competitive sporting event or that are set in a sporting venue, such as an arena, stadium, or field; usually focus on the training and rise of a character in a single sport (underdog genre) | *Everyone's Hero* (2006), *Cars* (2006) |
| Surreal | A story that is very strange, unusual, or unbelievable, or has the quality of a dream | *Yellow Submarine* (1968) |
| War | Stories that use combat or military conflict as the main background for the events that occur | *Valiant* (2005) |
| Western | Stories set in the American Old West of the nineteenth century; themes of honor, redemption, revenge, and finding identity | *Fievel Goes West* (1991), *Rango* (2011) |

# Developing Story Around: Theme

A theme is the central idea or message of the story. It's not only the subject of the story, but it is also the predicate. For example, love (subject) conquers all (predicate). A theme may be a lesson, but it does not have to be. Stories may have more than one theme, and the longer the story, the more themes it may have. The interpretation of the theme by the audience is subjective. The audience may see something in a story that wasn't necessarily intended.

Like genre, choosing a theme also brings the chicken or the egg scenario. Selecting a theme from the beginning will allow you to craft the story with specifics that directly relate to the theme. Writing a first draft of the story first, however, and then allowing the theme to evolve can open other possibilities that have not been considered during the initial story development. These possibilities can be added during the necessary rewrites.

To identify a theme of any story, think about a single word that can summarize the entire story. This is usually the subject. Then expand that word into a message. For example, the theme for *Partly Cloudy*: friends (subject) sometimes inadvertently hurt us (predicate).

There is an infinite amount of themes, but here are the themes from some of the Pixar shorts to get you started:

- *Geri's Game*: Imagination (subject) is needed in order to triumph, no matter how old you are (predicate).
- *For the Birds*: He who laughs last (subject) laughs longest and loudest (predicate).
- *Boundin'*: When life gets you down (subject), just rebound (predicate).
- *One Man Band*: Greed (subject) gets you nowhere (predicate).
- *Presto*: Cooperation (subject) leads to success (predicate).
- *Day & Night*: Our differences (subject) should be respected and celebrated (predicate), and we are usually more alike (subject) than we care to admit (predicate).
- *La Luna*: Dare (subject) to be your own person (predicate).
- *The Blue Umbrella*: Love (subject) will find a way (predicate).

The following, while not exhaustive, is a list of common subjects that can begin the theme. Don't forget to add the predicate. A subject alone is not a theme, it is a topic.

| | |
|---|---|
| alienation | language |
| anger | literature |
| beauty | loss |
| bullying | loyalty |
| catastrophe | manipulation |
| chaos | memory |
| chase | money |
| circle of life | motherhood |
| communication | nature |
| companionship | oppression |
| conspiracy | parenthood |
| corruption | persecution |
| crime | plans |
| customs | power |
| darkness | prejudice |
| deception | progress |
| desire | race |
| difference | reality |
| discrimination | rebirth |
| displacement | rejection |
| doubt | religion |
| dreams | responsibility |
| education | secrecy |
| emptiness | self-awareness |
| evil | self-reliance |
| failure | sexuality |
| faith | simplicity |
| fate | society |
| forgiveness | stages of life |
| freedom | struggle |
| fulfillment | suffering |
| greed | supernatural |
| growing up | suspicion |
| happiness | temptation |
| hazards | the present |
| heroism | traditions |
| home | trust |
| hope | vanity |
| identity | vision |
| illusion | war |
| individual | will |
| injustice | women's issues |
| intolerance | work |
| jealousy | youth |

**Figure 2.7**
A still image from the short film *Celestial* (2014), when Gan Vogh is forced by Titan to look differently at the planets he is destroying (timecode 04:36–05:18). Courtesy of the University of Central Florida Character Animation Specialization.

If you are still having trouble identifying a theme, they can easily be found within inspirational quotes. One of the themes for the short film *Celestial*, for example, is found in this quote by Wayne Dyer:

"When you change the way you look at things, the things you look at change."

# Developing Story Around: Characters

Many times it is best to come up with the protagonist or antagonist first and build the story around those characters. Maybe you have collected an image of a person who sparks a story idea, or perhaps you have met someone who would make a great character for a story. Maybe an idea comes from the experiences of a person, or something that they want to learn. These images and notations should be kept in your idea file or notebook as you come across them, and can be drawn upon when trying to develop your story idea.

Other times, you will have a general story idea and will be searching for the best characters to fit into the plot. Whichever approach you decide to use, always rewrite the story or different scenes from the viewpoint of different characters. Doing so opens possibilities to see the story from different perspectives and usually reveals character personalities that were not apparent during the first draft. Sometimes changing character perspective creates a much more interesting story.

A character is a person in a story. In an animated story, a character can also be anthropomorphized, that is, an animal or inanimate object that takes on the characteristics of a human being. As the story unfolds, the personalities of the characters are revealed through their thoughts, words, and actions. In an animated story, the audience must see the personality of the character through his or her actions, especially if dialogue or a voice-over narrative is not used. Behavior, as well as his or her effect on other characters, can help expose a character's personality traits throughout the story. In addition, how a character is physically represented can also reinforce his or her personality. Examples of this would be Donkey in *Shrek* and Randall in *Monsters, Inc.*

There are two basic characters that are necessary for a short story: a protagonist and an antagonist. That's it, and they can even be the same character.

A protagonist is the main character in the story. He or she is the hero or heroine who is

Figure 2.8
Character
archetypes.

confronted with a problem or desires to achieve a goal. The protagonist is not always an admirable character (i.e., an anti-hero).

An antagonist, however, does not need to be a character. The antagonist represents the problem the hero wants to solve or a character that gets in the way of the protagonist achieving his or her goal. Additional characters in a short story are usually flat and treated more like props than characters. For a variation, however, you can also have multiple protagonists, multiple antagonists, or characters that switch roles.

For example, in Pixar's *One Man Band*, there are three characters: the little girl, the one-man band Bass, and the one-man band Treble. It can be argued that any of the three are the protagonist or the antagonist. The little girl wants to place her coins in the fountain, but the one-man band competition prevents her from achieving her goal. Each of the one-man band characters want a coin from the little girl, but the other prevents her from giving her coin away. This is one example of what makes Pixar storytelling so brilliant. They are not afraid to break "the rules."

As mentioned in Chapter 1, Swiss psychiatrist Carl Jung identified the many character archetypes that are present in myths and dreams throughout all times and cultures. In the book *The Writer's Journey*, author Christopher Vogler builds off of Joseph Campbell's writings in that there are seven archetypes that occur most frequently in stories: Hero, Mentor, Threshold Guardian, Herald, Shapeshifter, Shadow, Ally, and Trickster.

Hero: The Hero is the protagonist and the main or central character to the story, whose dramatic function is to be a window through which the audience sees the story. This character or characters must be relatable because the audience must be able to identify and care about the Hero. The Hero must be universal, possessing some admirable qualities, common emotions, as well as flaws that are shared by the audience. The Hero must grow and change by the end of the story. There are two categories of heroes: willing (active and brave) and unwilling (passive and doubtful), and there are many varieties that can be combined with other archetypes. Gus from *Partly Cloudy*, Treble and Bass from *One Man Band*, and Alec Azam from *Presto* are all examples of heroes in Pixar's short films.

**Figure 2.9 Hero character Namid.** Concept drawings by Kelly Herbut for the short film in development, *Dreamweaver* (2015). Courtesy of the University of Central Florida Character Animation Specialization.

Mentor: Also known by Joseph Campbell as the Wise Old Man or Woman, the Mentor provides training, teaching, and help to the hero, usually giving a gift of supernatural abilities to assist along the journey. In Pixar's *Boundin'*, the jackalope acts as the Mentor for the little sheep.

**Figure 2.10**
**Mentor character Kaashi.** Concept drawings by Grace Cusimano, Kelly Herbut, and Erica Johnson for the short film *Dreamweaver* (2015). Courtesy of the University of Central Florida Character Animation Specialization.

Threshold Guardian: A Threshold Guardian is a minor antagonist that is symbiotic with the Villain and provides the first conflict, which tests the Hero's willingness and skill. Tippy, in Pixar's *One Man Band*, acts as Threshold Guardian.

Herald: Heralds provide a challenge, make an announcement, deliver a message, or provide motivation for the Hero. Heralds may be a person or a force of nature, and can be positive, negative, or neutral. In Pixar's *Presto*, a simple knock at the door acts as the Herald.

**Figure 2.11**
**Threshold Guardian/Trickster character Kaimana.** Concept drawings by Jenin Mohammed for the short film *Cuddle Fish* (2016). Courtesy of the University of Central Florida Character Animation Specialization.

**Figure 2.12**
**Herald/Ally character Good Dreams.** Concept drawings by Katherine Ryschkewitsch for the short film *Dreamweaver* (2015). Courtesy of the University of Central Florida Character Animation Specialization.

Shapeshifter: The Shapeshifter changes appearance or mood and may mislead the Hero, bringing doubt or suspense to the story. Usually a romantic interest or ally, their personality is two-faced and their loyalty is questionable. In Pixar's *Partly Cloudy*, the stork character, Peck, shows qualities of Shapeshifter when his attention is taken by another cloud early in the story and when he flies off to meet up with that cloud later.

Shadow: The Shadow is the antagonist of the story. They can be the Villain or Enemy of the Hero (or even a force of nature) but can also be an ally after the same goal. The Shadow's purpose is to challenge the Hero by creating conflict, and in turn bring out the best in the Hero by forcing the Hero to rise to the challenge in a life-threatening moment. The best Shadows are not completely evil or wicked, but also show a touch of goodness or some admirable quality, which can make them vulnerable, as well as make them a more rounded character. Since the Antagonist usually acts as a mirror of the Protagonist, time must be spent revealing the Villain so that the Hero is not flat. Often it is said that a story is only as good as its Villain, because the Villain can easily be the most interesting character of them all. In Pixar's *Day and Night*, both Day and Night are shadows of each other, as they both create conflict in the other and they both mirror each other.

**Figure 2.13**
**Shapeshifter character Keala.** Concept drawing by Jenin Mohammed for the short film *Cuddle Fish* (2016). Courtesy of the University of Central Florida Character Animation Specialization.

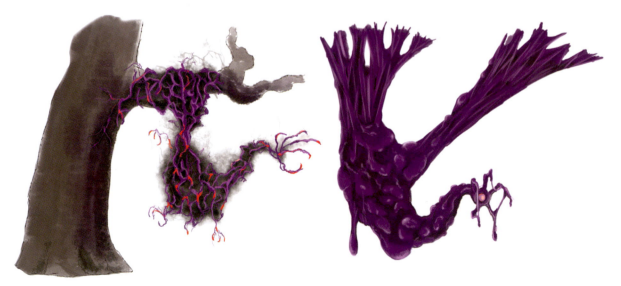

**Figure 2.14**
**Shadow character Nightmare.** Concept drawings by Erich Schulz for the short film *Dreamweaver* (2015). Courtesy of the University of Central Florida Character Animation Specialization.

Ally: The Ally is the sidekick who advises, fights alongside, and sometimes challenges the Hero. The Ally serves a necessary function such as companion, conscience, or comic relief, and can be used to advance the plot. The Ally can be utilized by the Hero as a scout, messenger, or errand boy. In Pixar's *Partly Cloudy*, the stork, Peck, serves the cloud, Gus, as his Ally to deliver the babies to their parents.

Trickster: The Trickster is the clown or comic relief of the story. In stories that are extremely serious, suspenseful, or tense, the Trickster is necessary to revive an audience's interest with moments of laughter.

Vogler uses these archetypes to describe both male and female characters. He writes that once he identifies a character's archetype in a story, he expects him or her to remain that archetype. However, after working as a story consultant for Disney Animation, he "encountered another way of looking at the archetypes—not as rigid character roles but as functions performed temporarily by characters to achieve certain effects in a story." This way of looking at the archetypes allows flexible character roles. This is especially important in short stories, as it permits one character to temporarily manifest characteristics, as they are needed, to advance the story. These character archetypes are integral in feature length films and not truly necessary to the animated short.

Vogler also looks another way at the archetypes, as different aspects of the Hero's personality that are brought forth from encounters with other characters she meets as the story progresses. The Hero learns something from every character she meets, gathering traits and energy to grow into a complete human being by the end of her journey.

Now that we understand the major archetypes of characters and their purposes in the story, we can begin to think about different types of characters. The following, while not an exhaustive list, are common types and stereotypes of characters and can be used as starting points to spark story ideas:

| | | | |
|---|---|---|---|
| absent-minded professor | feral child | maverick cop | straight talkin' lawman |
| action hero | friend of all people | mercenary | stupid orc |
| alien invaders | gentle giant | monster | super villain |
| angry male | gentleman thief | new kid | superhero |
| barbarian | girl next door | noble savage | swashbuckler |
| believer | grande dame | officer fresh from the | the chosen one |
| black knight | grumpy warrior | academy | tortured artist |
| boastful soldier | hardboiled detective | paladin | town drunk |
| boy next door | hero | petrushka | tragic hero |
| broker | hotshot | princess | treasure guardian |
| brute | hustler | professor | tycoon |
| cat lady | ingénue | pseudo-evil witch | urban villain |
| conspiracy theorist | jive-talking wizard | redeemed hero | village idiot |
| crone | joker/jester | roommate | vixen |
| dark lady | knight | school girl | wise fool |
| elderly martial arts master | lone vigilante | secret identity | yokel |
| everyman | lost love | shoulder angel | zombie |
| fall guy | lovers | sidekick | |
| farmer's daughter | machismo man | spear carrier | |
| father figure | mama's boy | spoiled child | |

# Developing Story Around: Locations

Sometimes stories can be created around a location. Whether it is a place you have been in reality or your dreams, locations can be the foundation of great stories. The location can be any size, from a planet to a country, from a city to a building, from a house to a cookie jar. Perhaps it is the inside of a fish tank or a town where everyone who lives there are clowns. Describe the details of this place. How does it look? What are the colors? Are there any smells? How do you feel when you are there? Think about the objects within the space. Take photos everywhere you go. Again, collected images and notations of interesting locations should be kept in your idea file or notebook as you come across them and can be drawn upon when trying to develop your story idea.

Below are some images I took of a farmhouse that I drove past one day. I turned the car around and stopped to take these images. I could just imagine the story of the farmer who lived there and the family that sat on that huge porch looking over the sea of cotton, not to mention the creatures that lived in those fields.

**Figure 2.15**
Cotton fields in Georgia, USA, 2008.

**Figure 2.16**
Farmhouse porch in Georgia, USA, 2008.

**Figure 2.17**
Cotton in Georgia, USA, 2008.

The following, while not an exhaustive list, are common locations that can help you get started:

abbey
adult bookstore
air force base
airport
alien planet
alligator farm
ancient pyramid
Angkor Wat, Cambodia
animal shelter
apothecary's shop
archaeological dig
art museum
artist colony
auto wrecking yard
bank
barn
beach
bed and breakfast
blood bank
botanical garden
boutique
bowling alley
Buddhist temple
cabin
casino
cave (bat, collapsed, crystal)
cheap hotel
Chinatown (any city)
city dump
city rooftop(s)

city street
coal mine
coffee house
colony world
concert hall
corporate board room
dance club
day care center
delicatessen
discount store
dome city
dungeon
elementary school
farmhouse
fishing boat
forbidden city
freighter ship
garden
ghetto
golf course
Grand Canyon
graveyard
greenhouse
grocery store
haunted house
hermit's cave
Hollywood
hospital
house of ill repute
hyperspace
inhospitable planet

insectarium
jazz club
junior high school
Kashmir valley
lighthouse
Machu Picchu
magic shop
market
middle school
monastery
motel
museum
newspaper office
nunnery
ocean liner
opera house
palace
parking lot
pet grooming salon
pet store
pharmacy
planetarium
police station
Potala Palace, Tibet
previously undiscovered Island
priory
prison
pyramids of Giza and great Sphinx
radio station

rainforest
restaurant
roadkill pickup truck
ruins
salt mine
schoolroom
Serengeti
sewer
shoe store
shrine
small town
sparsely populated planet
stadium
starship
steamship (or boat)
swamp
tattoo parlor
theater
tower
train station
treehouse
TV station
underwater dome
university
Venice (canals)
walled town
windmill
winery
YMCA
zoo

# Developing Story Around: Events

An event is something important that happens. A significant event that turns the story into a new direction is known as a plot point. Events in stories have a cause-and-effect relationship and in turn, build the plot and should influence later events (these are called causal events).[2] Causal events build tension because they either contain conflict or occur as the protagonist attempts to solve a problem or achieve a goal and fails. All causal events that occur in a short story must build in intensity as the story progresses and eventually lead to the climax. If an event does not increase in intensity from the previous event, then it is not a necessary part of the short story.

Events can be created related to a specific genre or theme. If you have chosen the genre, then think about the events that go along with that genre. Always be on the alert for interesting news stories and events from your life. Daydream. Imagine. Wonder.

As events are established in the story, be sure to include each character's struggle. There are two categories of conflict possible:

1. External Conflict
   a. Character vs. Another Character: A struggle with a character who is an opposing force, such as a villain, enemy, or competitor. The two musicians in Pixar's *One Man Band* have a competition going throughout the story as to who is the better musician.
   b. Character vs. Society: A struggle with the confrontation or attempt to overcome laws, traditions, and/or institutions of a culture or civilization. In Pixar's *Your Friend the Rat*, Remy and Emile argue that rats contribute to human society and therefore are valuable.
   c. Character vs. Nature: A struggle with Mother Nature, such as animals or natural hazards (earthquakes, volcanoes, tornadoes, etc.). In Pixar's *The Blue Umbrella*, the weather interferes with the umbrella owner's descent into the subway. What appears as conflict actually aids in steering the blue umbrella towards the resolution of the story.
   d. Character vs. Supernatural: A struggle with fate, the gods, or supernatural forces. An example would be *Alma*, when the little girl encounters an inexplicable self-transformation.
   e. Character vs. Technology: A struggle with the attempts of computers, artificial intelligence, or machines taking over. An example would be in Pixar's *WALL-E*, when the captain must fight Auto to regain control of the ship.
2. Internal Conflict
   a. Character vs. Self: A struggle in the mind; emotions, prejudices, doubts, beliefs, or flaws—both physical and emotional. The little girl in Pixar's *One Man Band* has an emotional internal struggle with herself throughout the story, trying to decide what to do with her coin.

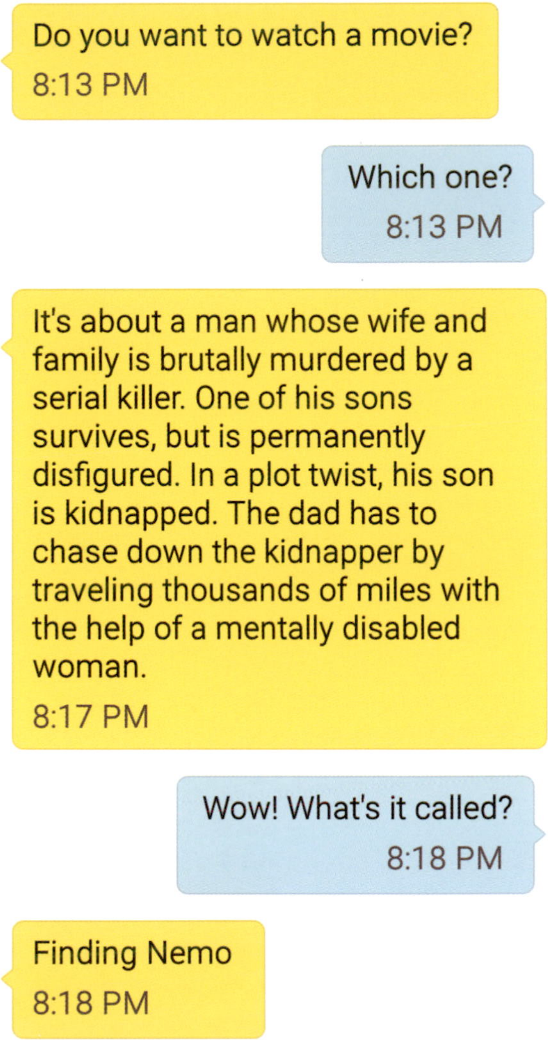

> Do you want to watch a movie?
> 8:13 PM

> Which one?
> 8:13 PM

> It's about a man whose wife and family is brutally murdered by a serial killer. One of his sons survives, but is permanently disfigured. In a plot twist, his son is kidnapped. The dad has to chase down the kidnapper by traveling thousands of miles with the help of a mentally disabled woman.
> 8:17 PM

> Wow! What's it called?
> 8:18 PM

> Finding Nemo
> 8:18 PM

**Figure 2.18**
Re-created internet meme stating events of the Pixar film *Finding Nemo*.

The following, while not an exhaustive list, are common major life events that can help you get started:

acquiring a visible deformity
addition of someone to family
becoming a full-fledged member of a church
beginning or end of school
being a senior in high school
breaking up with boyfriend or girlfriend
business readjustment
change in acceptance by peers
change in eating habits
change in frequency of arguments
change in living conditions
change in parent's financial status
change in residence
change in schools
change in social activities
change to different line of work
childhood fears
death of a brother or sister
death of a close friend
death of parent
decrease in arguments with parents
dismissal from work

divorce
exploring a hobby
family reunions
foreclosure of mortgage or loan
getting married
having a visible congenital deformity
hospitalization of a sibling
increase in arguments between parents
jail sentence of parent
loss of job by parent
marital separation
marital separation of parents
marriage of parent to stepparent
minor violation of law
outstanding personal achievement
personal injury or illness
retirement
serious illness requiring hospitalization
spouse starts or stops work
trouble with boss
unplanned pregnancy

# Developing Story Around: Music

Story ideas can be developed around music. Whether it is an existing lyrical song that has a great narrative or an instrumental piece, music can be a great inspirational source for atmosphere, mood, or story. In most animated shorts, the music is created after production is complete or in tandem at various points of production. However, it can be beneficial to create the music before the process begins.

In Pixar's short film *Boundin'*, Bud Luckey had already begun shaping the song before the idea had been pitched. He created a scratch track by playing the banjo and then laid out the storyboards into the story reel.[3] Another example of a story idea developed around music is the animation created by Ryan Woodward entitled *Thought of You* to the song "World Spins Madly On" by the Weepies. The idea for his short film was inspired during a plane flight as he listened to the song.[4]

Remember, if you choose to use music, you must get the correct permissions from the composer and/or musician, record label, or publishing company.

After following the suggestions given in this chapter, hopefully you have generated some ideas worthy of pursuit and development. The next chapter will take a look at possible complications you may encounter along the way.

**Figure 2.19**
**University of Central Florida Character Animation students created a short film around music composed by Dr.** Stella Sung and performed by the Milwaukee Youth Symphony Orchestra for *Atlas' Revenge* (2009). Courtesy of the University of Central Florida Character Animation Specialization.

## Bibliography and Further Reading

Desowitz, B. (2004). *A Pixar vet gets directing shot with "Boundin'" short*. Retrieved from https://www.awn.com/vfxworld/pixar-vet-gets-directing-shot-boundin-short.

Forster, E. M. (1956). *Aspects of a novel*. New York: Mariner Books.

Vogler, C., & Montez, M. (2007). *The writer's journey: mythic structure for writers*. Studio City: Michael Wiese.

Wood, M. (2004). *The pocket muse: ideas & inspirations for writing*. Cincinnati, OH: Writers Digest.

Woodward, R. (2010). *Ryan Woodward: Art & animation*. Retrieved from http://ryanwoodwardart.com/my-works/thought-of-you/.

Young, J. W. (2012). *A technique for producing ideas: The simple five-step formula anyone can use to be more creative in business and in life!* Charleston, SC: CreateSpace Independent Publishing Platform.

## Resources

Brainstorm and mindmap online. (2018). Retrieved from https://bubbl.us/.

Heffner, J. (2018). *Story starters*. Retrieved from http://thestorystarter.com/.

Internet Archive: Wayback Machine. (2018). Retrieved from http://archive.org/web/.

XMind: The Most Popular Mind Mapping Software on the Planet. (2018). Retrieved from http://www.xmind.net/.

## Notes

1. This can also be referred to as "lather, rinse, repeat," a popular idiom of the directions found on a bottle of shampoo that create an endless loop of the same steps until one runs out of the shampoo.
2. Forster, E. M., (1956). *Aspects of a novel*. New York: Mariner Books.
3. Desowitz, B. (2004). *A Pixar vet gets directing shot with "Boundin'" short*. Retrieved from https://www.awn.com/vfxworld/pixar-vet-gets-directing-shot-boundin-short.
4. Woodward, R. (2010). *Ryan Woodward: Art & animation*. Retrieved from http://ryanwoodwardart.com/my-works/thought-of-you/.

# Creative Obstacles

The path between getting an idea and producing the end product can be a long and winding one. There are many books and discussions available about idea generation, but very few when it comes to idea execution. Many obstacles can get in the way, but they can be summed up into three categories: money, time, or other excuses, mainly fears and distractions. This chapter will explore all of these obstacles and give ideas on how to overcome them.

# Money

Money is an obstacle for any project, and it always seems like there is never enough available. Because of this, it is imperative that the project is planned as thoroughly as possible. Planning well will reduce costs and the time needed to complete the project. Most animated short films are self-financed, unless you pitch your idea to a large studio (after working there for years) and it gets picked up for the next short film production. Raising money for the budget is always difficult but can be accomplished more easily using crowdfunding and fundraising websites such as GoFundMe, Kickstarter, or Indiegogo. Creating a short, animated film can be a huge financial undertaking. Many people go to school or back to school to create because of the available resources, but then the cost of the classes and living expenses while studying must also be considered.

When creating your budget, be sure to take the following into consideration:

- Computer hardware
- Software
- Ergonomic furniture
- Materials and supplies (if creating stop-motion or traditional animation)
- Learning
- Additional help
- Time
- Percentages for crowdfunding website and incentive costs, shipping, and packaging
- DVDs/BluRays
- Film festival submission fees

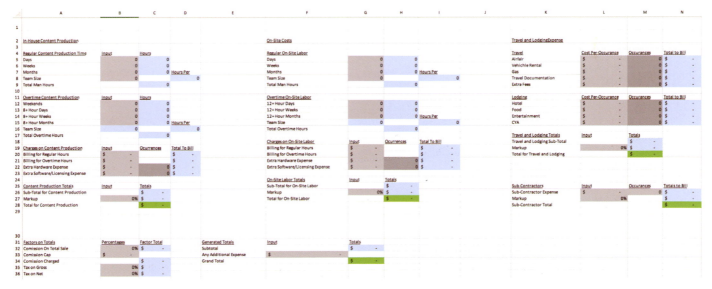

**Figure 3.1**
**Sample project budget spreadsheet.** Courtesy of Heather Knott of Ninjaneer Studios, 2016.

# Time

Like money, time is an obstacle because there is never enough of it. Unlike money, however, there usually is not a way to get any more time, unless you postpone a deadline. Complexity of story and style as well as your skill level are elements that will help determine how long it will take to complete a project. In addition, outside factors also play a part in making progression towards your goal. Learning how to budget and manage time effectively is the best way to move forward on any project.

## Complexity of Story

One must consider how much time will be needed to complete production. More often, the time frame is given and you must complete the project within the allotted time. Every animated story takes time to create. Stories that are more complex with many characters, environments, and other elements, such as realism or creating a specific artistic style, will take longer to produce. Because of this, it is important to remember what was established in Chapter 1: Every element used in the animated short story should drive the story forward. Everything must have a purpose. Limiting the elements will force more creativity during story development. Characters and settings can play multiple roles, allowing for the less-is-more approach. Consider your medium as well. All types of animation take time, whether it's hand drawn, clay, found object, or computer generated. Knowing where you can reduce elements makes the final product easier to complete while also challenging creativity and problem-solving skills. A great example of this is Pixar's short film *Geri's Game*. With only one character and one environment, we are drawn into the competitiveness and trickiness of Geri's mind.

Breaking the elements of the story into time blocks can help you figure out how much time it will take to complete different elements of production. By keeping a work log you can use current schedules to predict future estimates. More information on production scheduling can be found in Chapter 9.

## Skill Level

Skill level is one of the many factors to consider when deciding on the time frame it takes to complete an asset, sculpture, or drawing. The more experience you have, the more efficient you can be and therefore the faster you will get. This generally is true, although, not always.

Here is an example of how long it takes a beginner to animate a first pass in 3D.

One major key pose per character usually takes around 20–45 minutes. If working on a 5-minute film, with approximately one keyframe every 6 frames, animating at 24 fps, on the low end it will take

> 20 minutes × 4 frames per second
>
> = 80 minutes × 60 seconds per minute
>
> = 4800 minutes × 5 total minutes
>
> = 24000 minutes / 60 minutes
>
> = 400 hours or 10, 40-hour work weeks!

Ten 40-hour work weeks, just to animate one character for a 5-minute film.

When asking industry professionals how long they are given to complete a task, the answer is always one day to several weeks, depending on the project, complexity, quality level, and due date. This is standard across all different animation techniques, whether it be stop motion, 2D, or 3D. There are many variables and factors to consider, so there really is no formulaic answer. It is imperative that you keep a log book so that over time you will know how to budget your time based on your abilities.

| 3D Basic Pipline | Estimated Hours | Actual Hours | Balance |
|---|---|---|---|
| **PreProduction** | | | |
| Script | 20 | 30 | -10 |
| Art Direction | 16 | 20 | -4 |
| Storyboards | 20 | 15 | 5 |
| Animatic | 10 | 12 | -2 |
| Rough SFX/Music | 15 | 8 | 7 |
| PreViz | 20 | 21 | -1 |
| Production Schedule | 5 | 2 | 3 |
| ReWrite | 10 | 0 | 10 |
| ReDesign | 10 | 0 | 10 |
| **Total** | 126 | 108 | 18 |

| Production | Estimated Hours | Actual Hours | Balance |
|---|---|---|---|
| Modeling | 8 | 16 | -8 |
| UV layout | 8 | 16 | -8 |
| Texturing | 8 | 16 | -8 |
| Rigging | 32 | 64 | -32 |
| Research and Development | 14 | 28 | -14 |
| Animation Pass 1 | 36 | 72 | -36 |
| 1st Rough Cut | 2 | 3 | -1 |
| Animation Pass 2 | 18 | 36 | -18 |
| 2nd Rough cut | 2 | 3 | -1 |
| Animation Pass 3 | 9 | 18 | -9 |
| 3rd Rough Cut | 2 | 3 | -1 |
| Lighting | 72 | 144 | -72 |
| FX | 72 | 144 | -72 |
| Rendering | 72 | 144 | -72 |
| Compositing | 9 | 18 | -9 |
| 4th Rough Cut | 2 | 3 | -1 |
| Lighting and FX Fixes | 36 | 72 | -36 |
| Final Cut | 2 | 3 | -1 |
| Sound Mix | 50 | 65 | -15 |
| Final Mix | 40 | 45 | -5 |
| Print | 8 | 12 | -4 |
| **Total** | 502 | 925 | -423 |
| Construction Hours | 56 | 112 | |
| Animation Hours | 69 | 135 | |
| Lighting/etc hours | 344 | 685 | |

**Daily log averager for work**

| Day | Hours |
|---|---|
| Monday | 6 |
| Tuesday | 6 |
| Weds | 6 |
| Thursday | 8 |
| Friday | 4 |
| Sat | 4 |
| Sun | 8 |
| Average hours | 6.00 |

**How to determine how much time you have**

| | |
|---|---|
| Exercise | 1 |
| Lunch | 0.5 |
| Work to pay bills | 4 |
| Dinner | 0.5 |
| Sports | 2.5 |
| Fun time | 0.5 |
| Sleep | 4 |
| Total for one day | 13 |

Your average daily hours to work 6.00
How many days a week you can work 7
Total hours per week 42

**Figure 3.2**
Sample production schedule spreadsheet. Courtesy of Jason Maurer, Teaching Faculty, College of Motion Picture Arts at Florida State University, 2016.

# Limiting Elements for Animation

The first thing that could be limited to help create a feasible story in a short amount of time is the number of characters in a story. One character is plenty, and two characters can be used if absolutely necessary. Regardless of the medium, the time it takes to design, create, and animate a single character depends on your capabilities, but more often than not, you may be unable to complete the creation of more than one character in the designated time frame. If a second character is needed, the same character can be used again with minor changes, such as a different color, a head replacement, a change in scale, or another gender. Other characters can be incorporated into the story as long as they are not seen. An example of this would be a second character that can be heard from off camera, or if the main character speaks to another character

without the audience ever seeing them. Two characters in a story are not necessarily better than one, but you might have more plot options with a second, or even a third.

Keep the character designs as simple and stylized as possible. Realism is difficult on short production schedules. The more realistic the design, the more time is needed for preproduction, production, and postproduction. Everything is more difficult to accomplish when you deal with realism. Besides, a great story and believable motion is much more important in an animated short than a realistic look. In fact, artistic stylism is applauded in every avenue. Get creative and use your imagination. Sticking with bipedal anamorphic characters is also a great rule of thumb. There are exceptions to that rule, but bipeds are easier to study, observe, and ultimately

**Figure 3.3**
Character description and design for Gus, *Yours, Mime, and Ours* (2014). Courtesy of the University of Central Florida Character Animation Specialization.

**Figure 3.4**
Character description and design for Marcy, *Yours, Mime, and Ours* (2014). Courtesy of the University of Central Florida Character Animation Specialization.

animate. After all, we are bipedal. Create character model rotation sheets and sculptural maquettes, which can be used as reference when creating storyboards and animating.

Likewise, limiting the environment to simplified interiors or exteriors with the addition of one or two props is essential when dealing with a short deadline. Creative approaches to keeping the environment simple can include two-dimensional background elements with three-dimensional foreground elements. More often, however, having only a couple of foreground elements will keep the focus of the audience on the character and the action that ensues. After all, the character and the story should be the focal point and not the environment. Valuable time and energy should be spent on story development and animating the character. The environment should support the actions of the character and not steal the show. The exception to this can be when the environment *is* the character. An example of this is Pixar's 2015 short *Lava*.

In addition to limiting what will need to be created and animated, simplifying texturing and color is also a time and money saver, regardless of the medium. In 2D, it reduces the time spent inking. In 3D, using colored shaders on everything or limiting texture maps saves valuable time, as it forgoes the need to layout UVs on polygons. Keeping the environment colors muted, monochromatic, or in shades of gray while having the characters reflect a brighter, more intense color palette will keep the audience's attention where it needs to be, regardless of the medium. Color harmony is extremely important in any animation. Keeping the final palette limited to no more than three or four harmonious colors takes less time to create in 2D, is less expensive in stop motion, and regardless of the medium, will ensure that the audience is not distracted by the chosen colors.

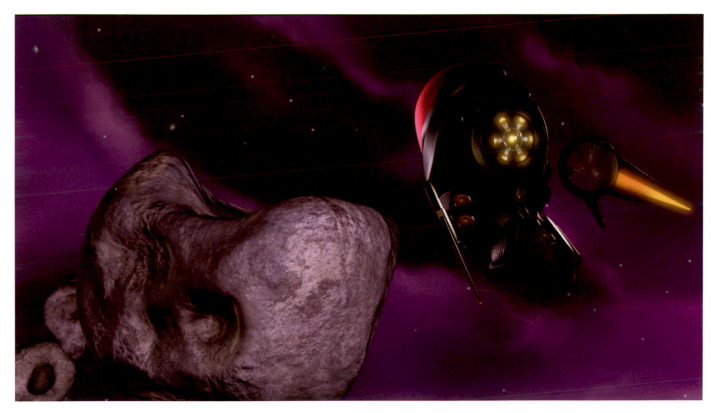

**Figure 3.5**
The simplified environment of *Celestial* (2014). Courtesy of the University of Central Florida Character Animation Specialization.

**Figure 3.6**
An example of a limited color palette.

As a 3D animator, if you already have an understanding of rigging, there are several tools available for speeding up the process of setting up the control rig for the characters that you create. Another idea is to take available free rigs from the internet and replace the model with your own. You should not use free rigs as they are for the main characters, because they are overused and seen too frequently, which lessons your chances of being accepted into film and animation festivals. Be sure to give end credits to the creator of the rig and try to alter the look using blendshapes to make it more personal. Creativity and self-expression is one of the key elements in creating a narrative short, which is much more difficult to do if everyone has seen the character model in many other animations.

In 3D and stop motion, lighting (and rendering in 3D) is always a time and technical challenge. Remember, the theme here is to keep it simple. Three-point lighting is usually sufficient. Be sure to add warmth to the key light and coolness to the fill light, which will provide an added dimension to the final render. In 3D, the addition of simulated global illumination, if time permits, will supplement the existing lighting. While rendering in separate passes may be a good idea for final manipulation of the finished look, it is not the simplified route. Do not be afraid to render in a single pass. Using command line rendering will free up valuable resources and allow multiple files to be listed in order to render sequentially and save time.

Do your research. Find creative ways to simplify your project and always remember to set realistic expectations. Cut corners when needed (also referred to as stylistic streamlining) and do not be afraid to refocus your efforts in order to complete the project.

## Time Management

Chapter 9 discusses production scheduling in detail, but it is important to mention here that even the most carefully planned schedule should be flexible enough to allow for unexpected issues that arise. This project may or may not have a solid deadline, such as in a client delivery date or a class assignment. Always specify a due date. Endlessly working towards perfection with no end in sight usually means that the project will never get completed. All projects need to be planned thoroughly in order to make progress toward completion in an organized and timely fashion.

As a creative person, our minds tend to constantly jump around from one idea to the next. Because of this, it is important to not only have a plan and a schedule for the overall project, but also one for daily, weekly, and monthly goals. The main element that I find the most useful is the

**Figure 3.7**
Logging everything you do in a day planner takes a little effort, but having a record of the time it takes to complete your work is helpful in the long run.

routine. Establishing a pattern for working helps keep focus on what is really important. Setting a daily and weekly routine will ensure that progress is made towards your goals. At the end of the day, however, Nike provides the best advice for time management: Just Do It!

There are plenty of books available for different productivity methods, but I have used the following methods to juggle everything related to a project:

- Calendar: A calendar is used to schedule due dates and time blocks to make progress towards project completion. A calendar is the first level of productivity organization because it allows you to step back and see the big picture in terms of time frame of completion. I use Google Calendar because it works with my email (I can easily add events from my email to the calendar) and sends email and text reminders. It also has a task list built in. You can create a project-specific Google account and calendar if you are working with a team, allowing for more efficient collaboration with the additional help of Google Hangouts.

- Trello (https://trello.com/): Trello is a free web-based collaboration tool that organizes your projects into boards, lists, and cards. Users can be assigned to cards, and cards can be dragged from one list to another. Cards can accept comments, attachments, due dates, and checklists. Trello supports most mobile platforms as well as web browsers. Trello is used as the second level of project organization because it allows the ability to break things down into lists: daily, weekly, and monthly routines as well as to-do, doing, and done.

- Pomodoro technique (http://pomodoro technique.com/): This is a pretty simple time management technique developed by Francesco Cirillo. The foundation of this technique is to break large tasks into smaller increments and use a timer to keep focus. Award yourself with mini-breaks to recharge your brain. During the break, you must completely refocus your thoughts away from the project. This gives your brain time to reboot, so to speak, and allows you to come back for the next segment recharged. Plenty of variations exist, but this one spells things out pretty clearly.

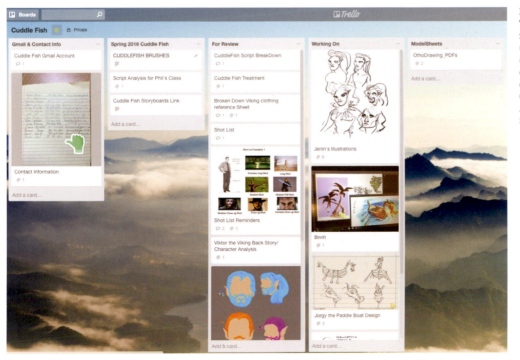

**Figure 3.8**
Trello board for short film *Cuddle Fish* (2016). Courtesy of the University of Central Florida Character Animation Specialization.

- The Pomodoro technique is used as the third level of productivity because it focuses on "doing" and not just creating lists. I use this process during each time block to complete tasks related to the current project, especially when having a difficult time getting work done.
  - Keep an inventory list of things to do.
  - The night before, choose three items on the list to complete the next day and place them on the daily activity sheet. Anything new that comes to mind gets placed on the bottom of the sheet to deal with at the end of the block. (I use Trello to keep track of my inventory list and activity sheet.)
  - Work in 25-minute "pomodoros" until the task is complete
  - Take a 5-minute "short break" in between each 25-minute "pomodoro."
  - After every 4 "pomodoros," take a longer 20-minute break as a reward.
  - Continue until the task is completed.
  - Use online timers to help you track your work. TomatoTimer (http://tomato-timer .com/) and Moosti (http://www.moosti .com) are two examples.

While it is imperative to manage your time in order to get work completed, it is also imperative to schedule other activities to keep the internal creative fuel burning and also enjoy life. By working these activities into your daily routine, you will always continue to grow and be inspired. Most of these are great to do during the "short break" if using the Pomodoro technique.

- Read: Reading books, newspapers, magazines, or websites on a regular basis helps keep you informed, reduces stress, improves your memory, provides entertainment, improves focus and concentration, and provides inspiration. Using a Kindle or a Nook ensures that reading material is always handy, especially if the app is on your phone. Audible (http:// www.audible.com) allows you to "read" while you are doing other things like driving, cleaning the house, and exercising.
- Log: Keep a record of your daily activities, how long it takes to complete tasks, and new ideas that come to mind. Add these to your idea notebook or create a journal for specific daily entries.
- Exercise: At a minimum, during each break, stand up and stretch to get blood flowing. Add a few jumping jacks or pushups on a regular basis and the benefits add up. Go for a 15 minute brisk walk after every meal. You will feel more alert and your body will stay flexible and strong.
- Clean: Regardless of whether you are home or at work, spend some time cleaning, decluttering, or organizing your space.
- Socialize: Spend a few minutes talking to a friend on the phone, write someone a letter, or meet somebody for lunch or coffee. Surround yourself with people who are like-minded but also spend time with people who are different.
- Nap: A short nap has been shown to boost productivity and improve focus. NASA research has created an app that optimizes the ability to nap for the perfect amount of time for a power nap (http://www.nap26.com).

**Figure 3.9**
The Pomodoro technique.

# Fear

Fear is certain, but it can be very dangerous. Everyone experiences some type of fear when beginning a new project, as well as during the project itself. We have a tendency to be harsh critics of our work and ourselves. Because of this, our negative thoughts infiltrate our daily lives and prevent us from making progress on our projects. Learning how to keep fears from paralyzing your actions is the key to overcoming them.

One of my favorite quotes about fear comes from the movie *After Earth*:

> Fear is not real. It is a product of thoughts you create. Do not misunderstand me. Danger is very real. But fear is a choice.

Fear is a choice. Overcoming a fear happens by meeting it head-on. First you have to identify what the fear actually is that is interfering with your progress. Then you have to overcome that fear.

## It's All Been Done Before

It has all been done before. Actually, this is probably true. Someone probably has done what you are about to do. The solution is to get a new idea. A new idea is simply the pairing of two or more things that have never been joined before. Put a new spin on an old idea and you have a new idea. I always laugh when critics and others say, "Well that was just a retelling of a story that has been done before." Of course it was! Every story has been told already. The key to crafting a new idea and a new story is to borrow the ingredients and come up with a new recipe.

During production you have the opportunity of re-creating an old story in a new way. *Avatar*, to many critics, borrows heavily from *Pocahontas*, *Fern Gully*, and *Dances with Wolves*, while adding a splash of *Aliens*. *Avatar* is mentioned here because amidst all the negative criticism out on the internet, this film was breathtakingly beautiful when seen as James Cameron envisioned it in an IMAX theater.[1] He took a well-known story about environmental conservation and added his own mark. Avatar took 15 years and more than 2,300 people to create, from original writing to the actual release of the film. Cameron chose to wait until the technology was able to properly create his vision before going into production, and he chose to work on other projects until this happened.

**Figure 3.10**
Negative thoughts that run through our heads.

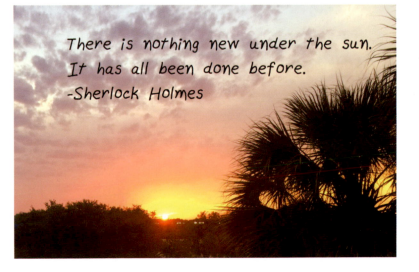

**Figure 3.11**
Nothing new under the sun.

## Self-Doubt: What I Create Won't Be Good

Being afraid that people, including yourself, will laugh at your project and criticize it for not being good enough can be debilitating. Whenever a creative person completes any project, and puts that project out into the public, it opens the doors to criticism, ridicule, and rejection. At the same time, however, the same project can create a connection with the audience that touches their hearts and their minds. The solutions for this fear is do it anyway. Make progress. Chip away at your production task list day after day until it is finished.

Going ahead and completing your project will provide you with a few things. First, you will have completed a project. Second, you will have gained experience. Third, you will soon realize that not everyone is as critical as you are. Fourth, you might be pleasantly surprised at the end result.

However, your finished project may not be the way you envisioned it. You may want to throw it out and start all over again. Send it to film festivals anyway. Put it in the public eye. This will lead to rejection, yes. But it may also lead to acceptance.

A film I completed, *Put to Rest*, was started in graduate school with the working title *Spinning Still*, and never sent out to festivals because I was not happy with the way it turned out. Thirteen years later, I finally revisited the project, but still was not happy with it. I sent it out anyway. It won an Audience Choice Award and has been accepted into three festivals to date. Of course, the rejection list is much longer, but the important message is that it has been accepted into festivals.

It is important to toughen up and get a thicker skin. Rejection is not personal. Rejection simply means that whomever is looking at your work does not connect with it for some reason. Perhaps your project does not meet the requirements for running time, subject matter, or style. Perhaps your project doesn't meet the quality level for that particular venue. Maybe your work truly is not "good enough" in the opinion of a certain juror for a festival. Do not take it personally. Keep applying to festivals, and begin work on your next project.

"To avoid criticism, do nothing, say nothing, be nothing."

Elbert Hubbard

# Distractions

While fear can definitely be an internal distraction, most other distractions are external: Demands from work, family, or friends can sidetrack even the most dedicated individual and sometimes even completely halt a project. Sometimes, simply changing your environment can help you regain focus and get away from external distractions. If you have a laptop, try going to a coffee shop, restaurant, library, hotel lobby, or park. Use noise-canceling headphones and listen to instrumental or ambient music to block out any sound in the environment. Physically getting away from familiar surroundings and people can help you stay on task and not get distracted.

Trying to balance working towards a project alongside a regular work schedule can be very difficult. If the project has a set deadline, the amount of time needed can be calculated to a certain degree, as mentioned earlier, so the amount of progress you need to make is set according to the schedule. However, if there is no hard deadline, it is important to make progress on a daily basis, no matter how small. Remember, all progress is progress. As we have learned from Aesop's fable of the *Tortoise and the Hare*, with steady progress you will eventually cross the finish line. This is where the timer comes into play. Make a pact with yourself to work for at least 15–30 minutes a day towards your project. On the weekends, alternate 15–30 minutes of work with the project and 15–30 minutes of family time, chores, or any other external distraction. You will be surprised at how much you can accomplish in such a short amount of time.

# Intended Audience

Disney's intended audience was not just children, but also the child within the adult. As Walt Disney said, "You're dead if you aim only for kids. Adults are only kids grown up, anyway."

From the beginning of your concept idea throughout the production pipeline, the intended audience should be considered. How you tell the story, and how you tell that story visually, will be affected by the intended audience. What is acceptable for one audience may not be acceptable for another and all of your hard work may end up, as it once was said, on the editing room floor. For example, the *Looney Tunes* series from the 1950s had to be edited because so many of the antagonists ultimately committed suicide and their intended audience was for children. The syndicated series has continued to be edited to remove the negative stereotypical portrayal of various races and ethnicities as well as the removal of characters doing dangerous stunts, smoking cigarettes, drinking alcohol, and popping pills. Knowing the parameters for your intended audience before you begin production, and keeping that in mind throughout, will save time, money, and creative heartache.

**Figure 3.12**
**Know who your intended audience is going to be.** Courtesy of the University of Central Florida Character Animation Specialization.

# Independent vs. Collaborative Filmmaking

Animated film creation can be divided into two categories: independent filmmaking, where one person creates every aspect of their animation or is responsible for finding additional help where necessary, and collaborative filmmaking, where a group of people work together as a production team to create an animated film. While there are definite advantages and disadvantages to both approaches, the disadvantages create additional obstacles to the creative process.

The clear disadvantage of individual projects is that they are smaller in production and scope. When making an independent film, a filmmaker works at his or her own level and is responsible for their own project, which can be as simple or as complex as they can manage. This can be a disadvantage, because one's artistic vision may be unattainable alone. The filmmaker must be keenly aware of their abilities and the feasibility of their projects. The main problems deal with concepts, stories that lack appeal or executions that lack quality. Individuals, however, are more self-directed than if they are working as part of a team, but this can be a frightening concept for some people. When working independently, it is a great idea to seek feedback from other filmmakers in order to obtain creative advice, rather than relying solely on self-critique. An individual can design their project so that it is directly geared to where they would like to enter the industry, if this is a desired goal.

If entering the animation industry is a desired goal, and since most studio productions are collaborative, it is a good idea for filmmakers to learn to network and assist one another. Working collaboratively is a way for filmmakers to get the experience of working as a team over the development of the project from start to finish. They get a thorough understanding of the dynamics of working as a team on a deadline. The biggest advantage of a collaborative project is that filmmakers can do more in a project. The film can be longer or have more characters, environments, or complexity. Many filmmakers also enjoy the ability to brainstorm ideas and work with others on a project. While all filmmakers should be able to understand the entire production pipeline, collaborative projects allow filmmakers to specialize. One filmmaker can lead in animation, while another might be the environment lead, etc.

The disadvantages that have surfaced during collaborations include inconsistencies with work ethic, abilities, and talent. Some filmmakers are aggressive when volunteering for workload, while others like to skim by with the minimum amount. This leads to a core group carrying the project forward. There are filmmakers who are eager but lack the talent and ability to meet the quality level; this results in inconsistencies throughout that must be refined by others. In school and in the studio, some links in the collaborative chain are stronger than others. It is important that each filmmaker be able to clearly define what they have done on a project for the credits and for their demo reel, for future projects and potential employment.

**Figure 3.13**
**Collaborative filmmaking.** Courtesy of the University of Central Florida Character Animation Specialization.

The use of both the independent and collaborative modes of working provides a wonderful opportunity to create a production. Filmmakers should regularly participate in critiques or problem solving of other projects in online forums. Each project has its own parameters, and like animation itself, there is no "one way" that works in all instances. Each area addresses a particular set of parameters. Collaboration and independent productions are equally important. Even when filmmakers are creating an individual project, a culture of collaboration exists if seeking feedback or help with resources and problems from others, or lending support to other's projects.

In conclusion, the many obstacles we encounter can never overpower our passion to pursue the development of an idea. We must tackle these challenges and overcome them. The next chapter will guide you through the steps to take and make this idea better as it evolves into a stronger, more solidified concept.

## Bibliography and Further Reading

Glei, J. K., Belsky, S., & Ariely, D. (2013). *Manage your day-to-day: Build your routine, find your focus, and sharpen your creative mind*. Las Vegas, NV: Amazon Publishing.

Keller, G., & Papasan, J. (2014). *The one thing: The surprisingly simple truth behind extraordinary results*. London: John Murray.

## Resources

Audible: Listening is the new reading. (2018). Retrieved from https://www.audible.com/.

Cirillo Consulting GmbH. (2018). The Pomodoro Technique®. Retrieved from https://francescocirillo.com/pages/pomodoro-technique.

Jung, E. (2018). Moosti. Retrieved from http://www.moosti.com/.

Nap26: Rest and rejuvenate in 26 minutes. (2018). Retrieved from http://www.nap26.com/.

TomatoTimer. (2018). Retrieved from https://tomato-timer.com/.

Trello. (2018). Retrieved from https://trello.com/.

## Note

1. I had the fortunate experience of watching *Avatar* at the Regal Pointe Imax in Orlando, Florida, which has a five-story-high 3D screen.

# 4

# Development of an Idea

Once an idea is identified as worthy of pursuit, the next step is to continue to evaluate the idea and explore all possibilities, critiquing, rewriting, revising, and refining until you either run out of money or run out of time. This process can take several weeks to several years, depending on the length of the story.

As Ed Catmull, president of Walt Disney and Pixar Animation Studios, states:

> Creativity has to start somewhere, and we are true believers in the power of bracing, candid feedback and the iterative process—reworking, reworking, and reworking again, until a flawed story finds its throughline or a hollow character finds its soul.[1]

Pixar has used the adage "story is king" as their guiding principle since their very beginning. The development of an idea at Pixar is protected by not forcing a timeline onto the story formation. In fact, Pixar does not move a project into production until the script is considered finished. However, throughout the production process, they remain open to candid critiques and make changes to the story when necessary. So, as you work through the following chapters and preproduction for your animation, remain open to changes. Keep making your idea better. Trust the process.

In the 1940s, Walt Disney coined the term "plussing." To him, the word "plus" was a verb. It meant tinkering with something and adding to it, to make it better and better, in order to deliver more than what is expected. It is not enough to have a great idea for your story. After writing a first draft or even settling on the final one, one must evaluate the idea, identify the weak areas, and add to it to make it better. Take the idea a step further. Then take it another step. This chapter explores how to start that process.

Figure 4.1
Story is king.

# Creating Interest, Setting Mood

"I've learned that people will forget what you said, people will forget what you did, but people will never forget how you made them feel."

Maya Angelou

The best way to create interest in a story is to develop an emotional connection from the characters to the audience. Walt Disney knew that emotional connection was the most important aspect of an animated story, because he knew that the emotional connection would draw an audience in.

> Walt was no cynical manipulator of other people's emotions. He didn't resort to trite formulas to wring an audience's tear ducts. He demanded that his films affect his emotions first, genuinely and deeply. He knew that if a scene made him laugh or cry, then his audience would be affected as well. "In everything he did," Roy O. Disney once said, "my brother had an intuitive way of reaching out and touching the hearts and minds of young and old alike."[2]

Pixar knows this as well, and they learned this from Disney. As John Lasseter said, "We make the kind of movies we want to see, we love to laugh, but I also believe what Walt Disney said 'for every laugh there should be a tear'. I love movies that make me cry, because they're tapping into a real emotion in me, and I always think afterwards 'how did they do that?'"

In addition to laughing and crying, Andrew Stanton identifies wonder and anticipation as two emotions that drive the story. In his TED talk, Stanton quotes William Archer in saying "Drama

**Figure 4.2**
**A great story should tap into real emotion.** The above image is from the animated short film *Heartstrings*, 2009. Image courtesy of Rhiannon Evans.

is anticipation mingled with uncertainty." He then goes on to ask the following:

> When you're telling a story, have you constructed anticipation? In the short term, have you made me want to know what will happen next? Have you made me want to know how it will all conclude in the long term? Have you constructed honest conflicts with truth that creates doubts in what the outcome might be?[3]

Stanton also goes on to say, "The magic ingredient in storytelling is: can you invoke wonder? The best stories infuse wonder." He should know. Stanton helped establish Pixar as one of the world's leading animation studios. He was writer and director for *A Bug's Life* (1998), *Finding Nemo* (2003), and *WALL-E* (2008). He also co-wrote all three *Toy Story* films and *Monsters, Inc.*

# Why Animation?

There needs to be a reason to animate your story. If nothing unusual is happening, then it can simply be created in live-action video. One of the easiest ways of ensuring there is a reason to animate a story is to make your characters anthropomorphic animals, giving them human forms and characteristics. More reasons to animate a story are when something happens within the story that is simply not possible in real life (like riding on a flying dragon, jumping into a portal, or using balloons to fly your house), or is too dangerous (like blowing up your character, falling off a cliff, or being rolled over by a car). Reasons are as follows:

- An artistic visual style of the finished film can also be a great reason to create the story as an animation.
- Sometimes, it can be less expensive to create something in animation than if it were created in real life.
- You can use camera motions that are impossible to create in the real world.
- You will have 100% control over what is happening visually.
- If your story occurs in a different time period or different world.
- If your story has impossible or imagined characters and locations.
- If you have a long-running show (like *The Simpsons*)—characters never age.
- For stunts that are too dangerous.
- If something happens within the story that is simply not possible in real life.

**Figure 4.3**
*Celestial* (2014) was a story perfect for animation because it is about a winged heavenly being named Gan Vogh, who creates planets and lives in a nebular cloud. Courtesy of the University of Central Florida Character Animation Specialization.

# Developing Character

In every story, the hero character has a problem to solve or a goal to achieve. The character's desire to solve their problem or achieve their goal is the driving force which causes them to go out into the world, which in turn, drives your story. In Chapter 2, we established that single character in a short animated film could assume various archetypal roles in order to keep the characters to a minimum. We also identified that characters can also be included and treated as props if essential to moving the story forward. It is also noteworthy to mention that to make a short story more intriguing, both the antagonist and the protagonist could have a problem to solve or a goal to achieve. Returning to Pixar's *Partly Cloudy*, the stork (Peck) had a problem to solve (how to deliver the babies without getting hurt) and the dark cloud (Gus) had a goal to achieve (creating dangerous baby animals for delivery).

In Pixar's *One Man Band*, the little girl wanted to put her coin in the fountain, while the performers (Treble and Bass) wanted to get the coin from the little girl. The number of characters in the story can establish the possible direction of the emotional graph.

## Creating Backstory

The backstory is a narrative history of events and circumstances that occurred before the story you are about to tell. The backstory (or parts thereof) is usually revealed selectively to the audience in order to make the narrative more believable, complex, or intriguing. However, many times, the backstory (or parts thereof) is not revealed at all to the audience. Instead, the backstory can be used as a device to give depth to the characters and help make the audiences care about the characters.

**Figure 4.4**
**Kaashi Maquette, Katherine Ryschkewitsch, *Dreamweaver* (2016).** Photo credit: Anthony Balinas. Courtesy of the University of Central Florida Character Animation Specialization.

Making the characters more emotionally appealing can be achieved by figuring out what drives them to act the way they do. What are their motivations? What is the character thinking? Why is the character acting this way? This is called the *character spine*.

As Andrew Stanton states:

> I took a seminar with an acting teacher named Judith Weston. I learned a key insight to character. She believed that all well-drawn characters have a spine, and the idea is that the character has an inner motor, a dominant, unconscious goal that they're striving for, an itch that they can't scratch.[4]

Stanton also points out, "These spines don't always drive you to make the best choices. Sometimes you can make some horrible choices because of them."

Stanton gives some examples of character spines in Pixar films:

| | |
|---|---|
| WALL-E | To find the beauty |
| Marli (*Finding Nemo*) | To prevent harm |
| Woody (*Toy Story*) | Do what was best for his child |

Other characters:

| | |
|---|---|
| Superman | Truth, justice, and the American way |
| Spiderman | With great power comes great responsibility |
| Ralph (*Wreck-It Ralph*) | To be a hero |
| Baymax (*Big Hero 6*) | To take care of people |

You can discover a character's spine by developing a good backstory and by getting into the minds of the characters. Get into character. Become the character. *Method acting*, which was developed by Konstantin Stanislavski, is used by actors to create lifelike performances and can also be used by storytellers to enhance the emotional reality of a character. A method actor will draw from life experiences, personal emotions, and memories in order to become their characters and make them believable. Careful consideration is given to the character's psychological motivations, identifying how

and why the character would act in different situations. Actors spend time "in character," going about their daily routines imagining as if they were that character, acting or responding to situations while always thinking and asking "How would this character respond and why?" so that later, on stage or in front of a camera, actions and reactions are more "honest" and real.

## Character Descriptions

In addition to the backstory, it is helpful to analyze the characters and create a detailed character description. Stereotypes are a great place to start. They are easily identifiable and do not need much explanation to an audience. While many preach on the "stay away from stereotypical characters!" bandwagon, the majority of successfully appealing and loveable animated characters are, in fact, based on a stereotype or the direct opposite of one. Even the unappealing characters are, too.

Some examples would be:

- Dory (*Finding Nemo*), the "ditzy blonde"
- The Mayor of Halloween Town (*Nightmare Before Christmas*), the "two-faced politician"
- Carl Fredricksen (*Up*), the "grumpy old man"

A character analysis includes both character traits (a character's behaviors, motivation, personality type, history, and relationships) and character description (age, gender, height, ethnicity, and other physical characteristics). All of the answers will impact how a character behaves and can give you clues to your character's spine.

You should ask not only questions like color, gender, and height, but also questions that answer background information, such as whether the character has brothers, sisters, or is an only child. How old is the character? Is he a child? Is she a teenager? Is he a parent? Are they androgynous? Schizophrenic? All of these answers have a huge impact on how the character behaves and will actually help you come up with ideas for how they look. It is really not important that your audience knows the answer to these questions. As an animator, however, the more you understand your character, the more believable your character will become. As you answer the questions in the next section, try to visualize your character. Keep a sketchbook handy and begin preliminary sketches.

## Analyze Your Character

On a sheet of paper, answer the following questions about your character. As you answer, begin to visualize and keep your sketchbook handy to draw preliminary sketches of ideas that come to mind. As your story develops, reconsider these categories (especially the morals and values) and figure out what drives the character; what exactly is their spine? You may also notice that the character spine usually aligns with one of the underlying themes of the story.

Character's Name:
Location
Address (where do they live? City, country):
Nationality (are they from a different planet?):
Driver's License?:
Vehicle Type (year, model, condition, special notes):
Socioeconomic Status
Education (degree, universities attended, Greek):
Current student?:
Criminal?:
Military Service:
Occupation:
    Skills:
    Trades:
Income:
Investments:
Debts:
Physical Characteristics
Age:
DOB:
Zodiac Sign:
Gender:
Height:
Weight:
Body Type and Shape (pear, column or rectangle, apple, hourglass, strawberry):
Facial Shape (oval, oblong, round, square, triangle, diamond, heart, rectangle):
Nose Size and Shape:
Ear Size:
Tail?:
Antennae?:
Posture:
Hair Color:

Hair Style/Length:
Facial Hair:
Eyes (color, glasses):
Shape of Eyes:
Shape of Mouth:
Skin Condition (color, acne, tattoo, piercing, scars, birthmarks):
Plastic Surgery:
Teeth (condition, braces, etc.):
Race:
Ethnicity:
Jewelry:
Distinguishing Features (big feet, big hands, big head):
Relationships
Relationship to Other Characters (antagonist, protagonist, etc.):
Sexual Orientation:
Relationship Status (single, married, divorced, living together, lives with roommate, commune, lives with parents, still a child, etc.):
Children (how many, how old):
Do Children Live with Character?:
Relationship with Children:
Siblings:
Likes and Dislikes
Food and Drink Preferences (vegan, vegetarian, carnivore, lactose intolerant, eats only junk food, drinks only local craft beers, etc.):
Pets (how many, type, sizes):
Hobbies:
Collections:
Political Affiliations:
Charities:
Sports Teams Fan:
Sports Team Player:
Clubs:
Psychological Makeup
Religion:
Phobias:
Neuroses:
Prejudices:
Bad Habits (smokes, chews, drugs, gambles, drinks, spits, etc.):
Good Habits (church goer, volunteer, etc.):
Values:

## Character Analysis: Viktor - The Sailor

Viktor is a young man, 23 years old, from coastal Scandinavia. He was born to a working class Viking family, who earned their living by herding red-cattle in the pastures of his native Norway. He is not a professional sailor, but left home to prove he could be something great.

Viktor has a stocky build, standing at 5'7" tall with broader shoulders, thick hairy muscular arms, and a firm and long torso. His legs are slightly thin and disproportionate to the rest of his body. Viktor's face is more square and bigger in proportion to the rest of his body. He has a slightly stubbled face and messy orange hair, which is mostly covered by a red bandana.

**Figure 4.5**
Character analysis description for Viktor, *Cuddle Fish* (2015). Courtesy of the University of Central Florida Character Animation Specialization.

## Character Analysis: Kaimana -  The Kraken

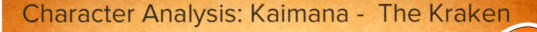

Kaimana has been alone in the sea for a long long time. A native of the seafloors of Greater Polynesia, his perspective on love has become distorted and now he'll take just about anything he can get. He enjoys deep sea diving and pulling ships to the crushing black depths.

He has a very elastic body. The character has 8 short tentacles and 2 very long ones with heart shaped tips at the bottom. Kaimana has a 4' body and his 2 long tentacles are 9ft making him a grand total of 13' long. He is also able to camouflage his colors and patterns to change based on his emotions.

**Figure 4.6**
Character analysis description for Kaimana, *Cuddle Fish* (2015). Courtesy of the University of Central Florida Character Animation Specialization.

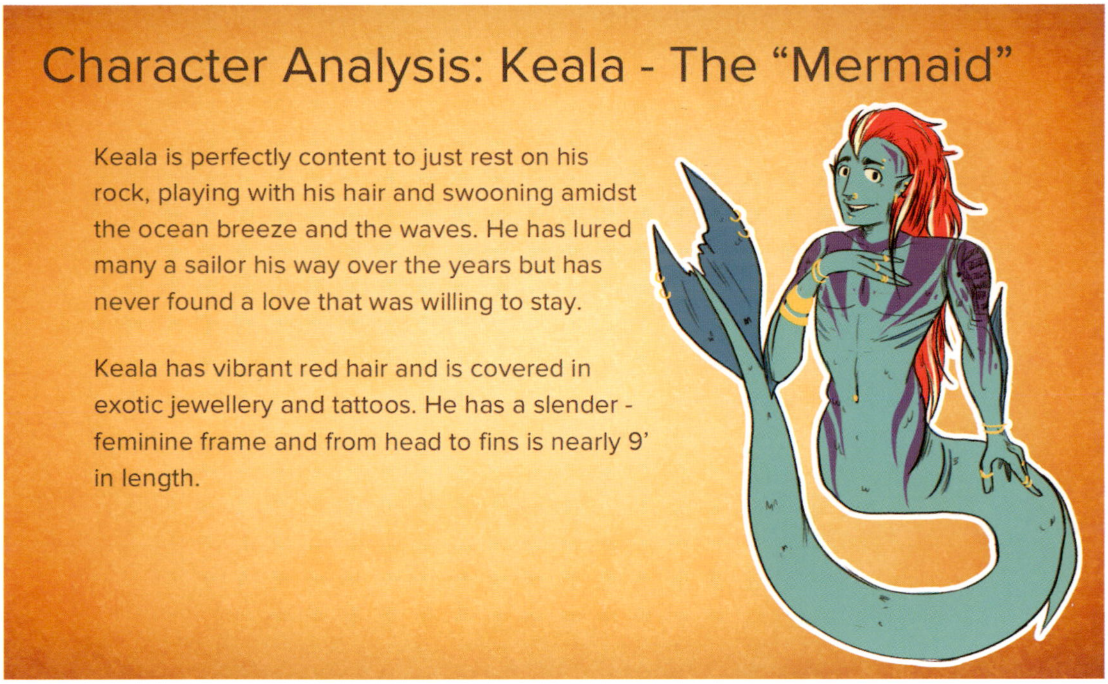

## Character Analysis: Keala - The "Mermaid"

Keala is perfectly content to just rest on his rock, playing with his hair and swooning amidst the ocean breeze and the waves. He has lured many a sailor his way over the years but has never found a love that was willing to stay.

Keala has vibrant red hair and is covered in exotic jewellery and tattoos. He has a slender - feminine frame and from head to fins is nearly 9' in length.

**Figure 4.7**
Character analysis description for Kaela, *Cuddle Fish* (2015). Courtesy of the University of Central Florida Character Animation Specialization.

## Examples of Values

You can use the chart below to find the core values of what matters most to your character. These will guide their conduct, performance, and decisions. As stated in Chapter 2, use what you know and draw from it. Capture a truth from your experiences and give your characters values you personally feel deep down to your core.

You should also begin drawing character model sheets depicting various emotions related to the story. The model sheet should reflect the range of motion that the character needs for the action of the film. At least five full-body drawings of body poses from various angles and five close-ups of the face with different facial expressions should be drawn. A silhouette of the character in a neutral pose is helpful to see if the character design reads well. Be sure to consider the appeal of your characters. Even villains can be visually appealing.

## Using Props, Location

An object can give insight into a character's past or personality, become an intricate detail that adds depth to the story, and can also be part of the look and appeal of the character. A prop can be something that the character wears, for example, glasses, jewelry, or hats; or it can be something the character always carries with them, such as a musical instrument, a walking cane, a backpack, or a weapon. In Pixar's *Presto*, the magician Presto has a magic hat, as all magicians do. The addition of Mickey's sorcerer's hat adds the explanation of how that magical hat works, giving depth and uniqueness to the story.

A location can also help us develop a character's behavior and shape the story. We, like our characters, tend to be more confident and comfortable in places that are more familiar, such as a friend's house or home. However, place us into an environment that is a break from

| | | | |
|---|---|---|---|
| Above and Beyond | Depth | Inquisitive | Realistic |
| Accomplishment | Development | Inspiration | Recreation |
| Accurate | Different | Intensity | Relaxation |
| Adaptability | Diligence | Intuitive | Resilience |
| Affection | Discipline | Inviting | Resolve |
| Agility | Diversity | Joy | Respect |
| Alertness | Dreaming | Knowledge | Responsiveness |
| Amusement | Ease of Use | Legal | Results |
| Anticipation | Effective | Listening | Rigor |
| Approachability | Efficient | Logic | Rule of Law |
| Assertiveness | Employees | Loyalty | Sanity |
| Attentiveness | Encouragement | Maximizing | Security |
| Awareness | Engagement | Meaning | Self Responsibility |
| Being the Best | Enthusiasm | Members | Selfless |
| Best People | Equality | Meticulous | Sensitivity |
| Bravery | Exceed Expectations | Modesty | Service |
| Calm | Exciting | Neatness | Shrewd |
| Capability | Experience | Obedience | Silliness |
| Carefulness | Explore | Openness | Skill |
| Change | Faith | Original | Speed |
| Citizenship | Famous | Passion | Stability |
| Clear-Minded | Ferocious | Patients | Stewardship |
| Comfort | Fitness | People | Success |
| Community | Fluency | Performance | Sympathy |
| Competition | Formal | Refined | Teamwork |
| Comprehensive | Fresh Ideas | Personal Development | Thoughtful |
| Contentment | Gratitude | Potency | Understanding |
| Control | Guidance | Practical | Unity |
| Cordiality | Helpful | Prepared | Valor |
| Craftiness | Honesty | Proactive | Variety |
| Creativity | Hospitality | Professionalism | Virtue |
| Customer Focus | Hygiene | Prosperity | Warmth |
| Daring | Impious | Purity | Welcoming |
| Dedication | Industry | Quality of Work | Wonder |

**Figure 4.8**
Location, *Dreamweaver* (2015). Courtesy of the University of Central Florida Character Animation Specialization.

the routine, and we change, becoming more introverted or extroverted. Placing a character in a comfortable or safe place opens the story to an intrusion by someone or of something, causing conflict and tension. Inserting a character into an unknown or scary location invites the opportunity for something amazing to happen, creating a character arc where they squelch their fears.

Both props and location can provide additional tools to add excitement and freshness to your story and characters. If you think everything has been done before and what you are doing is cliché, add a prop with meaning or change the location. Just remember, anything added to the story should serve a purpose and that is to drive the story forward.

# Creating the Environment

The environment is the space in which the story occurs; more than that, however, is has the potential to transport the audience into the world of the story. Creating a believable environment takes an incredible amount of detail. The best place to start is research.

For research, consider questions such as: does this place (or somewhere similar) really exist? Go to the location if possible. Take reference video and photographs. Perhaps a combination of several locations will create your own world. In *Big Hero 6*, Pixar created San Fransokyo as the setting, much like a mash-up of both San Francisco and Tokyo. If you cannot physically go to places to research the environment, explore other options. Watch travel videos on YouTube or go to the bookstore or library and find books about the culture, people, architecture, and sights. Use virtual reality to travel.[5] Explore multiple possibilities. As with any creative endeavor, do not just settle on your first idea.

When creating your environment, it is best to start with reference imagery to sketch floor plans and concept art. Building an architectural model from paper, cardboard, foam core, and wood can also be an incredible way to visualize location and help create storyboards later.

Figure 4.9
Environment design, *ALLEYOUP!* (2017). Courtesy of Koko Chou, Sheridan College Animation Thesis Film.

# Writing a Treatment

A treatment is a prose form of the story, written in the present tense, and reads like a short story. Written after the initial brainstorm session, the treatment is usually the full story in a simplified form, covering the theme, the characters, and a detailed synopsis summarizing the main idea. There are usually several rewrites of the treatment before the project moves into storyboard development.

A full-length feature film treatment is usually around 30–50 pages. Therefore, a 5-minute short film should be no longer than one or two pages.

Before beginning to write the treatment, one should go through the idea development covered in Chapter 2, and write a rough outline following the format explored at the end of Chapter 1. A good place to start is the framework provided by Algis Budrys (repeated here for your convenience):

1.  A character or characters
2.  in a situation
3.  with a problem or a goal
4.  makes two to three attempts to solve the problem or achieve the goal but
5.  does not succeed and usually makes the problem worse.
6.  A final attempt occurs at the climax of the story, and the main character or characters either succeed, by achieving the goal/solving the problem, *or* absolutely fails (Victory or Death).
7.  In the denouement (Affirmation), the result of the final attempt is confirmed as final.

Or, begin using the following, which the Pixar story department uses as prompts to write an initial outline:[6]

Once upon a time there was a (character)
Everyday (he or she did something—situational with a problem or goal)
Until one day, (inciting moment)
Because of that, (conflict) (and also, cause-and-effect, which drives the story forward)
Because of that, (conflict) (and also, cause-and-effect, which drives the story forward)
Until finally (crisis which leads to climax)
Ever since then (resolution)

Once you have a framework, expand the detail and flesh out the story in your treatment. Be sure not to over-explain to your audience. As Andrew Stanton said in his TED talk,

We are born problem solvers; we're compelled to deduce and to deduct because that's what we do in real life. It's the well-organized absence of information that draws us in. We can't stop ourselves from wanting to complete the sentence and fill it in. . . . Storytelling without dialogue is the purest form of cinematic storytelling. It's the most inclusive approach you can take. The audience actually wants to work for their meal; they just don't want to know that they're doing that. That's your job as a storyteller. To hide the fact that you are making them work for their meal.[7]

He calls this the Unifying Theory of 2+2. Provide the elements of the plot and be aware of the order you place them. Make the audience put things together. This is crucial to whether or not you succeed at engaging the audience. This is what holds an audience's attention to the story.

Be sure to research what has been done before that is similar to your idea. Google is a great tool to find out what else is out there. How is your idea different? What is similar? How can you change your idea to make it your own and not a repeat of what already exists? Present your idea to anyone who you trust and who might listen to get some feedback.

One of the story ideas that you have been seeing as examples is one that my students developed as part of the University of Central Florida's Emerging Media BFA Character Animation Specialization. The finished film was entitled *Yours, Mime, and Ours*, and was completed in May of 2017. It began, however, as *Urine Trouble* by Teresa Falcone.

After the initial pitch, the feedback was that the slapstick and exaggeration of the story was appealing, but the situation was pretty gross and unappealing. Several revisions later returned a much more appealing story. The final story is a heartwarming tale of a clown father trying to understand his mime daughter.

Above all, remember that storytelling has guidelines, not rules set in stone.

---

### "Urine Trouble" (working title)

**Inspired by true events . . .**

Thirteen-year-old Fiona is going to the doctor for a check-up. When she walks into the examination room, she sees a bowl of lollipops and goes to take one. With a sour look on his face, the doctor slaps her hand away and point to a sign that says "Lollipops are for after exams only!" She instantly dislikes him. The doctor proceeds with the not-so-gentle examination, including stabbing her too hard with a shot without warning and giggling at her little growing tummy on the scale. Fiona starts imagining lavish ways to get him back and give him a taste of his own medicine. The doctor hands her a cup and points to the bathroom. Fiona places the filled cup on the edge of the sink as she goes to wash her hands, and then, as if in slow motion, knocks the uncovered cup onto the ground, spilling its contents all over the single-bathroom floor. She frantically tries to soak it up with paper towels but it does nothing. She sheepishly walks back to the doctor with the empty cup saying she didn't really have to go. Annoyed, the doctor excuses himself to use the restroom. As he enters the bathroom he slips and falls on the wet floor and returns back to Fiona sopping wet and red with anger. He points to the door for her to leave. Fiona grabs a lollipop out of the bowl and leaves the room with a sly smile on her face.

Theme: Be nice, or it'll come back to bite you!
Characters: Fiona and the doctor
Inciting moment: The doctor slaps Fiona's hand away from the lollipops
Conflict: Fiona doesn't like the doctor and needs to get back at him

---

Figure 4.10 Treatment for *Cuddle Fish* (2015). Courtesy of the University of Central Florida Character Animation Specialization.

## Treatment

When a Sailor spies a pretty Mermaid in the distance, he sets sail to meet her. However, little does he know that a Kraken looming below his ship was cuddling his Kraken-like anchor. The hoisting of his anchor quickly turns into a tug-o-war between him and the Kraken. After losing the tug-o-war, the Kraken pursues the ship speeding towards the mermaid. When the sailor realizes that a kraken is following him, he promptly freaks out. Cannon balls fired from his ship are met by ink balls fired by the Kraken. Just when the sailor thinks he is close to reaching the Mermaid, the Kraken creates a whirlpool. The Kraken makes off with the anchor while the rest of the ship is being destroyed. Despite the chaos, the Sailor survives. He washes up on the Mermaid's rock, only to find out that the Mermaid is actually a Merman. The Sailor ends up being ok with this and both the Sailor and the Kraken finally get their love.

## What Is the Premise?

Considering the premise during the writing of the treatment can help shape the story. Asking a "What if?" question can help establish the premise of the story. Answering the "What if?" question provides the events. Continuing with our example of Pixar's *Partly Cloudy*, the events that lead up to the climax are the cloud, Gus, making the babies and the stork, Peck, delivering them. These events answer the following premise questions that we established in Chapter 1: If storks deliver babies, where do the storks get the babies? What if clouds made them? Who is responsible for the dangerous animal babies?

Other prompts that work for this as well: "I wonder," "If only," "Wouldn't it be interesting if." To rephrase our premise questions: I wonder, if storks deliver babies, where do the storks get the babies? Wouldn't it be interesting if clouds made them? And if only the dark cloud is responsible for the dangerous animal babies?

The final premise for *Yours, Mime, and Ours* (2014) was: Why don't some parents pay attention to their children? Is it so difficult to understand what your children want? What if a father doesn't realize that he has something in common with his daughter?

The premise is also known as the "hook" of the story. The "hook" draws the audiences' attention and lures them in through interest or intrigue.

It can also be helpful to develop the log line during the process of writing the treatment. The log line is a one-sentence summary of the story which contains synopsis of the plot and the "hook" to stimulate interest.

**Figure 4.11**
**Premise for *Cuddle Fish* (2015).** Courtesy of the University of Central Florida Character Animation Specialization.

## What Is the Theme?

As established in Chapter 2, the theme is the central idea or message of the story. A strong theme is always running through a well-told story. The theme can be thought about at the beginning of idea development, or even used as a starting off point when coming up with a story idea, but the main theme usually emergences from the story as it is crafted. Remain flexible to the idea of the theme changing as the story evolves. After several rewrites of the treatment, take time to reconsider other possibilities and be open to feedback. As stated earlier, the audience may see something in the story that was not intentionally planned.

The themes for *Yours, Mime, and Ours* (2014) were: Connecting with your child is as simple as spending time playing with them; and, pay attention to your children or you will miss out when they need you the most.

**Figure 4.12**
Genre and theme for *Cuddle Fish* (2015). Courtesy of the University of Central Florida Character Animation Specialization.

# Story Beats and the Beat Board

Once a treatment has been written, the next step is to identify the most important elements to create the story beats and beat board. The segment or unit in which an actor divides each scene in a script is called a "beat." A "beat" is a specifically measured and spaced moment that helps pace the film and drive the story forward, usually an event, decision, or a discovery. It can be the introduction of a character, a crisis or conflict, or a change in location.

Russian actor and theater director Konstantin Stanislavski, who also developed method acting, wrote about the "bits" of a play, which was divided into large bits or "episodes" and small bits or "facts." A new "bit" begins whenever the action of the scene shifts. When pronounced in English with a Russian accent by émigré teachers, the word "bits" was described as beads strung on a necklace, and were understood as "beats." Each "beat" relies on the previous beat to support it, much like beads strung together on a necklace. One bead cannot hold its place without the others, much like a string of dependent events (beats or bits) that rely on the previous beat to drive the story forward into the next scene. The persistent mistranslation of the word "bead" to "beat" ultimately led to the metaphor now commonly used to compare a script to a musical score.

In a feature-length, American film, each beat occurs about every 5 minutes, creating a subliminal rhythm. Erratic or uneven beats can be placed specifically so that the audience notices them and makes the scene more remembered. The more action involved in the story, the more frequently beats will occur.

Identifying the story beats is the first step to storyboarding. Once the story beats have been identified, then illustrating each beat will in turn create the beat board. The beat board is used to create an illustrated summary of the story before the rest of the storyboard is developed and is usually used during the pitch process.[8] A good place to start would be the outline created in the previous section with the framework suggested (either by Pixar or Algis Budrys). Beats are summaries of many scenes, so they are usually drawn in medium to long shot.[9] Be sure to create them in the aspect ratio of your film.[10]

To help identify the story beats, it can advantageous to simultaneously create an emotional graph for the story structure, as well as each character. On the left side of the graph (vertical axis) is the emotional intensity level (0–100) and the bottom of the graph (horizontal axis) is time, where each of the events is listed from the story beats and eventually updated with the shot list after it is created. This process helps visualize the emotional level as it increases in intensity to the climax, much like Freytag's pyramid, as discussed in Chapter 1.

**Story Beats (from *Cuddle Fish*)**

1. Zooming in to epic-sized ship with many rowing oars.
2. Spyglass scanning the horizon.
3. Focus on Mermaid in the distance.
4. Boat snags as the anchor catches it.
5. Sailor sails off, Kraken rises to the surface.
6. Sailor is hit with ink, shot by Kraken.
7. The Kraken begins to form a whirlpool and the Sailor begins to move back, getting sucked in.
8. The Sailor parachutes out of the whirlpool.
9. The Sailor awakens against the Mermaid's rock.
10. Reveal that the Mermaid is a Merman.
11. The Sailor shrugs it off and smiles.

Figure 4.13
Illustrated story
beats, *Cuddle
Fish* (2015).
Courtesy of the
University of
Central Florida
Character
Animation
Specialization.

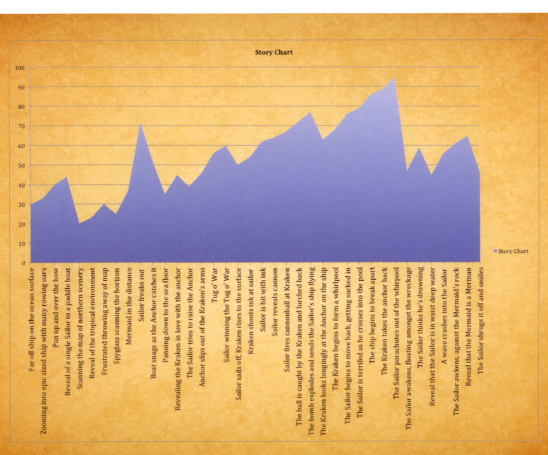

Figure 4.14
Emotional graph,
*Cuddle Fish*
(2015). Courtesy
of the University
of Central Florida
Character
Animation
Specialization.

# Creating a Shot List

A further expansion of the beats and treatment is the shot list. A shot list is essentially a detailed checklist that will give your film a sense of direction, organization, and efficiency.

It is important to note that the creation or filming of the shots is done in the order that is logical to create the film, not necessarily in the order of the story.

The best way to create a shot list is using a spreadsheet. Columns to include are:

1. A blank column to place an X in upon completion (or you can use highlighted cells)
2. Shot number (you may want to list these numbers in increments of 10 so that there is wiggle room later if needed to add additional shots)
3. Time length of shot
4. Shot description
5. Camera direction (camera motion, camera position, camera angles, possible transitions during editing)[11]
6. Action description (we also include if it is subtle, high action, or includes object interactions)
7. Characters in shot
8. Visual effects needed in shot
9. Sound effects needed in shot
10. Additional notes

If working as a team, you can create a Google sheet, which can easily be shared with all members of the team, so that it can be updated. Additional information can easily be added to customize the shot list, such as who has been assigned to each shot and which aspect of production to create. Additional columns for other areas of production can be added; suggestions for 3D animation include layout, camera, animation, effects, lighting, rendering, and compositing. Note that all columns do not need to be filled out initially, and they are always revisable and editable. Start by filling in the shot number and shot description. After writing the script, a revision of the shot list can include updated shot numbers and descriptions, as well as camera motion, camera position, and camera angles.

Upon completion of this chapter, your idea should be more fleshed out and forming into something more solid. Equipped with character descriptions, backstory, and environments, you have written a treatment and identified the premise and theme. You have created a list of story beats and illustrated a beat board culminating with the creation of the initial shot list. With these items in hand, you are ready to venture into the next chapter and write the first draft of your script.

## Bibliography and Further Reading

Catmull, E. & Wallace, A. (2014). *Creativity, Inc.: Overcoming the unseen forces that stand in the way of true inspiration*. Random House Publishing Group, Kindle Edition.

Coats, E. (2012, June 13). *22 #storybasics I've picked up in my time at Pixar*. Retrieved from http://storyshots. tumblr.com/post/25032057278/22-storybasics-ive -picked-up-in-my-time-at-pixar.

Stanton, A. (2012). *The clues to a great story*. Retrieved from https://www.ted.com/talks/andrew_stanton_the _clues_to_a_great_story?language=en.

Williams, P. & Denney, J. (2010). *How to be like Walt: Capturing the Disney magic every day of your life*. Health Communications, Kindle Edition.

## Resources

Korolov, M. (2016, July 13). *VR travel: 10 ways to see the world from your living room*. Retrieved from https:// www.gearbrain.com/vr-travel-samsung-gear-vr-google -cardboard-1737536488.html.

## Notes

1. Catmull, E. & Wallace, A. (2014). Creativity, Inc.: Overcoming the unseen forces that stand in the way of true inspiration. Random House Publishing Group, Kindle Edition.

2. Williams, P. & Denney, J. (2010). *How to be like Walt: Capturing the Disney magic every day of your life*. Health Communications, Kindle Edition.

3. Stanton, A. (2012). *The clues to a great story*. Retrieved from https://www.ted.com/talks /andrew_stanton_the_clues_to_a_great_story ?language=en.

4. Stanton, A. (2012). *The clues to a great story*. Retrieved from https://www.ted.com/talks /andrew_stanton_the_clues_to_a_great_story ?language=en.

5. Korolov, M. (2016, July 13). *VR travel: 10 ways to see the world from your living room*. Retrieved from https://www.gearbrain.com/vr-travel-samsung -gear-vr-google-cardboard-1737536488.html.

6. Emma Coats, a Pixar story artist, tweeted a series of #storybasics of things she learned about storytelling from various directors and coworkers. This was one of them, that I elaborated on for clarity. Coats, E. (2012, June 13). *22 #storybasics I've picked up in my time at Pixar*. Retrieved from http://storyshots.tumblr.com/post/25032057278/22 -storybasics-ive-picked-up-in-my-time-at-pixar.

7. Stanton, A. (2012). *The clues to a great story*. Retrieved from https://www.ted.com/talks /andrew_stanton_the_clues_to_a_great _story?language=en.

8. See Chapter 9 for more information about the pitch session.

9. See Chapter 6 for definition and explanation of camera positions for shots.

10. See Chapter 7 for more information about aspect ratios.

11. See Chapters 6, 7, and 8 for more information about camera motion, camera position, camera angles, and editing transitions.

Figure 4.15
Shot list, *Yours,
Mime and Ours*
(2014). Courtesy
of the University
of Central Florida
Character
Animation
Specialization.

| Shot Number | Corresponding Storyboards | Time Frame | Brief Description | Int/Ext |
|---|---|---|---|---|
| 001.00 | (IMG) 001 - 008h | 00:00.00 - 00:16.12 ; | Title Sequence; | Ext/Int |
| 002.00 | 009 - 014 | 00:16.13 - 00:38.07 ; | Marcy's Box; Moving | Int |
| 003.00 | 015 - 015a | 00:38.08 - 00:39.21 ; | Marcy's Ceiling; | Int |
| 004.00 | 015b - 015e | 00:39.22 - 00:42.09 ; | Marcy's Ceiling POV; | Int |
| 005.00 | 016 - 016b | 00:42.10 - 00:44.17 ; | Marcy's Right Wall; | Int |
| 006.00 | 017 - 017a | 00:44.18 - 00:46.12 ; | Marcy's POV | Int |
| 007.00 | 018 - 026 | 00:46.13 - 00:54.22 ; | Marcy is celebrating | Int |
| 008.00 | 027 - 027c | 00:54.23 - 00:56.19 ; | The duster and the | Int |
| 009.00 | 028c - 032c | 00:56.20 - 01:08.22 ; | Marcy is happy, | Int |
| 010.00 | 033 | 01:08.23 - 01:10.19 ; | Marcy laughs at Gus | Int |
| 011.00 | 034 - 037d | 01:10.20 - 01:21.17 ; | Gus pokes Marcy's | Int |
| 012.00 | 038 - 038e | 01:21.18 - 01:25.21 ; | Gus tries to hug | Int |
| 013.00 | 039 - 041d | 01:25.22 - 01:30.07 ; | Gus puts Marcy | Int |
| 014.00 | 042 - 045c | 01:30.08 - 01:40.09 ; | Gus thinks for a | Int |
| 015.00 | 046 - 047a | 01:40.10 - 01:42.17 ; | In the midst of Gus' | Int |
| 016.00 | 048 - 048f | 01:42.18 - 01:46.15 ; | Gus slings the rubber | Int |
| 017.00 | 049 - 049d | 01:46.16 - 01:49.11 ; | After many failed | Int |
| 018.00 | 050 - 050c | 01:49.12 - 01:52.18 ; | Humorous shot of | Int |
| 019.00 | 051 - 052e | 01:52.19 - 02:00.02 ; | Gus sits on Marcy's | Int |
| 020.00 | 053b - 053j | 02:00.03 - 02:01.21 ; | Gus leaps into his | Int |
| 021.00 | 054 - 055b | 02:01.22 - 02:07.03 ; | While Gus is inside | Int |
| 022.00 | 055c - 055h | 02:07.04 - 02:14.21 ; | Marcy presses up | Int |
| 023.00 | 055i - 055o | 02:14.22 - 02:19.02 ; | It appears to be a | Int |
| 024.00 | 055p - 056c | 02:19.03 - 02:22.03 ; | A large box lands in | Int |
| 025.00 | 057 - 057c | 02:22.04 - 02:23.18 ; | Marcy's POV as she | Int |
| 026.00 | 057g - 057r | 02:23.19 - 02:32.11 ; | Marcy wants to leave | Int |
| 027.00 | 058 - 058e | 02:32.12 - 02:36.20 ; | As Marcy tries to get | Int |
| 028.00 | 059 - 062b | 02:36.21 - 02:46.04 ; | Gus is rummaging | Int |
| 029.00 | 063 - 063d | 02:46.05 - 02:48.14 ; | Gus hops on the | Int |
| 030.00 | 064a - 064g | 02:48.15 - 02:51.01 ; | Gus continues to ride | Int |
| 031.00 | 065 - 065i | 02:51.02 - 02:57.00 ; | Gus honks his nose | Int |
| 032.00 | 066 - 066d | 02:57.01 - 02:59.23 ; | Marcy is still trying to | Int |
| 033.00 | 067 - 069e | 03:00.00 - 03:04.18 ; | Gus peddles above | Int |
| 034.00 | 070 - 070b | 03:04.19 - 03:07.15 ; | Marcy sees Gus fall | Int |
| 035.00 | 071 - 073d | 03:07.16 - 03:12.11 ; | Gus comes back up | Int |
| 036.00 | 074 - 075f | 03:12.12 - 03:17.17 ; | Marcy points to the | Int |
| 037.00 | 076 - 077c | 03:17.18 - 03:20.23 ; | Gus walks over to | Int |
| 038.00 | 078 - 078a | 03:21.00 - 03:22.06 ; | Marcy starts to get | Int |
| 039.00 | 079 - 082a | 03:22.07 - 03:35.11 ; | Gus opens up the | Int |
| 040.00 | 083 - 083b | 03:35.12 - 03:37.17 ; | Marcy's excitement | Int |
| 041.00 | 084 - 084e | 03:37.18 - 03:39.19 ; | Gus is framed to the | Int |
| 042.00 | 085 - 085c | 03:39.20 - 03:42.05 ; | Marcy is framed on | Int |
| 043.00 | 086 - 086b | 03:42.06 - 03:43.15 ; | The camera switches | Int |
| 044.00 | 087 - 092b | 03:43.16 - 03:52.22 ; | Begins with ECU on | Int |
| 045.00 | 093 - 094a | 03:52.23 - 03:55.06 ; | Gus is now focused | Int |
| 046.00 | 095 - 097 | 03:55.07 - 03:58.15 ; | Following the air | Int |
| 047.00 | 098 - 098a | 03:58.16 - 04:01.15 ; | Gus is still pumping | Int |
| 048.00 | 099 - 100a | 04:01.16 - 04:04.07 ; | Gus pumping the | Ext |
| 049.00 | 102e - 103 | 04:04.08 - 04:05.09 ; | Air bubble inflates the | Int |
| 050.00 | 104 | 04:05.10 - 04:07.21 ; | Marcy is still trapped | Int |
| 051.00 | 105 - 107g | 04:07.22 - 04:12.12 ; | Gus is furiously | Int |
| 052.00 | 108 - 108b | 04:12.13 - 04:13.18 ; | The cake is | Int |
| 053.00 | 109 - 109b | 04:13.19 - 04:14.18 ; | Gus executing the | Int |
| 054.00 | 112 - 112b | 04:14.19 - 04:15.08 ; | Air bubble from the | Int |
| 055.00 | 113 - 113e | 04:15.09 - 04:19.03 ; | Gus is concentrating | Int |
| 056.00 | 114 - 114c | 04:19.04 - 04:19.19 ; | Air bubble runs along | Int |
| 057.00 | IMG (Ext) | 04:19.20 - 04:23.01 ; | We see the house a | Ext |
| 058.00 | 117 - 117d | 04:23.02 - 04:27.03 ; | Gus' hand appears | Int |
| 059.00 | 118 - 118b | 04:27.04 - 04:28.20 ; | Marcy does not pay | Int |
| 060.00 | 123 - 128b | 04:28.21 - 04:39.08 ; | Gus dejectedly goes | Int |
| 061.00 | 129 - 129c | 04:39.09 - 04:41.03 ; | Marcy nods excitedly | Int |
| 062.00 | 130 - 130j | 04:41.04 - 04:44.20 ; | Gus jumps into the | Int |
| 063.00 | 131a - 131b | 04:44.21 - 04:45.15 ; | Marcy looks for Gus | Int |
| 064.00 | 132 - 132e | 04:45.16 - 04:47.11 ; | Marcy continues to | Int |
| 065.00 | 133 - 135a | 04:47.12 - 04:52.08 ; | Jack-in-the-box tune | Int |
| 066.00 | 136 - 136g | 04:52.09 - 04:57.16 ; | Marcy is surprised | Int |
| 067.00 | 137 - 138b | 04:57.17 - 05:00.00 ; | Gus ecstatically | Int |
| 068.00 | 139 - 139d | 05:00.01 - 05:01.18 ; | Marcy smiles back at | Int |
| 069.00 | 140 - 141b | 05:01.19 - 05:06.08 ; | Gus flips the box | Int |

| Effects | Effects Team | Characters | Camera | Camera Layout |
|---|---|---|---|---|
| Water coming from | Clinnie | Gus | Dissolve (Fading between | Cooper |
| Glow from her hands | Maral | Marcy | Rotate around Marcy as she | Cooper |
| Glow from her hands | Maral | Marcy | Top down on Marcy as she | Cooper |
| Glow from her hands | Maral | Marcy | POV of Marcy, Cut to the next | Cooper |
| Glow from her hands | Maral | Marcy | | Cooper |
| Glow from her hands | Maral | Marcy, Gus | | Clinnie |
| None. | N/A | Gus, Marcy | | Clinnie |
| None. | N/A | None. | | Clinnie |
| Glow from her hand | Maral | Gus, Marcy | | John |
| None. | N/A | Marcy | | Brian |
| Confetti | Bridges | Gus, Marcy | | Teresa |
| Glow from her hand | Maral | Gus, Marcy | | Piant |
| None. | N/A | Gus | | Teresa |
| None. | N/A | Gus, Marcy | | Cooper |
| Motion Blur | | Marcy | Pull Back from close up on | Juan |
| Motion Blur | | Gus | | John |
| None. | N/A | Gus, Marcy | | Clinnie |
| Glow from her hand | Maral | Marcy, Gus | | Teresa |
| Motion Blur, Dust | Chambless | Gus, Marcy | | Sheri |
| None. | N/A | Gus, Marcy | | Dalton |
| None. | N/A | None. | | Chambless |
| Glow from her hand | Maral | Marcy | | Chambless |
| Glow behind cake | Teresa | Marcy | | Chambless |
| Glow from her hand | Maral | Marcy | | Chambless |
| None. | N/A | Marcy | | Bridges |
| Glow from her hand | Maral | Marcy | | Piant |
| None. | N/A | Marcy | | Chambless |
| Action Lines | Cooper | Gus | | John |
| Glow from her hand | Maral | Gus, Marcy | | Sheri |
| Glow from her hand | Maral | Marcy, Gus | | Sheri |
| Pie Splatter | Dalton | Gus | | Bridges |
| Glow from her hand | Maral | Marcy | | Chambless |
| Glow from her hand | Cooper, Maral | Gus, Marcy | | Maral |
| Glow from her hand | Maral | Marcy | | Piant |
| None. | N/A | Gus, Marcy | | Bridges |
| None. | N/A | Marcy, Gus | | Brian |
| None. | N/A | Gus, Marcy | | Bridges |
| None. | N/A | Marcy | | Piant |
| Peanuts | Sheri | Gus, Marcy | | Bridges |
| None. | N/A | Marcy | Copy Shot 26 | Piant |
| Peanuts | Sheri | Gus, Marcy | | Brian |
| None. | N/A | Marcy | | Piant |
| Peanuts | Sheri | Gus, Marcy | | Brian |
| Cake Change Pop | Cooper | Gus, Marcy | Fast Pull Back | Juan |
| None. | N/A | Gus | | Juan |
| None. | N/A | None. | | Sheri |
| Peanuts? | Sheri | Marcy, Gus | | Juan |
| None. | N/A | Gus | | Juan |
| Action Lines | Cooper | None. | | Juan |
| Glow from her hand | Maral | Marcy | | Chambless |
| Sweat Drops | Brian | Gus | | John |
| Action Lines | Cooper | None. | | Clinnie |
| None. | N/A | Gus | | Teresa |
| None. | N/A | None. | | Sheri |
| Sweat Drops | Brian | Gus | | Teresa |
| None. | N/A | None. | | Sheri |
| None. | N/A | None. | | Brian |
| Cake Splatter being | John | Gus | | Brian |
| Cake Splatter | Juan | Marcy | | Dalton |
| Cake Splatter | Juan | Gus, Marcy | | Clinnie |
| None. | N/A | Marcy | | Dalton |
| Cake Splatter | Juan | Gus | | Maral |
| None. | N/A | Marcy | | Dalton |
| Cake Splatter | Juan | Marcy | | Brian |
| Cake Splatter (as it | Juan | Gus | | Maral |
| None. | N/A | Marcy | | Dalton |
| Cake Splatter | Juan | Gus | | John |
| None. | N/A | Marcy | | Dalton |
| Cake Splatter, Motion | Juan | Gus | | Maral |

| Shot Number | Corresponding Storyboards | Time Frame | Brief Description | Int/Ext |
|---|---|---|---|---|
| 070.00 | 142 - 142f | 05:06.09 - 05:11.07 ; | Marcy looks excited | Int |
| 071.00 | 142g - 142o | 05:11.08 - 05:16.19 ; 132 total frames | Gus crawls over to Marcy and puts his finger up against her box to help her get out. | Int |
| 072.00 | 142p - 142q | 05:16.20 - 05:18.09 ; 38 total frames | Marcy realizes Gus is trying to help her with her box. | Int |
| 073.00 | 142r - 142t | 05:18.10 - 05:20.19 ; 58 total frames | Marcy's hand comes into frames and moves to the spot on the box where Gus is pointing. Marcy places her finger where Gus' finger is, and then they start running their fingers down the box in unison. | Int |
| 074.00 | 142u - 142w | 05:20.20 - 05:22.23 ; 52 total frames | Gus and Marcy continue to run their fingers down the box in unison. Marcy's hand takes up the right side of the screen while Gus' hand takes up the left side of the screen. | Int |
| 075.00 | 142x - 142zzz | 05:23.00 - 5:25.18 ; 67 total frames | Marcy finishes the last bit of line on her own. Gus smiles even wider. He looks over his shoulder as he backs up into the cake box. Gus waves her over one last time. | Int |
| 076.00 | 142zzzz - 142zzzzz | 05:25.19 - 05:26.21 ; 27 total frames | Marcy's face lights up in excitement as a wide smile sweeps across her face | Int |
| 077.00 | 143 - 150 | 05:26.22 - 05:38.03 ; 270 total frames | Marcy pushes open flaps, screen turns from greyscale to color. Marcy crawls into the box with Gus. Gus pulls out a flower from his pocket and gives it to her. She takes it and squirts water in his face. They laugh. | Int |
| 078.00 | 150a - 151b | 05:38.04 - 05:44.09 ; 149 frames | Gus and Marcy are in a freeze frame, it is revealed that a photo was taken, as the camera moves it is revealed the new photo is in a frame and now located on the wall as it reveals surrounding frames | Int |

| Effects | Effects Team | Characters | Camera | Camera Layout |
|---|---|---|---|---|
| Glow from her hand | Maral | Marcy | | Dalton |
| Cake Splatter | Juan | Gus | | Maral |
| None. | N/A | Marcy | | Dalton |
| Cake Splatter, Glow from the line they are creating | Juan, Maral | Gus, Marcy | | Maral |
| Cake Splatter, Glow from the line they are creating | Juan, Maral | Gus, Marcy | | Teresa |
| Cake Splatter, Glowing line | Juan, Maral | Gus, Marcy | | Maral |
| None. | N/A | Marcy | | Dalton |
| Cake Splatter, Water coming from squirting flower | Juan, Clinnie | Gus, Marcy | | Dalton |
| None. | N/A | None. | | Teresa |

# Scriptwriting

Once you have completed your treatment and the first pass at the shot list, it is time to further develop the story through writing a script (also known as a screenplay). A script is a document written in the present tense that outlines every sound (music, effect, dialogue), behavior (action, thought), and visual (camera motion, position, transition, location, time of day) element necessary to tell a story. The speculation script (also called a reading script or spec script) is exceptionally simple, and crafting the best story possible should be the focus. During the first writing of your script, keep visual details to a minimum, especially if you are not aware of the possibilities. This information will be discussed in Chapters 6, 7, and 8, and can be added to both the script and shot list during the revision process.

This spec script (which is usually written on speculation with the hopes of getting it sold or gaining representation by an agent) will be scrutinized and transformed through countless rewrites. The shooting script is then further interpreted by the director of the story and will include revision dates, shot and scene[1] numbers, title sequences, and camera directions. Revisions to the script can be made and a new version of the document can be saved. However, if already in production, see Chapter 9 for further details about how to make the changes noticeable to the production crew. If you are writing as the screenwriter and director, then the inclusion of these additions is acceptable, since you will be the one directing and producing your screenplay, but a spec script should be written and finalized first.[2]

Depending on which screenplay books you read, formatting experts agree on three necessary parts of the script: scene headings, direction, and dialogue. Different words can be used to describe each of these areas and may also be further broken down into subcategories or elements of the screenplay.

1. Scene headings introduce a new scene, location, and/ or time of day (also called master scene heading, shot heading, or slugline).
   a. Subheadings are used when a new scene heading is not necessary, and perform a variety of functions, such as introducing a change in camera angles or moving a character from one location to another within a larger environment (i.e. room to room). These should be used sparingly (also called scene heading, shot heading, or secondary scene heading).
   b. Transitions[3] describe how the story will visually move from one scene to the next and are usually created during the editing of the film (also called scene ending).
2. Direction follows the scene headings and describes what is happening in the scene and how things look and sound, such as a description of the environment, where characters move throughout the scene, how characters relate to each other, and what sounds are heard (also called action, business, description, narration, narrative, scene description, or stage direction).
3. Dialogue is what characters say as well as when and sometimes how the actors deliver the lines of in the story, such as colloquial speech, dialect, slang, etc.
   a. Character headings precede all dialogue and cue the actor(s) to know when a line is delivered (also called character caption, character cue, or character slug).
   b. Parentheticals explain to the actor how a line of dialogue should be delivered or to whom they are speaking (also called actor instruction, character direction, or personal direction).

# Writing a Script

The physicality of actually writing a script means that you must format the script in a professional manner. Learning to format a script is one of the first obstacles beginning screenwriters have to overcome. The important thing to remember is that even though you are probably writing as screenwriter and director, the practice of writing in proper format provides practice and could possibly lead to future projects.

The easiest way to format a script is to use software designed specifically for that purpose.[4] However, all one really needs is a computer with a word processor with the ability to set the formatting to spec script industry standards (the difference between an amateur and a professional),[5] which are as follows.

## Paper

Three-hole punched, 8½" × 11", 20lb, each page printed only on one side of paper, later clasped in the top and bottom hole with two 1¼" brass brads with brass washers in back, card stock cover, 80lb. This brad length works whether you are writing a short, a television episode, or a feature-length film. If you are unable to get standard American paper, scripts on A4 paper are acceptable.

Why? Scripts will need to be photocopied, so two brass brads are easier to remove than three, saving time and money. Printing each page only on one side of the paper allows for notes to be taken on the back.

## Type Font

Font should be 12 point, 10 pitch, fixed pitch font, Courier style.

Why? 12 points allows for six lines of type for every vertical inch, 10 points allows for 10 characters for every horizontal inch, and fixed pitch because every letter occupies the same amount of horizontal space on the line, regardless of whether it is a capital W or lowercase i. Courier is the font that is associated with the typewriter, since screenplay format was developed in the typewriter era, and Courier is a very readable font—also, any version of Courier is acceptable, so long as it is 12 point, 10 pitch. Using this font, along with the standard margins listed below, creates a uniform amount of content per page that translates, on average, into 1 minute of finished film.

## Title Page Margins and Formatting[6]

"TITLE" appears on line 25, centered in quotes and in ALL CAPS bolded; 4 blank lines follow

written by on line 30, centered; 1 blank line follows

Writer(s)' name(s) on line 32, centered

Contact information (physical address, phone number), left and bottom justified, with the last line of the information an inch from the bottom of the page, line 60

## Main Page Margins

Right, top, and bottom margins: 1"

The first line of text should appear 1" from the top

Left justified: 1.5"

## Page Numbers

- The only thing in the page header, right justified, appears 0.5 inches from the top of the page, with a period following the number, starting on the second page of the script.
- No page numbers should appear on the title page or the first page of the script.

## First Page of Script

- The TITLE appears on the top, centered, and in ALL CAPS bolded (however, most formatting experts believe this is not necessary since the title is on the title page)
- 1 blank line follows (If you decide to put a TITLE on your first page)
- FADE IN: appears, bolded, left justified, line 3 if there is a TITLE, otherwise line 1, in ALL CAPS, followed by a colon

## Last Page of Script

- FADE OUT. appears, bolded, right justified, in ALL CAPS, followed by a period
- 3–5 blank lines follow
- THE END appears, centered, in ALL CAPS, and bolded

## All Other Script Pages

- Start on the top of the page, left justified
- Scene heading (shot heading, master scene heading, slugline)
  - Between main page margins, in ALL CAPS, bolded in this order:
    - camera placement (INT. or EXT. or INT./EXT.)
    - location (HOUSE, STREET, CHURCH, etc.)
    - time of day (DAY, NIGHT, MORNING).

### Example 1

INT. MEMORIAL HOSPITAL—MORNING

- Additional location information can be used to specify an area within a larger location

### Example 2

INT. MEMORIAL HOSPITAL—
PATIENT ROOM—MORNING

- Parentheticals can be added for time clarification so as not to create identical headings if the next scene takes place in the same location as the previous scene (DAWN, DUSK, LATER).

### Example 3

INT. MEMORIAL HOSPITAL (NEW ORLEANS)—
MORNING (DAWN)

- This example shows parentheticals used for locale specification, such as in a city
- The addition of a camera shot and subject of shot can be added before the time of day sparingly during the spec script and added here during the shooting script (establishing shot, closeup, extreme closeup, two shot, three shot, tracking shot, traveling shot, moving shot, aerial shot, etc.; character's hands, character's eyes, etc.)

### Example 4

INT. MEMORIAL HOSPITAL (NEW ORLEANS)—
CLOSEUP – CHARACTER'S HANDS—
MORNING (DAWN)

- An en dash separates location from time of day and other information (for Mac use Opt + Shift + hyphen; Windows use Alt + 0150) to create the en dash: —
- Triple-space blank lines before each new scene heading
- Double-space blank lines after each scene heading
- Single-space if the scene heading is longer than one line
- Never leave a scene heading as the last line of a page; move it to the next page *unless* it is an ESTABLISHING SHOT as indicated in the scene heading

## Subheading

- Between main page margins, in ALL CAPS
- Double-space blank lines before and after each subheading
- Used to prevent repeating the same information in the main heading by listing only the new information, such as a camera direction or a change in sublocation, such as a different room in the same house

## Transition

- Left justified 6", in ALL CAPS, bolded, followed by a colon, except for FADE IN: which is left justified 1.5" (FADE TO:, FADE OUT., FADE TO BLACK. , FADE TO WHITE., CUT TO:, TIME CUT TO:, SMASH CUT TO:, QUICK CUT TO:, DISSOLVE TO:, SLOW DISSOLVE TO:, RIPPLE DISSOLVE TO:, WIPE TO:, IRIS WIPE TO:, INVISIBLE WIPE TO:, IRIS FADE OUT., MATCH CUT TO:, etc.).
- If the transition is too long to fit on the line, back it off of the right margin.
- Do not end a page with a transition. Carry a transition to the top of the next page if there is not enough room.
- Double-space blank lines before and after each transition.
- Limit to 2–3 transitions in a spec script (in addition to the opening and closing, Fade In: and Fade Out.). Additional transitions are added to the shooting script.

## Direction

- Between main page margins
- Double-space blank lines before and after direction and in between direction paragraphs
- Single-space within the direction paragraphs
- A long direction paragraph should be broken into smaller paragraphs
- Written in present tense
- Written concisely, not wordy
- The names of key characters are in ALL CAPS the first time the character is introduced
- Sounds are in ALL CAPS, unless made by a character on screen, then the sounds are in lowercase and also treated as dialogue

## Dialogue[7]

- Left justified 2.5", right 2.5", 3.5" for dialogue
- Not centered
- Use underlines for emphasis
- Colloquial speech, dialect spellings, slang spellings, and poor grammar is acceptable
- Do not abbreviate any words
- All dialogue must serve the purpose of driving the story forward[8]
- Preceded by character heading
- Single-space lines before and within dialogue
- Double-space blank lines after dialogue

## Character Heading

- Precede any dialogue.
- Left justified[9] 4", bolded, and in ALL CAPS unless the name has a prefix (DaVINCI, McDOUGAL, MacMILLAN).
- Not centered. All character headings have a left margin of 4".
- Double-space blank lines before each character heading.
- Single-space blank line after each character heading.
- Abbreviate titles (DR., MRS., MJR., etc.).
- It is common practice to refer to good guys by their first name and bad guys by their last.
- If the character is off screen while delivering the dialogue, use (V.O.) or (O.S.) following the character heading. Use (O.S.) if the character is physically present in the scene, just not currently on camera. Use (V.O.) for everything else.
- When dialogue carries to another page of the script, indicate so by placing (MORE) with the same margins as the character heading on the last line of the page and at the top of the next page a new character heading with (cont'd) to the right of the character's name.

## Parenthetical

- Left justified 3.5", right 3", 2" for parentheticals
- Lowercase with no ending period
- Always enclose in parentheses
- Follow character heading, preceding the dialogue or imbed in the dialogue on their own line (*not* at the end of the dialogue)
- Single-space line before and after parentheticals
- Any action that the character is doing during the dialogue should be written as direction paragraphs, and the ongoing dialogue should be broken apart using Character Name (cont'd)
- preceding each section of dialogue. Do not use parentheticals for this.

*Omit the following* from the spec script, however, add them to the shooting script:

- The top CONTINUED and the bottom (CONTINUED) on the spec script
- Scene numbers

## Camera Directions

Do:

- Write in present tense.
- Write economically.
- Include camera directions that are absolutely necessary.
- Leave white space on the page.

Don't:

- Include pictures or illustrations.
- Use fonts other than Courier.
- Cheat the margins.
- Forget to spellcheck.
- Write more than the project requires. One page per minute. This means a short animated film would be 1–10 pages long. A feature-length animated film runs between 85 and 110 pages. A television episode averages 20–22 pages.

## Sample Scripts

A great resource for samples of scripts can be found on The Internet Movie Script Database. *WALL-E* is a great example since the first 20 minutes of the film have no dialogue (http://www.imsdb.com/scripts/Wall-E.html). You will notice that directions are written line-by-line one sentence at a time, as opposed to paragraph format. I personally think this makes the script easier to read.

What follows is a sample shooting script from Celestial, written in 2012. See if you can pick out all of the mistakes in this script.

```
                 CELESTIAL

                    By

  Zakk Bombka, Josh Janousky, Lindsey Jones, Daniel Lukas,
  Jacqueline Malvin, Ashley Morrow, McKenna Phillips, Chris
    Sanchez, Adrienne Seufert, David Silva, Ward Silverman,
         Philip Wigner, & Samuel Zilberstein,
```

Figure 5.1
First draft shooting script from *Celestial* (2014). Courtesy of the University of Central Florida Character Animation Specialization.

EXT. OUTER SPACE

FADE IN: LONG SHOT- Outer space with countless bright and colorful stars. PAN TO a nebula in the distance. BRIGHT LIGHTS FLASH LIKE LIGHTNING from within the nebula.

MID SHOT- The silhouette of an large, ominous figure is seen through the clouds of the nebula. The dark figure is moving its arms and body around a smaller silhouette of something round. The LIGHTNING CEASES and the silhouette sulks in front of the orb. The silhouette reaches for the orb and tosses it.

A PLANET BURSTS THROUGH THE CLOUDS OF THE NEBULA, moving towards camera and filling the frame. DOLLY around planet and ZOOM OUT TO MID SHOT. THE PLANET ROTATES RAPIDLY. ITS COLOR CHANGES TO GREEN AND BLUE AND OCEANS APPEAR ON ITS SURFACE. CLUSTERS OF LIGHTS APPEAR ON THE SURFACE OF THE PLANET. A space probe TITAN, is seen leaving the planet's atmosphere.

LONG SHOT- With a background of space and stars, the title, Celestial, is displayed.

CROSS FADE TO:

EXTREME LONG SHOT- A planet in the distance with Titan in the foreground. DOLLY AROUND to reveal a cluster of several other planets.

POV SHOT [TITAN'S HUD]- As he continues through space, he notices that the planets are becoming increasingly more barren.

LONG SHOT- After moving around a large planet, Titan stops.

EXTREME LONG SHOT- Titan has stopped in front of a large, colorful grouping of beautiful, large cloud-like pillars where a group of planets seem to have collected.

CLOSE UP [TITAN'S FACE]- The colors of the nebula reflect on Titan's amazed face. Intrigued, he travels towards the pillars.


INT. NEBULA

LONG SHOT- Particle clouds with SPECKS OF FLICKERING LIGHT throughout. The centers of these pillar-like clouds are dense, allowing very little light to pass through. Titan flies into frame and stops.

CUT TO several (3) MID SHOTS of Titan zooming around the nebula excited.

(CONTINUED)

CONTINUED:                                                    2.


MID SHOT- A large creature, MAKAR reaches out and grabs a
cloud of the nebula near Titan.

POV SHOT [TITAN'S HUD]- Titan's eyes follow Makar's arm as
it rises.

OVER THE SHOULDER [TITAN]- As Makar grabs a different cloud
with his other hand.

MID SHOT - Makar's hands are seen moving around A CLUSTER OF
SPINNING PARTICLES AND LARGE CHUNKS OF ROCK.

MID SHOT- Looking at the creation, he raises it.

RACK FOCUS - A look of hope is seen on his face.

LONG SHOT, LOW ANGLE - Glancing back at the stars behind
him, Makar continues to energize the planet. He raises the
planet once more as it PULSES WITH LIGHT. Makar's gaze moves
from the planet to the NEARBY STAR and then back to the
planet. A hint of frustration is seen in Makar as he charges
the planet with more aggression.

MID SHOT - Makar lowers his creation and resumes his work.

FULL SHOT - Intimidated but still intrigued, Titan hides
behind a cloud of particles and watches him.

MID SHOT, HIGH ANGLE - Makar is seen SWIRLING A CLOUD OF
PARTICLES AND COMPRESSING IT INTO A SOLID MASS.

CLOSE UP - As Makar's hands pass over the spherical form,
its surface gradually takes shape. ELECTRIC CHARGES pass
from his hands to the newly created planet and form
BILLOWING THUNDERSTORMS ACROSS ITS ATMOSPHERE.

RACK FOCUS - He moves his gaze to a NEARBY STAR behind it
and then back to the planet.

MID SHOT - A WARM GLOW IS SEEN ENGULFING THE PLANET. THE
GLOW INTENSIFIES AS LIGHT AND HEAT RADIATES FROM IT. Makar's
face fills with excitement as he holds the FLICKERING
CREATION up triumphantly.

LONG SHOT- The planet suddenly EXPLODES IN A FLASH OF LIGHT
AS PIECES SCATTER IN ALL DIRECTIONS. Makar recoils, covering
his face with his hands and arms. The BLAST SETTLES and he
lowers his hands and arms.

MID SHOT- Disappointment overtakes him as he slumps over the
FLOATING, SMOLDERING REMAINS.

LONG SHOT- Titan peeks out further from behind the cloud as
Makar raises his hands once more.

                                                  (CONTINUED)

CONTINUED:                                                      3.


CLOSE UP, LOW ANGLE- In Makar's hands, CHUNKS OF ROCK SLOWLY
COME TOGETHER IN A SPINNING MOTION. SWIRLING CLOUDS OF DUST
FORM AROUND IT.

MID SHOT- Titan's face in awe of Makar's creation
(reflection can be seen).

LONG SHOT- In the distance Titan is seen moving quickly
towards Makar. As he approaches, he enters the atmosphere of
Makar's newest creation.


INT. PLANET

POV SHOT [HUD]- Titan enters the atmosphere of the planet,
his eyes open wide with wonder at the beautiful landscape. A
GREEN BATTERY METER IS SEEN ON HIS DISPLAY HUD.

LONG SHOT, DOLLY- He CAPTURES PHOTOGRAPHS OF THE PLANET AND
RECORDS HIS VIEW OF THE ENVIRONMENT.

MID SHOT, LOW ANGLE- Titan looks up to see THUNDEROUS CLOUDS
ROLL IN FOLLOWED BY MONSTROUS WAVES THAT CRASH UPON THE
SHORELINE. LIGHTNING FLASHES IN THE DISTANCE.

LONG SHOT, HIGH ANGLE- As he is struggling to leave the
atmosphere of the planet, Titan is hit by some debris and
eventually struck by a bolt of lightning.


INT. NEBULA

LONG SHOT- Titan is seen quickly exiting the planet's
atmosphere on the opposite side of Makar.

POV SHOT [TITAN'S HUD]- Titan sees Makar destroying his
planet. The battery is now lower.

MID SHOT- Titan flies towards Makar's face and frantically
attempts to capture his attention.

MID SHOT- Titan flies further out in front of Makar and
FLASHES A BRIGHT PROJECTION OF LIGHT FROM HIS BODY. Makar
ceases his attempt at making a star as he sees a SMALL
FLASHING LIGHT.

MID SHOT- Makar extends his hand out beyond the object and
THE FLASHING LIGHT and brings it back toward him leading
Titan closer to his face.

ZOOM TO CLOSE UP- Makar's gaze is set on Titan who PROJECTS
A SMALL HOLOGRAM OF THE PLANET. Intrigued, Makar's attention
remains on Titan and the PROJECTION is unnoticed.


                                                      (CONTINUED)

CONTINUED: 4.

MID SHOT, LOW ANGLE- Titan drastically ENLARGES THE HOLOGRAM
and Makar quickly turns his gaze toward it. The PROJECTION
SHOWS THE SURFACE OF THE BEAUTIFUL PLANET AND THE PROCESS OF
ITS DESTRUCTION. Makar shakes his head and then points at a
star in the outer galaxy that shines brighter than the rest.

OVER THE SHOULDER SHOT [MAKAR'S]- Titan desperately PROJECTS
MORE IMAGES OF THE PLANET'S SURFACE. SEVERAL IMAGES ARE
DISPLAYED ONE AFTER ANOTHER. While one IMAGE IS BEING
DISPLAYED, THE PROJECTION BEGINS TO FLICKER AND STATIC IS
SEEN THROUGHOUT THE PROJECTION. A BATTERY METER APPEARS ON
(TITAN'S DISPLAY HUD). AS IS APPEARS IT IS YELLOW AND THEN
BECOMES RED AS IT SHORTENS IN LENGTH.

LONG SHOT- Side view of Titan and Makar. Makar reaches
towards the projection in amazement.

CLOSE UP- Makar's eyes widen as a look of realization
appears on his face.

LONG SHOT, SLOW PAN- He turns his gaze away from Titan
toward THE DAMAGED PLANETS FLOATING AROUND THE NEBULA. He
stares deeply at THE DAMAGED PLANETS and his expression
fades to complete remorse.

MID SHOT- Makar looks from the destruction back to the
hologram and a determined expression overtakes his face.

LONG SHOT- Makar purposefully moves his hands fluidly in a
spherical motion in front of him. CLOUDS OF PARTICLES AND
SPECKS OF LIGHT APPEAR.

POV SHOT [TITAN'S HUD]- Titan sees Makar's new creation. THE
BATTERY METER FLASHES AS ITS RED COLOR FADES AND BECOMES
EMPTY. Slowly the display fades to black.

CLOSE UP- Makar's amazed face as he stares proudly at the
planet he is creating. LIGHT FLASHES ON HIS FACE. He turns
away from the camera to show Titan his new creation.

LONG SHOT- Makar sees Titan floating lifelessly away from
the nebula. He trudges through the surface of the nebula
with great urgency to catch up to Titan, but his steps are
slow and heavy.

CLOSE UP- Makar's legs struggle to move through the nebula
material, bound to its surface. He attempts to lift them
further.

EXTREME LONG SHOT- Makar reaches the edge of the nebula and
extends his arms towards Titan, who is seen floating away
into the depths of space.

(CONTINUED)

CONTINUED:                                                            5.


CLOSE UP- Makar stares off into space with an expression of
utter devastation.

MID SHOT- Back inside the nebula, Makar looks from the
planet back to the place where Titan drifted away. With a
look of purpose and determination, Makar picks up the
planet.

LONG SHOT- Makar sends the planet out into space. He stands
proudly as he stares at the drifting, rotating creation.

CAMERA PANS BACK with the planet as it drifts away.


EXT. OUTER SPACE - LATER

EXTREME LONG SHOT- Space with Makar's nebula appearing small
in the distance.

CLUSTERS OF LIGHTS are seen in the darker regions of the
planet.

A satellite is launched from the planet.

                                              FADE TO BLACK:


          THE END


## Dialogue and Sound

Dialogue is mentioned in the scriptwriting section above, but I wanted to make an emphatic point on the reasons why dialogue should be avoided in the animated short film. Animation is a visual medium. A great, animated short film should be able to tell a story visually, without the aid of narration or dialogue. In addition, the absence of narration and dialogue is ideal in engaging an international audience.

There are other aspects of sound that need to be considered, however. Music, sound effects, and Foley are important parts of a finished animated story since they support the visuals created.[10]

At this point, however, it is important to include any thoughts on sound that might come up, especially if the sound is imperative to the story and moves the story forward. Add these to the spec script and shot list.[11]

Completion of this chapter should equal the completion of the first draft of your spec script. Your spec script should keep the visual details to a minimum, be written in the present tense, and outline the location, time of day, music, sound effects, dialogue, action, and thought necessary to tell your story. In the next chapter, basic cinematography rules along with camera lenses, motions, positions, and angles are discussed. Revisions should include the implementation of these details into both the script and shot list.

## Bibliography and Further Reading

Alex, T. (2012). Your CUT TO: is showing: The most complete spec screenplay formatting guide ever written. Seattle, WA: CreateSpace Independent Publishing Platform.

Beauchamp, R. (2005). *Designing sound for animation.* Burlington, MA: Elsevier/Focal Press.

Brown, M. R. (2018). Screenplay format guide. Retrieved from http://www.storysense.com/format.htm.

Brown, M. R. (2018). Script format: dialogue. Retrieved from http://www.storysense.com/format/dialogue.htm.

Internet Movie Script Database (IMSDb). (2018). *WALL-E*. Retrieved from http://www.imsdb.com/scripts/Wall-E.html.

Riley, C. (2009). The Hollywood standard: The complete and authoritative guide to script format and style (2nd ed.). Studio City, CA: M. Wiese Productions.

## Resources

Amazon Storywriter. (2018). Retrieved from https://storywriter.amazon.com/.

BPC-Screenplay for Windows. (2018). Retrieved from http://www.bpc-screenplay.com/screenplay/installing.html.

Celtx. (2018). Retrieved from https://www.celtx.com/index.html.

DubScript Screenplay Writer | A screenplay app for Android that works with Fountain, Final Draft (FDX), and PDF. (2018). Retrieved from https://www.dubscript.com/.

Final Draft Screenwriting Software. (2018). Retrieved from https://www.finaldraft.com/.

Open Source. (2018). Trelby: A free, multiplatform, feature-rich screenwriting program. Retrieved from http://www.trelby.org/.

Page 2 Stage. (2018). Retrieved from http://www.page2stage.com/.

Plotbot: Write screenplays online with friends. (2018). Retrieved from http://www.plotbot.com/.

Screenwriting: Downloads related to <fade in>. (2018). Retrieved from http://www.rolandstroud.com/Screenwriting-1.html.

Storytouch: Scriptwriting at your fingertips. (2018). Retrieved from http://storytouch.com/.

WriterDuet: Screenwriting software that will change your life. (2018). Retrieved from https://v4.writerduet.com/.

## Notes

1. A shot is defined as a visual structural unit for each camera change and is equivalent to the narrative beat. A scene is a series of shots that occur in a single location and during a continuous period of time. A change in location or time would result in a change of scene. A sequence is a series of scenes that form a section of the story, as an act or part of an act. To simplify the process and avoid confusion when working as a team on a short animated film, we have adopted the practice of only numbering shots without restarting the number for each scene. Our films have a typical shot number between 50–100 for a 5-minute film. We have also adopted the practice, especially working in 3D, to use the camera sequencer in Autodesk's Maya, which allows for continuity between shots. We break the files into sequences of shots that occur in the same scene. This practice will take a short film comprised of 50–100 shots and break them into 8–14 sequences, saving each into its own Maya file. This process speeds up the workflow by reducing the number of files that need to be lit and set up for render.

2. This chapter will begin your journey as you write your script, however, for a more detailed discussion of scriptwriting, additional books are listed in the bibliography of this chapter.

3. Transitions are usually a fourth category, however, it makes more sense to me to group them with scene headings since they close out the preceding scene and are rarely used in the spec script.

4. Finaldraft.com is probably the most commonly used software out there for both Mac and Windows, but it is quite pricey. Celtx.com has an inexpensive scriptwriting software for Mac, while also having a free online subscription that allows you to type up a script (among other paid subscriptions that do much more). Trelby.org is free for Windows or Linux. See the resources section of this chapter for more free screenwriting options.

5. Formatting information is compiled from these highly recommended additional reading sources: Brown, M. R. (2018). *Screenplay format guide*. Retrieved from http://www.storysense.com/format.htm; Riley, C. (2009). *The Hollywood standard: The complete and authoritative guide to script format and style* (2nd ed.). Studio City, CA: M. Wiese Productions; Alex, T. (2012). *Your CUT TO: is showing: The most complete spec screenplay formatting guide ever written*. Seattle, WA: CreateSpace Independent Publishing Platform.

6. You can also download a Microsoft Word Animation Script Template from the companion website for this book.

7. Dialogue has many rules and examples, too many to put in this book. For further questions and clarifications, I highly recommend reading the books already mentioned in footnote 4 or Brown, M. R. (n.d.). *Script format: dialogue*. Retrieved from http://www.storysense.com/format/dialogue.htm.

8. Keep dialogue to a minimum or none, especially in the animated short. The story should be told visually.

9. Professional scriptwriter formatting opinions vary anywhere from 3.5" to 4.1", but the majority settle on 4".

10. One of my former colleagues wrote a great book on designing sound for animation. I highly recommend it as a great addition to your reference library. Beauchamp, R. (2005). *Designing sound for animation*. Burlington, MA: Elsevier/Focal Press.

11. Find out more about sound in Chapter 8.

# 6

# Cinematographic Visual Techniques

Whether you are using a real-world camera to film your stop motion, drawing the layout in 2D, or using a virtual camera in a 3D software package, one must understand and consider the visual aspects of the frame as seen through the lens of a camera. Acting as both writer and director, and after writing your spec script and creating your first draft shot list, the next step is to identify the camera lens, motion, position, and angle that will be used for each shot during production, as these significantly influence the structure and meaning of a film through visual language. This next section will go over the terminology used for cinematography.[1]

**Figure 6.1**
Dave frames his subject through the viewfinder of the camera. Still image from *Squeaky Business* (2011). Courtesy of the University of Central Florida Character Animation Specialization.

# Cinematography Rules

First and foremost: Rules are meant to be broken. While there are certain rules to follow for everything, it is always important to remember: Never say never! There must be a reason to break a rule, and usually it is for emotional impact and dramatic affect. With that in mind, the following three rules are favored for effective cinematography.

The hero character (aka the good guy) usually enters screen left and exits screen right. Motion to the right is considered positive because we tend to view an image from left to right and thus movement in that direction seems natural. The villain character (aka the bad guy) typically enters screen right and exit screen left. Movements to the left of the screen feel uncomfortable and build tension.[2]

## 180° Rule

As a basic guideline, there is a physical relationship between two characters within the frame of the camera lens. An imaginary link between the two characters called the "line of action"[3] creates a connection from one character to the other. The camera must remain on one side of this defined line between one camera cut to another. By following the 180° rule, characters remain on the same side of the frame during the scene, which allows the audience to keep themselves oriented to the action happening on screen.

Reasons not to break the line:

- Moving Characters: If your character is walking, running, driving, etc., the line of action is the direction that the character is moving. Crossing the line confuses the audience because it looks as if the character has changed direction.
- Prevent Confusion: Changing the camera more than 180° will disorient the audience.

If the camera passes over the line (also called crossing the line or jumping the line), you are breaking the rule. As stated earlier, you must have a reason to break the rule if you are doing so.

Reasons to break the line:

- More Than Two Characters: Sometimes, the line must be crossed because it simply does not work for all of the characters in your scene.
- Emotional Tension: If you cut to a camera on the exact opposite side of the line, it is called a *reverse cut*, which causes disorientation in the viewer and confusion. A *reverse cut* should be avoided unless it provides an element of unease to the story.[4]

**Figure 6.2**
180° rule: Characters must remain on the same side of the frame from one camera cut to the next during the scene. This image shows Turt on screen left (boxed in green) and Gator on screen right (boxed in red). The screen does not need to remain equally divided from shot to shot. Still images from *Mustache Mayhem* (2011). (Timecode 04:11–04:19) Courtesy of the University of Central Florida Character Animation Specialization.

**Figure 6.3**
180° rule and 30° rule.

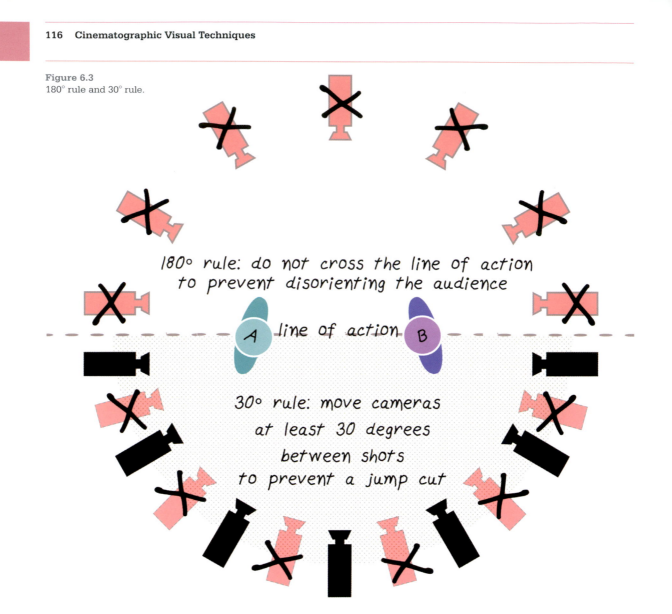

180° rule: do not cross the line of action
to prevent disorienting the audience

A   line of action   B

30° rule: move cameras
at least 30 degrees
between shots
to prevent a jump cut

If the camera must break the line, there are several ways to do so without causing confusion:

- Do not use a camera cut. Instead, use a horizontal tracking or tumbling movement to cross the line.[5]
- In between shots, use a cut to a wide shot or very wide shot to orient the audience to the whole scene.[6]
- Use a cut away.[7]

## 30° Rule

As a basic guideline, this rule explains that the camera should move at least 30° (but no more than 180°) between shots of the same subject occurring in succession; otherwise, a *jump cut*[8] occurs, which is very jarring to the audience.

By following the 30° rule, the cut is less jarring. The 30° rule also softens a change in camera position, such as changing from a medium shot to a close-up.[9]

## Eye-Level Rule

We live our day-to-day lives viewing the world around us at eye level. Because of this, the majority of your camera angles should be created at eye level, especially if you want no dramatic impact for the shot. Place the camera at the same height as the subject to achieve the eye-level rule, as if the character will be able to look directly into the camera lens. Deviating from eye-level creates an emotional impact directly related to the amount of difference in the angle.

# Camera Lenses

Again, no matter if you are using a real-world camera or a virtual one, the camera lens, or the digital virtual imitation thereof, should be considered as another element of cinematography when creating your shot list. It is important to note that there is no difference in definition between lenses used for a still camera or a video camera (or a virtual one in a 3D software). There is some preliminary camera terminology that should be understood.

*Depth of field* is the area of focus and can also describe how deep or shallow (depth) the area of focus (field) is. In a nutshell, the amount of light that enters the lens determines the depth of field: more light = shallower depth of field (less area of focus, more blur), and less light = deeper depth of field (more area of focus, less blur).

There are several ways of controlling the amount of light that enters the lens, which in turn affects the size of the depth of field. Combining these settings can give you varying results.[10]

- Aperture: The aperture is the opening of the iris (or shutter). The fStop is the setting that changes the size of the aperture. Most films are shot between f/4 and f/8 the majority of the time, using the lower fStop numbers lower lighting, extreme close-ups, and for specialty shots.
  - The lower the fStop number (f/1.4, f/2, f/2.8, f/4), the larger the aperture and the shallower the depth of field (less area of focus, more blur).
  - The higher the fStop number (f/5.6, f/8, f/11, f/16, f/22), the smaller the aperture and the deeper the depth of field (more area of focus, less blur).
- Focal Distance: This is the distance from the camera lens to the subject.
  - The further away from the subject is from the camera lens, the deeper the depth of field (more area of focus, less blur).
  - The closer to the subject from the camera lens, the shallower the depth of field (less area of focus, more blur).
- Shutter Speed (Still Camera) or Shutter Angle (Video Camera): This is the time that the shutter is open on a still camera or the size of the shutter angle[11] on a video camera. The shutter speed/angle determines the amount of motion blur.
  - The faster the shutter speed or the smaller the shutter angle, the shorter the exposure time and the less light enters, therefore moving objects appear less blurry.
  - The slower the shutter speed or the larger the shutter angle, the longer the exposure time, therefore moving objects appear more blurry.
- Focal Length: This is the distance from the film (or digital sensor) to the center of the lens and is measured in millimeters. Focal length is directly related to the angle of your lens. Changing the focal length gives you the ability to zoom into or away from your subject.
  - The smaller the focal length (8mm, 16mm), the wider the angle and the deeper the depth of field (more area of focus, less blur).
  - The longer the focal length (80mm, 300mm), the smaller the angle and the shallower the depth of field (less area of focus, more blur).

**Figure 6.4**
**Depth of field shows the foreground in focus and the background blurred.** Still image from *Snacktime* (2015). (Timecode 02:32) Courtesy of the University of Central Florida Character Animation Specialization.

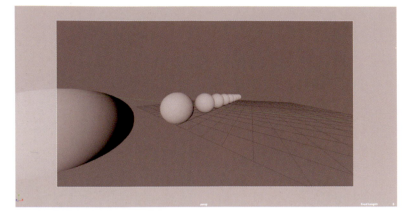

**Figure 6.5**
A super wide-angle lens of 8mm distorts and expands the field of view, elongating the length of the area while allowing for more of the width. Objects closer to camera are stretched.

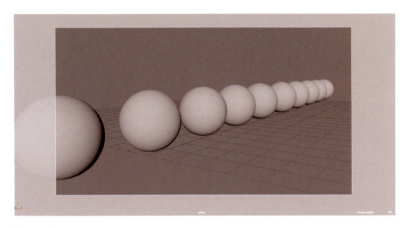

**Figure 6.6**
A wide angle lens with a focal length of 35mm has less distortion. This image, and those that follow, are of the exact same setting as the previous image showing the 8mm lens. The only thing that is changing is the position of the camera and the focal length.

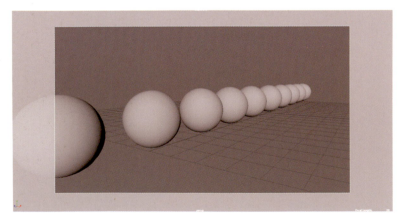

**Figure 6.7**
A wide-angle lens with a focal length of 28mm is versatile for creating depth and achieving the cinematic look of filmmaking.

## Wide Angle

Wide-angle lenses are able to capture more of the environment. The wider angle, however, distorts and expands the field of view, elongating the length of the area while allowing for more of the width. Wide-angle lenses are most commonly used for capturing landscapes, architecture, and wide groups of people. Traditionally, a super wide-angle lens is classified as anything with a focal length under 20mm. Wide-angle lenses have a focal length of 21–35mm.

Most filmmakers use either a normal standard lens or a 28mm for the majority of their film.

> When we go to the movies we want to have an experience that emulates reality in many ways, but also is fantastical and surrealistic. That's where a lens like the 28mm comes into play. It's just off center. Just barely wider than our regular field of vision, but not too wide that it becomes distracting. It's different enough from a 'normal' focal length like the 50mm that it lets us subconsciously feel like we're in a new world, but it's also close enough to realty that we aren't lost by any noticeable distortion that we would experience from a more extreme lens choice, like a 12mm. Conversely, shooting on a medium telephoto lens (like a 65mm), would also would [*sic*] be just off center from our normal field of vision, but it could never work as universally as the 28mm lens. If you had to shoot an entire film on a single lens, it would be a lot easier to use a 28mm than a 65mm, unless you're doing something really specific. The 28mm would allow for wides, close-ups, landscape shots

and more, all while maintaining a unique and original look. The 65mm would paint you into a corner in some cases, making establishing shots, masters, or medium-wides quite difficult. That said, a normal focal length like a 35mm or 50mm may seem to be the more natural choice as that field of view is closest to human vision, but the 28mm's ability to add that slight bit of surrealism to the picture is exactly what we want.[12]

## Standard Lenses (Normal)

Standard lenses are considered the "normal" view because there is little to no distortion. Standard lenses generally produce an image that looks natural to the human eye. Standard lenses have a focal length range of 35–70mm, and the most common lens is a fixed[13] 50mm lens.

## Telephoto

Telephoto lenses have a narrower angle so the subject appears closer to the camera. A forced perspective occurs because the field of view flattens in relationship to the longer focal length, so objects in the distance will appear closer to objects in the foreground.

- A medium telephoto lens focal range is between 80mm and 135mm and is ideal for framing the head and upper body (mid-shot). Pairing it with a lower fStop such as a 2.8 gives a beautiful depth of field so that the subject is clear and the surrounding field in the front and the back of the area of focus is a soft blur.
- A "true" telephoto lens has a focal length of between 135mm and 300mm.
- A "super" telephoto lens has a focal length of more than 300mm.

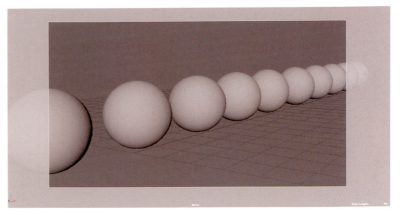

**Figure 6.8**
View through a 50mm standard lens "normal" view.

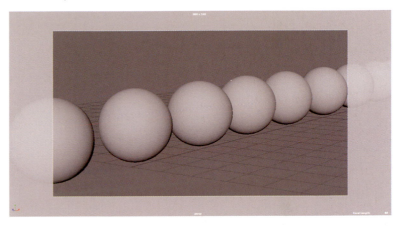

**Figure 6.9**
View through a medium telephoto lens of 80mm. The field of view is flatter compared to the 50mm.

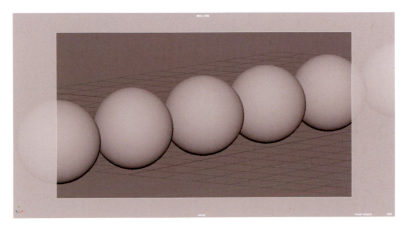

**Figure 6.10**
View through a super telephoto lens of 500mm. The field of view is noticeably flatter compared to the 50mm lens.

## Fisheye

Fisheye lenses are ultra-wide lenses, which produce a convex non-rectilinear distorted view. The center of the image appears magnified because all of the surrounding areas diminish in size. This view can be digitally created using a distortion filter or effect.

**Figure 6.11**
View through a digitally created fisheye lens. Still image from *Box Forts* (2012). (Timecode 2:28–2:31) Courtesy of the University of Central Florida Character Animation Specialization.

## Macro

Macro lenses provide the ability to focus on objects at an incredibly close range and create an image that is life-sized. They have a very shallow depth of field.

**Figure 6.12**
Macro lenses can also be simulated digitally using a shallow depth of field. Still image from *Flower Story* (2012). (Timecode 00:35) Courtesy of the University of Central Florida Character Animation Specialization.

## Looking Through Objects

While not a lens, a scene can be shot through an object such as a stained glass window, water, or translucent plastic to create a distorted image with emotional impact. In addition, if working in a 3D software, the camera can be placed in such a way that the as if the object was the camera itself, which works wonderfully for unique point of view[14] shots.

**Figure 6.13**
Looking through a monocular. Still image from *Box Forts* (2012). (Timecode 02:24 – 02:26) Courtesy of the University of Central Florida Character Animation Specialization.

## Reflecting from Objects

While not a lens, a scene can also be shot reflecting from an object's surface, such as a mirror, eyeball, or a chrome bumper, to create a focus on both the reflective object and the action in the scene.

**Figure 6.14**
The conquistador sees his reflection in the handle of his sword, showing his narcissistic tendencies. Still image from *Snacktime* (2015). (Timecode 01:27–01:31) Courtesy of the University of Central Florida Character Animation Specialization.

# Camera Motion

The following section describes the different types of camera motion that can be used when creating your film.

## Static

A static camera (also called stable or locked down) is stationary and does not move during the shot. The focal length may change, but the aim does not.

## Pan

A pan is when a stationary camera physically rotates from left to right, or right to left (x-axis). Pan is an abbreviation of panoramic and is used to show the environment or the contents thereof.

A whip pan (also called a flick pan, swish pan, or zip pan) moves the camera so quickly that the image becomes a full frame motion blur. This type of pan can be used as a transition between shots indicating passage of time or frenzied action.

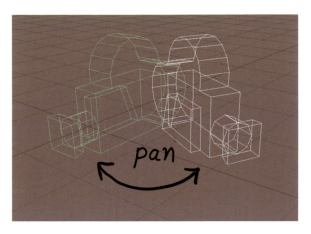

Figure 6.15
A camera pan motion.

Figure 6.16
**The camera pans to follow the Sputnik satellite as it travels in orbit.** Still images from *Box Forts* (2012). (Timecode 03:45–03:46) Courtesy of the University of Central Florida Character Animation Specialization.

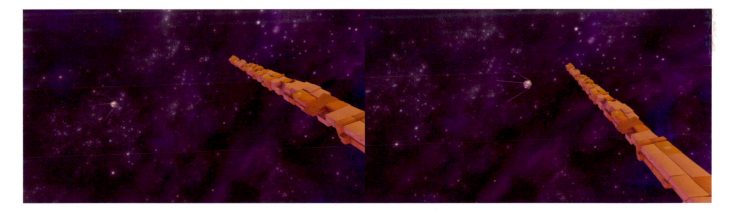

Figure 6.17
**The camera moves with a whip pan from Jake's box fort of the Eiffel tower over to Judy's frenzied action as she builds her next fort.** Still images from *Box Forts* (2012). (Timecode 03:01–03:02) Courtesy of the University of Central Florida Character Animation Specialization.

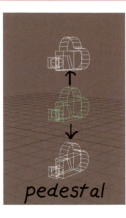

## Pedestal

A pedestal is when the camera physically moves from down to up, or up to down (y-axis), usually on a tripod in real life. This shot is useful when needing to raise or lower the camera to see "eye to eye" with the subject while adding emphasis to make a point.

**Figure 6.18**
A camera pedestal motion.

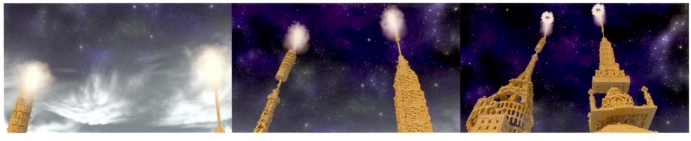

**Figure 6.19**
**The camera pedestals down to show the height of the two towers.** Still images from *Box Forts* (2012). (Timecode 03:21–03:24) Courtesy of the University of Central Florida Character Animation Specialization.

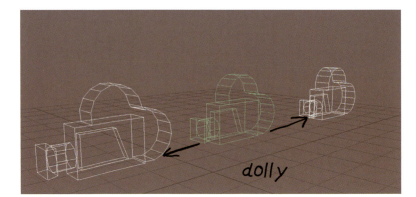

**Figure 6.20**
A camera dolly motion.

## Dolly

A dolly is a camera movement closer to the subject (dolly in) or backing away from subject (dolly out) (on the z-axis).

A push-in/push-out is when the camera dollies in towards the subject causing the scene to narrow, and then out away from the subject, causing the scene to widen. This shot is usually used to change location while the subject remains the same.

**Figure 6.21**
**A dolly in to show the statue transform into the living and breathing Winston.** Still images from *Snacktime* (2015). (Timecode 00:49–00:51) Courtesy of the University of Central Florida Character Animation Specialization.

## Tracking

A truck or tracking shot is a camera movement, which follows a moving subject while moving left to right and maintaining a perpendicular relationship to the subject.

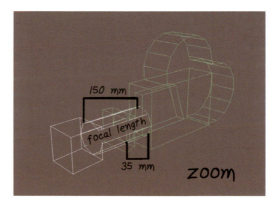

Figure 6.22
A camera track motion.

**Figure 6.23**
The camera pans to follow the arrival of the school bus. Still images from *Box Forts* (2012). (Timecode 00:11–00:17) Courtesy of the University of Central Florida Character Animation Specialization.

## Zoom

A zoom is where the subject appears to move towards the camera to a close-up or away from the camera from a close-up to a wide shot by changing the focal length. The camera does not physically move.

**Figure 6.25**
The camera zooms in to focus on Judy's stunned expression. Still images from *Box Forts* (2012). (Timecode 02:31–02:33) Courtesy of the University of Central Florida Character Animation Specialization.

Figure 6.24
When the camera zooms, the focal length changes but the camera does not move.

## Circular

A circular shot (also called shooting in the round) is created while tumbling the camera around the subject in a circle.

**Figure 6.32**
The camera circles around the intense poker game between Turt, Mustache, and Gator. Still images from *Mustache Mayhem* (2011). (Timecode 03:26–03:36) Courtesy of the University of Central Florida Character Animation Specialization.

## Crane

A crane shot is traditionally filmed with a device that is use to move a camera up above and away from the subjects or starts high above and moves vertically downward into the scene. Any shot, digitally or otherwise, which mimics this motion, is also considered a crane.

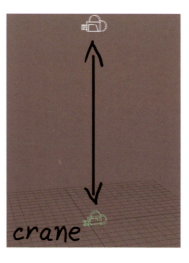

**Figure 6.33**
A camera crane motion.

**Figure 6.34**
The camera cranes down the outside of the building where Dave lives to show the New York landscape as it reflects in the windows. Still image from *Squeaky Business* (2011). (Timecode 00:06–00:11) Courtesy of the University of Central Florida Character Animation Specialization.

## Handheld

A handheld camera motion is an unstable image created by the physicality of holding the camera, or digitally mimicking the same look and feel. The emotional effect is instability, especially when following a stable, locked-down camera. The bumpier the movement, the more the instability is felt.

**Figure 6.35**
**The camera following Turt is handheld to add to the emotional instability of his frantic search for Gator.** Still images from *Mustache Mayhem* (2011). (Timecode 05:25–05:30) Courtesy of the University of Central Florida Character Animation Specialization.

## Shake

While real-world cinematographers try to avoid a shaky camera, shake is sometimes added to a digital camera to enhance the believability of a shot. When something monumental is being shown, such as the speed of a car passing by or the fast and quick movement of a camera as it follows something plummeting from the sky to the earth below, an added camera shake, either simulated by moving the frame or physical by moving the camera, adds impact and plausibility.

**Figure 6.36**
**Shake is added to magnify the speed and instability of the camera as it follows the falling box holding Jake and Judy.** Still images from *Box Forts* (2012). (Timecode 04:01–04:05) Courtesy of the University of Central Florida Character Animation Specialization.

## Steadicam

Traditionally, a steadicam device[16] allows a camera to move as if it were handheld and track a subject, but without the bumpiness or physical track, making the camera appear as if were floating. Animating digital cameras do this from the outset.

## Aerial

An aerial shot is taken from the sky level,[17] giving an extreme bird's-eye perspective.

**Figure 6.37**
**Still image of the opening shot from** *Box Forts* **(2012).** (Timecode 00:05–00:09) Courtesy of the University of Central Florida Character Animation Specialization.

# Camera Position

The location of the camera and the width of the angle of the lens impact the composition of the frame, what the audience can see, and how the audience reacts emotionally to what is being seen.

The closer the camera is to the character, whether physically or forced by camera angle, the more intimate, engaged, and focused the audience will be with the subject. It is much easier to specify where the audience should focus. The farther the camera is from the character, the more the audience will feel they are observers and are less involved, because the characters become part of the background. The location, however, becomes more significant to the audience because more of it can be seen. The visual field becomes more complex as there is much more for the audience to take in and process.

The final display size of the screen also affects the emotional impact of a shot and must be considered. A film designed for a mobile device has different considerations than a film designed for the silver screen. Wide shots have much more dramatic power on a large theater screen than on a small mobile device, where closer shots are needed more.

## Extreme Wide Shot

An extreme wide shot (EWS; also called an extreme long shot [ELS] or extreme full shot [EFS]) is a really broad panoramic view of an exterior location taken from a significant distance.

## Very Wide Shot

A very wide shot (VWS; also called a very long shot [VLS] or very full shot [VFS]) shows a broad view of the environment and the full character.

## Wide Shot (LS/FS/WS)

A wide shot (WS; also called a long shot [LS] or full shot [FS]) shows an entire character from head to toe and a good view of the environment.

**Figure 6.38**
**Extreme wide shot.** Still image from *Celestial* (2014). (Timecode 02:57–02:59) Courtesy of the University of Central Florida Character Animation Specialization.

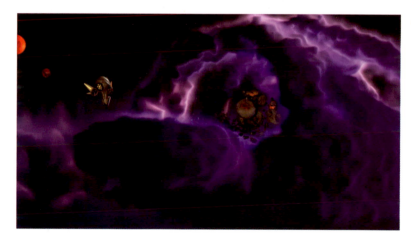

**Figure 6.39**
**Very wide shot.** Still image from *Celestial* (2014). (Timecode 02:21–02:27) Courtesy of the University of Central Florida Character Animation Specialization.

**Figure 6.40**
**Wide shot.** Still image from *Expend* (2018). (Timecode 03:10–03:16) Used with kind permission from Bismark Fernandes, Savannah College of Art and Design.

## Medium Wide Shot

A medium wide shot (MWS; also called a medium long shot or medium full shot) shows a character from the knees and above, and is wide enough to see the physical setting and facial expressions.

**Figure 6.41**
**Medium wide shot.** Still image from *Celestial* (2014). (Timecode 04:28–04:29) Courtesy of the University of Central Florida Character Animation Specialization.

## Mid Shot

A mid shot or medium shot (MS) shows the character's upper body, arms, and head.

**Figure 6.42**
**Mid shot.** Still image from *Celestial* (2014). (Timecode 00:26–00:34) Courtesy of the University of Central Florida Character Animation Specialization.

## Medium Close-Up

A medium close-up (MCU) shows the character filling half the screen.

**Figure 6.43**
**Medium close-up.** Still image from *Celestial* (2014). (Timecode 02:43–02:46) Courtesy of the University of Central Florida Character Animation Specialization.

## Close-Up

A close-up (CU) shows the character's face and shoulders.

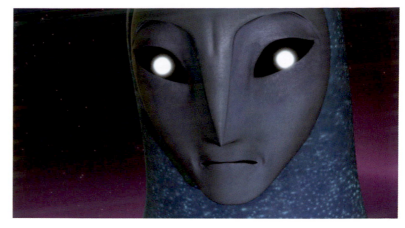

**Figure 6.44**
**Close-up.** Still image from *Celestial* (2014). (Timecode 06:13–06:15) Courtesy of the University of Central Florida Character Animation Specialization.

## Extreme Close-Up

An extreme close-up (ECU) focuses on a part of the face or body that fills up the screen.

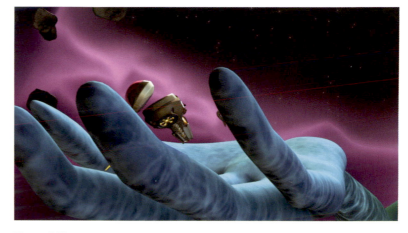

**Figure 6.45**
**Extreme close-up.** Still image from *Celestial* (2014). (Timecode 05:48) Courtesy of the University of Central Florida Character Animation Specialization.

## Cut-In

A cut-in is an interruption of a continuous shot with an insert view of a close-up of the subject, showing some part of the subject in detail, followed by a cut back to the first shot, used to emphasize emotion. This is an editing technique but should be considered and planned while creating the shot list.

**Figure 6.46**
**A cut-in is used to focus on the seed.** Still images from *Flower Story* (2012). (Timecode 05:01–05:17) Courtesy of the University of Central Florida Character Animation Specialization.

## Cut-Away

A cut-away is interruption of a continuous shot with an insert view of something else, followed by a cut back to the first shot, used to add interest or information. This is another editing technique, but should be considered and planned while creating the shot list.

**Figure 6.47**
A cut-away is used to see that Priscilla is reacting to the conquistador's arrival in her lair. Still images from *Snacktime* (2015). (Timecode 02:49–02:57) Courtesy of the University of Central Florida Character Animation Specialization.

## Establishing Shot

An establishing shot is usually the first shot of a new environment and shows the relationship between the environment and the characters, to show where the story is taking place. Usually an extreme wide shot or a very wide shot.

**Figure 6.48**
**Establishing shot.** Still image from *Yours, Mime, and Ours* (2014). (Timecode 00:13–00:14) Courtesy of the University of Central Florida Character Animation Specialization.

## Two-Shot

A two-shot frames two characters and is used to establish a relationship between them. Most two-shots are either mid shots of two characters, side by side, or shots that have one character in the foreground and the other in the background. A three-shot (group shot) is the same, except with three (or more) characters in the frame.

**Figure 6.49**
**Left: A two-shot of Winston and Priscilla.** (Timecode 02:19–02:21) Right: A three-shot establishing Winston's location as he watches the standoff between Priscilla and the conquistador. (Timecode 03:14–03:18) Still images from *Snacktime* (2015). Courtesy of the University of Central Florida Character Animation Specialization.

## Over-the-Shoulder Shot

An over-the-shoulder shot (OSS) is taken from an angle behind the shoulder of one person so that the back of the head and shoulders is used to frame the image of whoever or whatever the camera is pointing toward.

**Figure 6.50**
**Over-the-shoulder shot.** Still image from *Yours, Mime, and Ours* (2014). (Timecode 01:17–01:24) Courtesy of the University of Central Florida Character Animation Specialization.

## Shot Reverse Shot

A shot reverse shot (also called a reverse) is a shot sequence where the first shot is a camera angle that focuses on one character who is looking at a second character (either off-screen or on-screen as an over-the-shoulder shot), followed by a second shot with the other character looking back at the first character.

**Figure 6.51**
Shot reverse shot. Still images from *Ukelayla* (2018). (Timecode 02:36–02:41) Courtesy of the University of Central Florida Character Animation Specialization.

## Point-of-View Shot

A point-of-view (POV) shot is taken from the angle of the first-person viewpoint of a character, as the name indicates. Point-of-view shots are usually preceded by a close-up of the character.

**Figure 6.52**
Point-of-view shot of Gus looking at his daughter, Marcy. Still image from *Yours, Mime, and Ours* (2014). (Timecode 03:13–03:15) Courtesy of the University of Central Florida Character Animation Specialization.

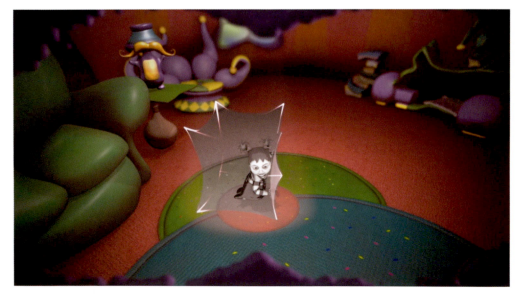

# Camera Angle

The emotional impact of the film is also affected by the angle of the camera during the shot. Below are the types of angles that should be considered when creating your shot list.

## Eye Level

An eye-level camera lens angle is perpendicular to the ground and parallel to the character's eyes. The camera is not tilted in any direction (no angle), and the character is not looking up or down into the lens. As stated earlier in the eye-level rule, most of the shots in a film will contain no angle, since this conveys a normal or neutral emotional impact. This non-angle provides no dramatic power and is ideal for most shots.

## High-Angle

A high-angle or down-shot camera is located above the subject of focus, tilted downward. This creates a great point-of-view shot from a taller character to a shorter one. Emotionally, it also removes power from the subject, making the subject seem scared, subordinate, or feeble. High-angle shots are also great for establishing shots.

## Low-Angle

A low-angle or up-shot camera is located below the subject of focus, tilted upward. Emotionally, it gives power to the subject, making the subject seem larger, dominant, or strong. Low angles are also great for framing a character looking downward, so that the entire face is in frame.

Combining a low-angle shot with a high-angle shot during an encounter between two characters establishes which character is considered more powerful (the one filmed at the high angle), and which character is considered to be weaker (the one filmed at the low angle). While easier to establish with larger angles, using smaller angles makes this subtler to the audience, but still sends the message.

**Figure 6.53**
Eye-level camera angle. Still image from *Mustache Mayhem* (2011). (Timecode 01:07–01:15) Courtesy of the University of Central Florida Character Animation Specialization.

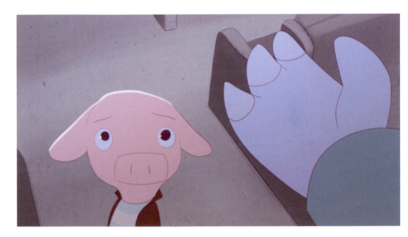

**Figure 6.54**
A high-angle camera. Still image from *ALLEYOUP!* (2017). (Timecode 00:40) Courtesy of Koko Chou, Sheridan College Animation Thesis Film.

**Figure 6.55**
A low-angle camera. Still image from *ALLEYOUP!* (2017). (Timecode 00:39) Courtesy of Koko Chou, Sheridan College Animation Thesis Film.

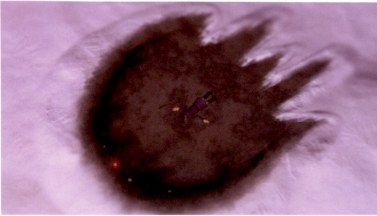

**Figure 6.56**
**A bird's eye angle.** Still image from *Ember* (2013). (Timecode 05:56–05:60) Courtesy of the University of Central Florida Character Animation Specialization.

## Bird's Eye

A bird's eye or overhead shot is filmed above the subject looking down, as if the camera's point of view was from a bird. Using this angle gives you another way to show how things in the scene relate to each other. The distance and angle from the subject matter changes the emotional impact. Framing the subject closer with a steeper angle (looking almost directly down) is rather powerful.

**Figure 6.57**
**A Dutch-angle camera.** Still image from *Box Forts* (2012). (Timecode 04:05–04:08) Courtesy of the University of Central Florida Character Animation Specialization.

## Dutch Angle

A Dutch angle (also called a canted angle, Dutch tilt, German angle, or slanted angle) has the camera leaning sideways, tilted on its roll axis, making the horizon line no longer parallel within the frame. A Dutch angle, usually shot as a static shot, creates a dynamic composition due to the diagonals created. Emotionally, it creates a feeling of instability or uneasiness. When paired with a close-up, it can suggest the mental instability of a character. Dutch angles should be used sparingly.

**Figure 6.58**
**A worm's eye angle.** Still images from *Mustache Mayhem* (2011). (Timecode 03:21–03:23) Courtesy of the University of Central Florida Character Animation Specialization.

## Worm's Eye

A worm's eye shot or undershot is filmed below the subject looking up, as if the camera's point of view is from a worm and the ground. It's usually used to show the enormity of an environment, such as when looking up at skyscraper buildings.

# Revising the Shot List

Chapter 4 suggested that you create a shot list after writing your treatment. Now that a first draft of the script is made and basic cinematography has been covered, it is time to revisit the shot list and make some changes.

First and foremost, be sure to add additional shot descriptions, including anything new that developed while writing the script. Once this is completed, an update of the shot numbers is usually needed if increments of 10 were not used for additional room to add new shot numbers. Add the action description and identify which characters are in each shot. This information is helpful when considering your camera direction. If working in a spreadsheet, this is easily done by adding additional rows where needed.

Next, consider each shot as you visualize what is occurring in the shot description. Enter the camera direction as you progress through the shot list. Additional columns can be added for position, motion, angles, and focal length.

Remember that this list, as well as the treatment and script, is a malleable object. Nothing is ever set in stone until the project is complete. Make decisions but stay open to changes. Upon completion of these updates to the shot list, you may want to also revise both the treatment and script as well. In the next chapter, we will further the development of visual design in your story by deciding on the art direction and creating storyboards while considering screen design.

## Bibliography and Further Reading

Ebert, R. (2008, August 30). *How to read a movie*. Retrieved from https://www.rogerebert.com/rogers-journal/how-to-read-a-movie.

Mascelli, J.V. (1965). The five Cs of cinematography: Motion picture filming techniques simplified. Hollywood: Cine/Grafic Publications.

NoamKroll.com. (2018). *28mm lenses: The secret ingredient for achieving a film look*. Retrieved from http://noamkroll.com/28mm-lenses-the-secret-ingredient-for-achieving-a-film-look/.

Sijll, J.V. (2010). Cinematic storytelling: The 100 most powerful film conventions every filmmaker must know. Studio City, CA: Michael Wiese Productions.

## Notes

1. Chapters 7 and 8 will discuss other aspects that will need to be considered, such as composition and editing.
2. Ebert, R. (2008, August 30). *How to read a movie*. Retrieved from https://www.rogerebert.com/rogers-journal/how-to-read-a-movie.
3. Also known as "the line" or the "action line" and not to be confused with one of the principles of animation also named the line of action.
4. The bathroom scene in *The Shining* is a great example of this.
5. See the section in this chapter on camera motion for explanation of tracking and tumbling.
6. See the section in this chapter on camera position for explanation of wide shot and very wide shot.
7. See Chapter 8 for explanation of *cut away*.
8. See Chapter 8 for explanation of *jump cut*.
9. See the section in this chapter on camera position for explanation of medium shot and close-up.
10. You can also always add depth of field in post, during compositing, especially if using a 3D package. Make sure to render the z-buffer for this purpose.
11. A shutter angle is a metal disc with a pie slice opening that rotates at a constant rate to allow light onto the film (or digital sensor). The larger the angle, the more the light can enter.
12. NoamKroll.com. (2018). *28mm lenses: The secret ingredient for achieving a film look*. Retrieved from http://noamkroll.com/28mm-lenses-the-secret-ingredient-for-achieving-a-film-look/.
13. Fixed means that there is no focal range, therefore, no ability to zoom the lens in or out of the subject.
14. See the section in this chapter on camera angle for explanation of point of view.
15. The dolly zoom can be seen during the stampede in *The Lion King*.
16. A wearable camera mount device invented in 1971 by cameraman Garret Brown in conjunction with Cinema Product, Inc.
17. Such as from a helicopter, building top, or drone.

# Art Direction, Storyboarding, and Screen Design

# Art Direction

Art direction for animation is the process of taking the story to an entirely different visual level. Most importantly, the art direction establishes the artistic style of the film. Art direction evokes emotion from the audience by making the story look beautiful, which in turn, adds meaning.

By choosing certain elements, such as color and texture, art direction adds psychological appeal to the story by evoking a particular response and mood. The time period and location of the story heavily influence the art direction. The time period and location should be chosen before or in conjunction with the style.

*Mise-en-scène* is a French term that developed in the theater and literally means "placing on stage," but has evolved into two meanings for film production. The first meaning describes how anything seen through the camera lens should be telling the story in a visual and artful way with a purpose defined by the director. In other words, mise-en-scène is the art direction of the film. Some also include the cinematography in this definition. The second meaning defines mise-en-scène as one long, uninterrupted take that allows the action to play and the composition to rely only on camera movement and zooms instead of editing different cuts together.

# Choosing and Developing a Style

As with any part of the production process, one should begin with a brainstorming session followed by research. Begin by visualizing what the finished film might look like. Look back into your idea files that were created, as suggested in Chapter 2. Peruse through the files or notebook for items that relate to a style that works. Start a new idea notebook or file specifically for the art direction. Use the steps outlined in Chapter 2 to help you find ideas. This time, however, collect imagery specifically geared towards the art direction of your film.

art supply store. Take photos. Research the time period. Research the location. Visit the location if possible. Take a trip to learn about the world in which your story unfolds. If no such world exists, find influences that are similar. If you cannot physically experience these locations, become an armchair traveler. Search the internet for the location. Many places have great 3D walkthroughs available online. Watch the Travel Channel. Go to TravelChannel.com. Google Maps street view is a great way to experience a location.

## Research

Once you have a style in mind, gather as many books, magazines, or images as you can find about your style, furniture design, and the architecture of your time period and location. Use the internet. Go to the library. Visit the local

## Artistic Style

Perhaps a particular artist, artistic medium, or artistic style inspires you. Incorporating that look into your film will add depth and beauty to your story. The following, while not an exhaustive, is a list of art movements to help spark an idea.

| | | | |
|---|---|---|---|
| Abstract Art | Art Brut | Abstract Expressionism | Abstract Illusionism |
| Academic Art | Action Painting | Aestheticism | Altermodern |
| Arbeitsrat für Kunst | Art Deco | Art Informel | Art Nouveau |
| Assemblage | Les Automatistes | Auto Destructive Art | Barbizon School |
| Baroque | Bauhaus | Classical Realism | Color Field |
| Context Art | Conceptual Art | Constructivism | Cubism |
| Dada | Expressionism | Fantastic Realism | Fauvism |
| Figurative Art | Figuration Libre | Folk Art | Fluxus |
| Harlem Renaissance | Humanistic Aestheticism | Hypermodernism | Hyperrealism |
| Impressionism | Institutional Critique | International Gothic | International Typographic Style |
| Lyrical Abstraction | Magic Realism | Mannerism | Massurrealism |
| Maximalism | Metaphysical Painting | Mingei | Minimalism |
| New Objectivity | Northwest School | Op Art | Orphism |
| Photorealism | Pixel Art | Plasticien | Plein Air |
| Qajar Art | Rasquache | Realism | Remodernism |
| Renaissance | Rococo | Romanesque | Romanticism |
| Samikshavad | Shin Hanga | Shock Art | Sosaku Hanga |
| Symbolism | Synchromism | Tachisme | Toyism |
| Transgressive Art | Ukiyo | Underground Comix | Vancouver School |
| Verdadism | Vorticism | | |

The following, while not exhaustive, is a list of Art Materials and Techniques that may also prove to inspire.

Assemblage (beads, cardboard, found objects, glue, paper, textiles, wire, wood)

Carving (granite, ice, ivory, marble, wood, plaster, stone, wax)

Casting (aluminum, bronze, cement, gold, pewter, plaster, plastic, silver, synthetic resin, wax)

Ceramics

Cartooning

Comic book

Design (advertising, architecture, fashion, furniture, graphic, industrial, interior, jewelry, production)

Drawing (chalk, charcoal, Conté crayon, graphite, ink, marker, pastel)

Finishes (enamel, patina, polychrome, wax)

Graffiti

Illustration

Mixed media

Modeling (clay, digital, papier-mâché, plaster, sand)

Painting (acrylic, digital, finger paint, fresco, gouache, latex, oil, tempera, watercolor)

Paper cut

Photography (black and white, color, tint, film, fisheye, hand-colored, Hipstamatic, infrared, Instagram, Polaroid, sepia, tilt-shift)

Printing

Printmaking (3D, aquatint, embossing, engraving, etching, inkjet, intaglio, laser, letterpress, linocut, lithography, metalcut, mezzotint, moku hanga, monotype, relief etching, screen, Styrofoam, printing, woodcut, wood engraving)

Tattooing

**Figure 7.1**
**A graphic illustration art direction style.** Notice the halftone pattern and the black ink outlines. Still image from *Squeaky Business* (2011). (Timecode 03:00–03:09) Courtesy of the University of Central Florida Character Animation Specialization.

Figure 7.2

Style guide page, *Yours, Mime, and Ours* (2014). Courtesy of the University of Central Florida Character Animation Specialization.

# Creating a Style Guide

Once a style is decided, a style guide should be made. A style guide, essentially, is a rulebook for the film. The contents will include the answer to any questions that may be asked about how the visuals will be created, since everything in an animated film must be created.

Some suggestions for contents:

- How to draw or model the
  - setting
  - environment
  - characters
- How the lighting will look
- How to animate the characters
- How to set up shots
- What colors are used (color palettes)
- What textures will look like
- A collection of reference images

Creating a style guide forces the creator to establish the rules of the world where the story unfolds, flesh out the way the characters look and act, and determine the look of the film. Every detail must be considered. The style guide is extremely beneficial when working with a team of people so that the film is created cohesively. Figures 7.3 through 7.8 show examples of style guide pages.

# Scale

Gan is much larger
than Titan. Gan creates
planets which range in scale
from a small ball to a large yoga ball
in comparison to a toddler.
Titan is about the size of
a large bug in comparison
to Gan [small enough to enter
the atmosphere of one of the larger
planets but large enough
to still be seen by Gan]

Figure 7.3
Style guide page from *Celestial* (2014). Courtesy of the University of Central Florida Character Animation Specialization.

# Staging

Titan always moves from left to right,
emphasizing his transient nature
and the fact that he enters and exits
Gan's life (leaving a significant impact)

Figure 7.4
Style guide page from *Celestial* (2014). Courtesy of the University of Central Florida Character Animation Specialization.

# LIGHTING
## Sources

In the outer reaches of the nebula, the star serves as a strong rim light, shining behind the cloud structures and giving them the appearance of being back-lit. Inside the clearing with Gan's workshop and within the planet, the star is the key light, generally illuminating the scene

Figure 7.5
Style guide page from *Celestial* (2014). Courtesy of the University of Central Florida Character Animation Specialization.

# COLOR
## Palettes

Overall, our palette is mainly cool colors with hints of warm colors. Throughout the film, the value of the colors increases when information is being revealed or something is being realized

### Intro

The colors of the nebula are bright as the star is revealed to Gan

### Space

Space is dark because it represents the unknown

### Canyon

The canyon is unexplored and therefore mostly in shadow

### Flaming Planet

The flaming planet scene begins bright to represent Gan's false hope

### Workshop

The workshop is dim, representing Gan's pursuit of misguided goals

### Planet, Rock

The planet is brighter than the nebula, indicating an imminent shift

### Planet, Cave

The cave is dark because it is Titan's initial exploration of the new planet

### Planet, Forest

The bright forest represents the knowledge of Gan's creative potential

### Planet, Storm

The storm decreases the value drastically signifying the dramatic irony that Titan does not know what is happening

### Realization

Once Gan realizes his mistake, the nebula becomes much brighter

Figure 7.6
Style guide page from *Celestial* (2014). Courtesy of the University of Central Florida Character Animation Specialization.

# TEXTURES

### Photographic Reference

### Illustrated Texture

**Figure 7.7**
Style guide page from *Celestial* (2014). Courtesy of the University of Central Florida Character Animation Specialization.

**Figure 7.8**
Final storyboard, *Celestial* (2014). Courtesy of the University of Central Florida Character Animation Specialization.

Once you have a script, a shot list, and an overall art direction, the next step in the preproduction process is to create a storyboard. A storyboard is a sequential series of individually drawn frames that look much like a comic strip and are a visual representation of the story, showing the planned shots of a film. Each storyboard can be drawn on paper, index cards, or directly into a computer using software and a digital drawing tablet. If created digitally in Photoshop, for example, each shot or sequence can be created in one PSD file with many layers, allowing for ease in making adjustments to boards when assembling the shots in an animatic. Each board would then be saved out as a TARGA. A good file naming convention is something like the following: shotNumber.boardNumber.ext.

The shot number of the storyboard is taken from the shot list. Each shot may need several boards to visually describe the action taking place. Therefore, if there are 110 shots in the 5-minute film being created and the first shot has five boards, these boards would be labeled as 001.00.tga, 001.20.tga, 001.40.tga, 001.60.tga, and 001.80.tga. the board numbers allow for adding new shots in between if more boards are added to the shot. Some studios use alphabet letters, such as 001a.tga, 001b.tga, 001c.tga, 001d.tga, and 001e.tga. Whichever you use is fine, as long as you are consistent.

Storyboarding, much like story writing, is also an iterative process until the story is ready for production. In addition, during production, there are times when certain aspects of the story must be re-boarded for one reason or another. For example, the story may need refinement or the action may not be clear to the audience.

This question always arises: "How many storyboards does one need?" The answer, of course, depends on the quality of animation you want to create. According to Ed Catmull,[1] Pixar story artists create around 12,000 storyboards to make a 90-minute film. This means that approximately 667 are needed for a 5-minute short. When a team of people is creating an animation, storyboarding becomes even more important, so that everyone on the team knows what is happening visually. Since every storyboard image will be used to produce one of a succession of images that create your film, the position and movement of the viewer's eye must be considered. Therefore, before you begin storyboarding, you should have a strong understanding of screen design and composition.

Later in this chapter, camera techniques and movements are discussed in relation to screen composition, along with some consideration of editing as it relates to continuity between camera cuts and transitions. In traditional filmmaking, these things can be addressed during the editing process. Typically, a director can shoot multiple takes of the same scene and choose the best option during the editing process. This is not how it is done in animation. Different takes would be a complete waste of time in animation. Camera techniques and movements must be considered during the planning phase because each element must be created. This is the reasoning why these parts of cinematography are explained this chapter.

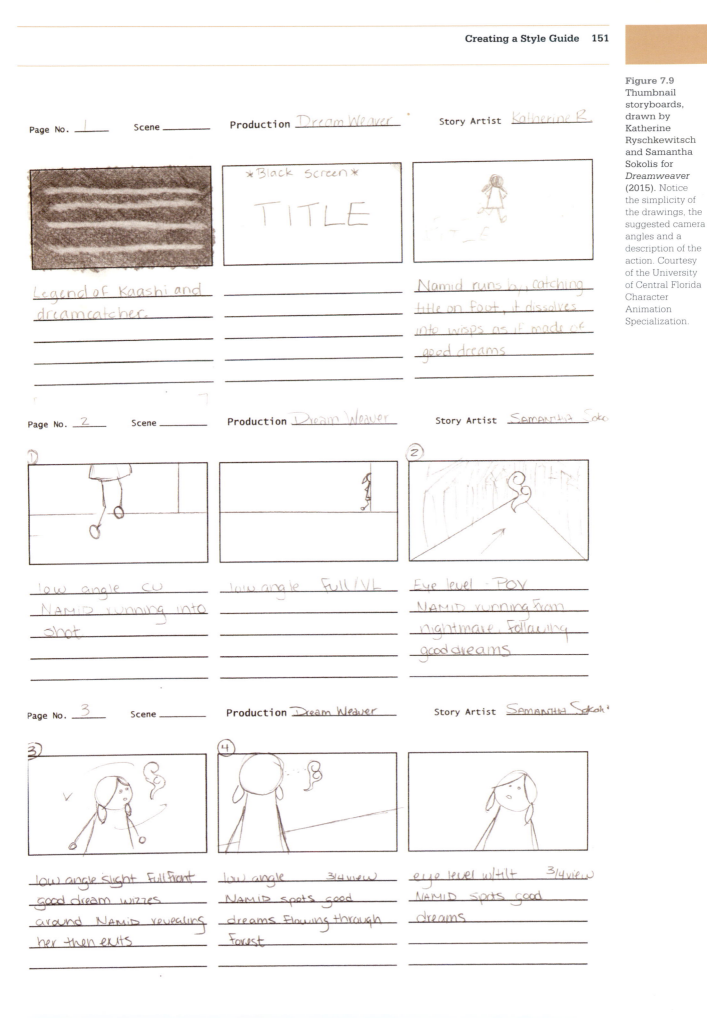

Page No. 1    Scene _____    Production *Dream Weaver*    Story Artist *Katherine R*

Legend of Kaashi and dreamcatcher.

*Black screen*

TITLE

Namid runs by, catching title on foot, it dissolves into wisps as if made of good dreams

Page No. 2    Scene _____    Production *Dream Weaver*    Story Artist *Samantha Soko*

low angle CU NAMID running into shot

low angle Full/VL

Eye level - POV NAMID running from nightmare. Following good dreams

Page No. 3    Scene _____    Production *Dream Weaver*    Story Artist *Samantha Sokoli*

low angle slight Full front good dream wizzes around NAMID revealing her then exits

low angle    3/4 view NAMID spots good dreams Flowing through Forest

eye level w/tilt    3/4 view NAMID spots good dreams

Figure 7.9 Thumbnail storyboards, drawn by Katherine Ryschkewitsch and Samantha Sokolis for *Dreamweaver* (2015). Notice the simplicity of the drawings, the suggested camera angles and a description of the action. Courtesy of the University of Central Florida Character Animation Specialization.

**Figure 7.10**
Storyboard panels for storyreel, drawn by Brianna Jaeger for *Cuddle Fish* (2016). Notice that these storyboards are more detailed than the thumbnails. (Timecode 1:20–1:50) Courtesy of the University of Central Florida Character Animation Specialization.

# Framing (Aspect Ratios)

Every screen in which we view an animation is rectangular in shape, regardless of whether the film is projected in a theater, viewed on a television, displayed on a computer monitor, streamed on a tablet, or played on a cellular phone. The size of the screen directly changes the visual impact that a film has on an audience. Because of this, deciding which screen size will be used for presentation is important before you begin the storyboarding process.

Screen layout is a term used in television and web design and is how something is placed within the dimensions of the film space, or edges of the frame. In cinematography, the term "framing" is used synonymously as the way subjects are placed amongst objects within the space of the frame using the camera angles and positions discussed in Chapter 5. Framing communicates to the audience just as much as anything a character might say; therefore, its impact is even more essential when the story has no dialogue.

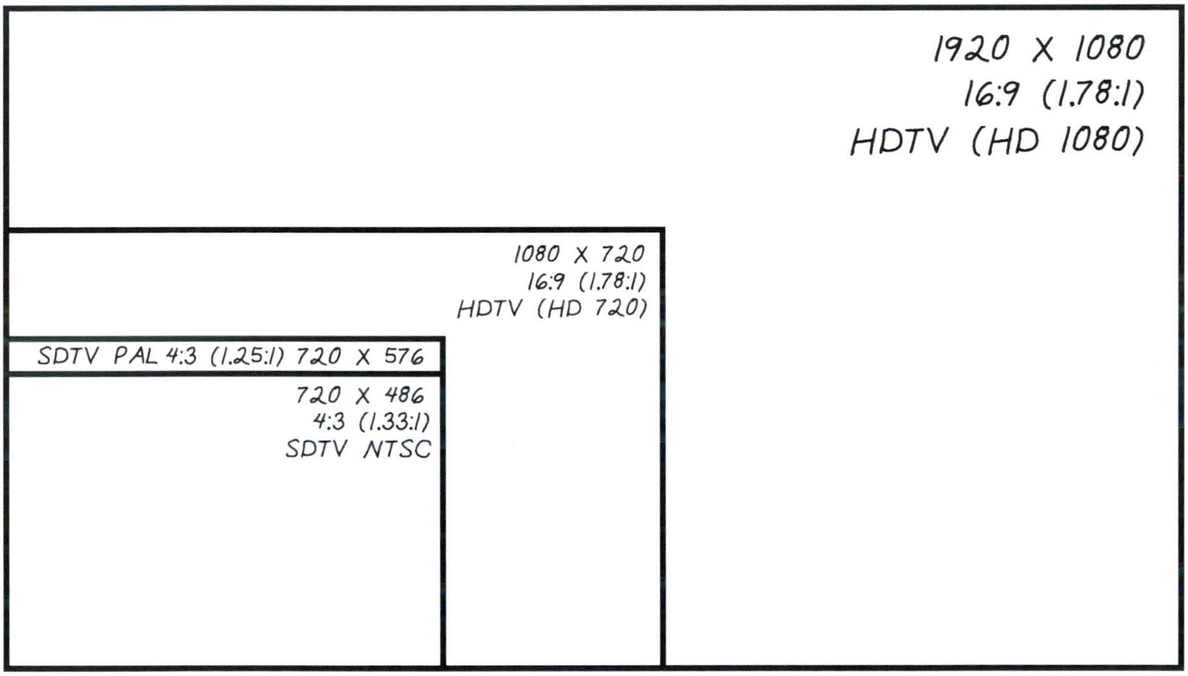

1920 X 1080
16:9 (1.78:1)
HDTV (HD 1080)

1080 X 720
16:9 (1.78:1)
HDTV (HD 720)

SDTV PAL 4:3 (1.25:1) 720 X 576

720 X 486
4:3 (1.33:1)
SDTV NTSC

Figure 7.11 Standard television resolution compared to high-definition television resolutions.

7680 X 4320
16:9 (1.78:1)
UHD Television (8K)

10240 X 4320
21:9 (2.33:1)
UHD Television (10K)

3840 X 2160
16:9 (1.78:1)
UHD Television (4K)

1920 X 1080
16:9 (1.78:1)
HDTV (HD 1080)

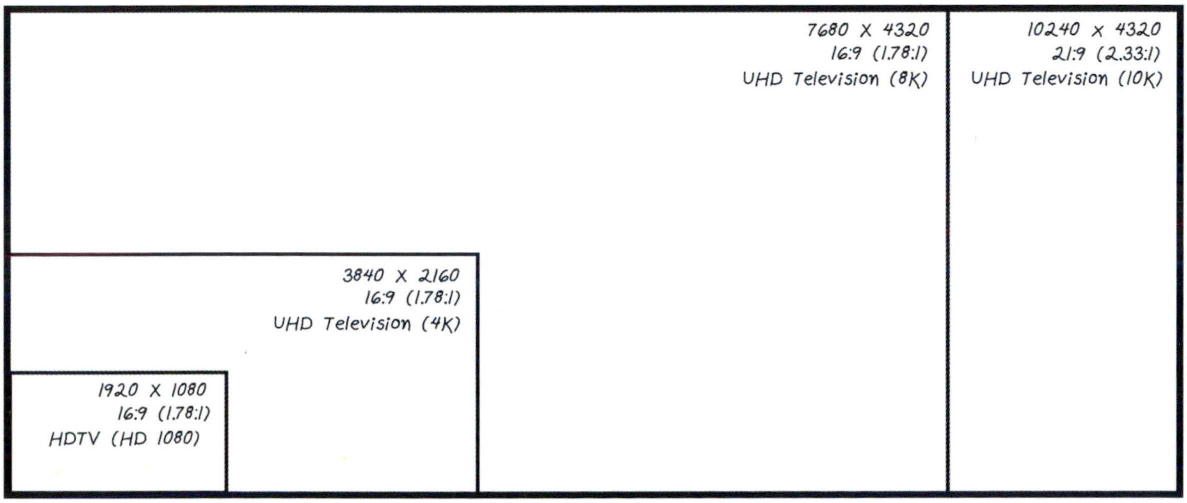

Figure 7.12 High definition television resolution compared to ultra-high-definition television resolutions. 10K UHD is currently only used in art museums.

The surface area of the frame is dependent upon the scale of the height and width, which is known as the aspect ratio. When working digitally, the display aspect ratio (DAR; also known as device aspect ratio or image aspect ratio) is indicated in the W:H format and the storage aspect ratio (SAR; also known as the frame aspect ratio or resolution and in film as the negative aspect ratio) is the number of pixels indicated in W × H, where W is the width and H is the height. This is usually a very confusing topic for most to understand because there are so many different descriptions of the same thing.

In addition, the displayed image is dependent on which display aspect ratio (DAR) the film image (SAR) is actually displayed on, as this affects whether the image is stretched or squished. For example, if an image is created digitally with a SAR of 720 × 576 (PAL), it has a DAR of 5:4. However, if it is displayed on a 4:3 standard television screen, the image is then squished. To fix this problem, the pixel aspect ratio (PAR) needs to be considered and adjusted.

A pixel is a square. If a film is created digitally and the SAR and DAR are equivalent and display DAR is the same, the image displayed will be square pixels (the PAR would be one pixel high by one pixel wide or 1:1). To fix the squished problem above, we would need to change the PAR to 1.07:1. The equation would be:

$$PAR = DAR / SAR$$

Fortunately, software settings consider these calculations when exporting your project based on your export or render settings. This is another reason why it is imperative to know what type of device your project will be shown or projected from. Therefore, working in square pixels at the highest resolution your computer and storage can handle is the best solution, and exporting any changes out of software like Premiere is the best practice.[2]

The chart below shows some of the aspect ratios that are most commonly used. The first and second column is the display aspect ratio. Please note that this chart may change as technology improves.

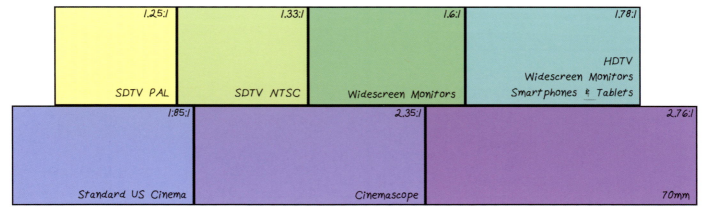

**Figure 7.13**
Pixel aspect ratio comparisons.

| DAR W:H | PAR W:H | SAR W × H | Film Format | |
|---|---|---|---|---|
| 4:3 | 1.25:1<br>1.33:1 | 720 × 576<br>720 × 486<br>2048 × 1536<br>1024 × 768 | | Standard Television (SDTV) PAL<br>Standard Television (SDTV) NTSC<br>Tablet (iPad) |
| | 1.37:1<br>1.43:1 | | 4p/35mm<br>15p/70mm | Academy Ratio (1932)<br>IMAX original (horizontal orientation format) |
| 16:10 | 1.6:1 | 2560 × 1600<br>1280 × 800<br>1440 × 900 | | Widescreen Computer Monitor (2K)<br>Tablets |
| 16:9 | 1.78:1 | 7680 × 4320<br>3840 × 2160<br>1920 × 1080<br>1080 × 720<br>960 × 540<br>3840 × 2160<br>2560 × 1440<br>1136 × 640<br>1334 × 750 | | Ultra HD Television (8K) (Widescreen)<br>Ultra HD Television (4K) (Widescreen)<br>High Definition Television (HD 1080) (Widescreen)<br>High Definition Television (HD 720) (Widescreen)<br>High Definition Television (HDTV 1080) (Widescreen)<br>Widescreen Computer Monitor (UltraHD)<br>Widescreen Computer Monitor (2K)<br>Smartphones and Tablets (Widescreen) |
| | 1.85:1 | 1998 × 1080 | 3p/35mm<br>5p/35mm<br>8p/35mm | 2K Flat Digital Cinema Package (DCP) (Widescreen)<br>IMAX digital (Flat) (Widescreen)<br>Super 35 (Anamorphic)<br>Super 35 (Widescreen)<br>VistaVision (horizontal orientation format) (Widescreen)<br>Standard US format (1956) |
| 256:135 | 1.9:1 | 4096 × 2160 | | 4K Digital Cinema Standard |
| 21:9 | 2.33:1 | 10240 × 4320<br>2560 × 1080 | | Ultra HD Television (10K)<br>Widescreen Computer Monitor (2K) |
| | 2.35:1 | | 5p/70mm | Cinemascope (Scope) (Anamorphic) |
| | 2.39:1<br><br>2.40:1 | 2048 × 858 | 4p/35mm<br>5p/70mm<br>2p/35mm | 2K SKOPE Digital Cinema Package (DCP) (Anamorphic)<br>Cinemascope (Scope) (Anamorphic)<br>Cinemascope (Scope) Two-Four-Oh (Anamorphic)<br>Techniscope (Anamorphic) |
| | 2.59:1 | | 6p/35mm<br>(times 3<br>cameras) | Cinerama (Anamorphic) (film run horizontally) |
| | 2.76:1 | | 4p/65mm | MGM 65 (Anamorphic)<br>Ultra Panavision 70 |

As you can see, there are varying general aspect ratios that are used for video and film creation. Determining how your project will be displayed before you begin is beneficial because your framing will be affected by the display size. However, there are several techniques available if the display size is intended or becomes necessary for more than one aspect ratio.

1.  Shoot and Protect: The concept of "shoot and protect" was originally developed for television. Shoot and protect keeps the important material inside a protected area within the frame. Since television screens were either 4:3 or 16:9 when this method was created, a compromised aspect ratio of 14:9 was determined as the safe area for framing.[3] The video or film is then created consciously, with all of the action happening in the safe area so that nothing is lost when changing from one display to another using a center cut, which cropped equally on both sides of the frame.

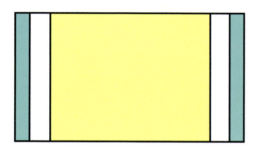

**Figure 7.14**
The shoot and protect area encompasses the yellow and white surface area.
Yellow = 4:3 + White = 14:9 + Teal = 16:9.

2.  Pan-and-Scan or Tilt-and-Scan: Cropping widescreen film images to standard definition aspect ratio without using a protected 14:9 area results in the loss of important aspects of the film's composition. The pan-and-scan method uses panning left and right or cutting to focus the attention to the important action in a shot; using this method, cropping the image does not remove the most important visual information. Tilt-and-scan (also known as reverse pan-and-scan) is the method use when converting 4:3 to 16:9. These methods were developed when widescreen movies were scanned and formatted for standard definition television. However, it is important to note that film directors dislike this method because it changes the way an audience sees the action of the screen, since almost half of the image is cropped from view.

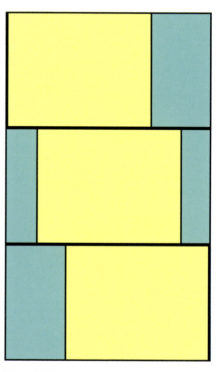

**Figure 7.15**
Tilt-and-scan is the method use when converting 4:3 to 16:9. The yellow surface area is kept while the teal area is cropped off, dependent upon the location of the important area of the shot.

3.  Letterboxing or Pillarboxing: If a film is framed with a display aspect ratio of 16:9 (widescreen) and then shown on a screen with an aspect ratio of 4:3 (standard width), horizontal black bars (mattes) can be added to the top and bottom of the image to create a 4:3 display aspect ratio and preserve the film's original width without stretching the height. This process is called letterboxing. The opposite scenario is called pillarboxing, when vertical black bars are added to the left and right of a standard 4:3 image, maintaining the original height while creating a 16:9 display aspect ratio without stretching the width.

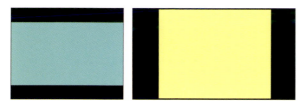

**Figure 7.16**
Letterbox (left) and pillarbox (right).

## Composition: The Golden Rectangle and the Rule of Thirds

### The Golden Rectangle

Pythagoras was a Greek philosopher who is considered to be the father of math, most noted for his proof of what has become known as the Pythagorean theorem. Pythagoras is also credited with identifying the Golden Section, Golden Ratio, and Golden Rectangle. The Golden Section had the Golden Ratio of 1:1.6180339887.[4] The Golden Rectangle is created with this aspect ratio.

The Greeks considered the Golden Rectangle as the mathematical basis for beauty and architecture. The Golden Rectangle is a universal rule used in design and art because the proportions are pleasing to the eye.

### The Rule of Thirds

The rule of thirds is a compositional tool, which is basically a simplified version of the Golden Rectangle. The major difference is that this rule can be used on any aspect ratio. The rule of thirds states that dividing a composition into nine equal parts using two equally spaced horizontal

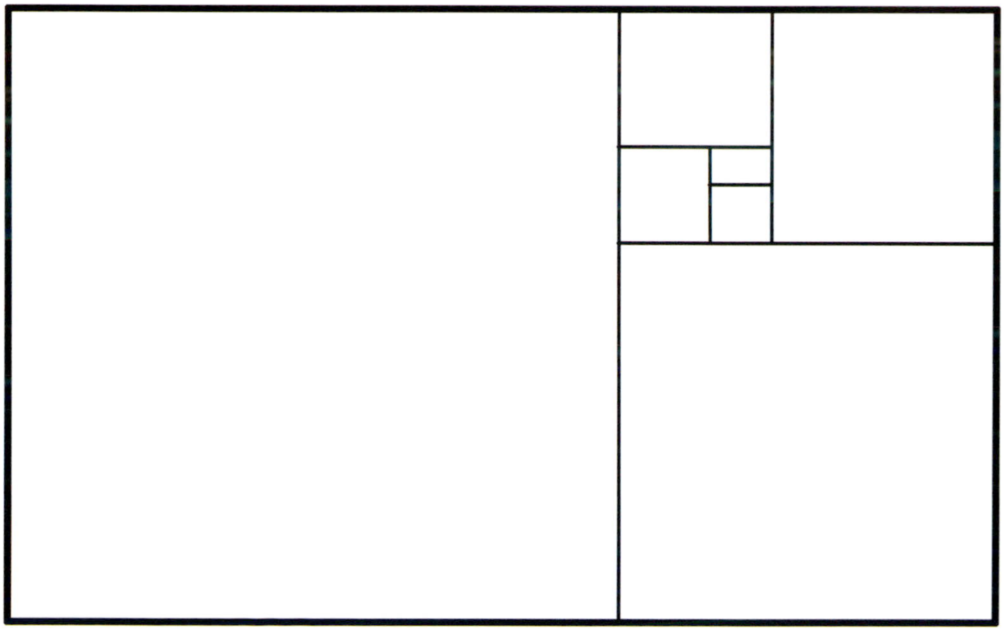

**Figure 7.17**
The Golden Rectangle.

and vertical lines can create a visually interesting composition by placing important compositional elements along these lines or at the point of their intersection.[5]

When creating your storyboards, you should create an overlay grid. For overlaying a rule-of-thirds grid automatically for all work in Photoshop, all that needs to be done is to set the grid preferences and view the resulting grid. Begin by creating a document set to the pixel dimensions of your chosen SAR. An example would be 1920 × 1080, 72pixels/inch[6] for HD1080. To set grid preferences on a Mac:

1. From the Photoshop menu, select Preferences, then Guides, Grids, and Slices.
2. In the Preferences dialogue box, set the Grid Line to 33.33% and the subdivisions to 1.
3. You can also choose a more prominent color, like red, instead of gray.
4. Click OK.
5. From the View menu, select Show > Grid.[7]

Creating an interesting composition, however, is much more than considering the rule of thirds. A great composition in filmmaking is one that communicates the story visually while making the action easy to read, controlling the focal point to emphasize what is important on screen, all while connecting moving imagery from shot to shot in a way that makes sense to the audience and affects their emotions.

### Safe Areas

Action safe and title safe zones were created to prevent images on old tube televisions from being cropped. We continue this practice today, since not everyone has upgraded their televisions. In addition, not all TVs are created equally, so cropping does still occur from one display to the next and even on new technology. Compositionally, using action safe and title safe also helps avoid tangency problems with the edges of the frame.[8]

Action safe traditionally is 10% from the edge of the frame, both horizontally and vertically. Today, most producers have changed this to 5%. Any important action or the position of the characters should be within this central 90% of the screen area.

Title safe traditionally is 20% from the edge of the frame, both horizontally and vertically. Today, most producers have changed this to 10%. Any text or logos should be kept within this central 80% of the screen area.

**Figure 7.18**
An overlay grid in red. The cyan lines are the title and action safe areas.

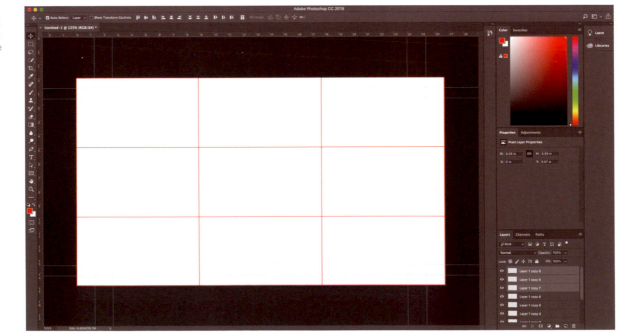

Figure 7.19
Title and action
safe areas
displayed in
Maya.

## Avoid tangents

In mathematics, a tangent is a straight line that touches a curve or curved surface at a point, but never crosses beyond that point. In art and design, a visual tangent occurs when two objects touch, when an object touches the edge of the frame, or when an object intersects with the corner of the frame. Visual tangents create a flattened image and a visual uncomfortableness, causing spatial confusion. In animation, visual tangents also cause confusing silhouettes.

Figure 7.20
In this frame, a visual tangent is created with the middleground rock pieces floating above Gan Vogh's head. They almost make him look like he is wearing Mickey ears. Still image from *Celestial* (2014). (Timecode 04:53) Courtesy of the University of Central Florida Character Animation Specialization.

## Avoid Frontal Angles

A frontal angle causes the subject and environment to flatten, and should be generally avoided in most shots. However, as with most rules, there are times when this rule should be broken.

The eye-level, head-on frontal angle of a subject can be used dramatically to make the audience feel as if they are looking through the eyes of another character. This angle engages the audience fully for the most emotional impact, particularly when combined with camera positions that are close-up or extreme close-up, because the subject is usually looking directly into the camera and therefore, at the audience.

Another use for this angle can be to "break the fourth wall." The fourth wall is an imaginary wall that exists between the audience and the action taking place. Breaking the fourth wall is when a character directly looks at, engages, and speaks to the audience.

## Controlling the Viewer's Eye

There is an order to where the audience looks on the screen.[9] Understanding how the viewer perceives an image is critical when designing the composition of each shot. Knowing where the focal point is located as each shot progresses is important when telling visual stories to ensure the viewer is experiencing what is intended. Failure to do so leads to visual miscommunication, and the story elements that you so painstakingly crafted will not be understood. Our peripheral vision allows us to still understand what else is happening on screen. However, it should be noted that details are lost unless they are part of the focal point, and even then, sometimes completely missed by the viewer.

**Figure 7.21 Frontal angle of Layla.** *Still image from* Ukelayla *(2018). (Timecode 04:00 – 04:09) Courtesy of the University of Central Florida Character Animation Specialization.*

1. Faces: If there is a face on screen, it becomes the first and foremost focal point. More specifically, we focus on the eyes. Because we are social creatures, we look mostly at the eyes of people who are communicating with us. We pick up nuances and clues to what people are actually saying from the emotion they emit through facial expressions. If multiple characters are on screen, we will focus on the dominant character and then shift back and forth during interactions.

2. Movement: If something is moving, our attention is drawn to focus on it, especially if there is a juxtaposition between the object that is moving and a static background. The greater the contrast between the motion and the stillness, the more attention is focused on the motion. Because of this, it is important to make the focus of a shot be the object or subject with the most movement. If more than one character is on screen, one character is the dominant character while the others are peripheral with subtle movement. If the focus is originally on one area of the screen, peripheral movement can cause the viewer to shift focus to another area. Camera movement can also aid in providing direction to the focal point.

**Figure 7.22**
In this shot, we can see a focused gaze on Gan Vogh's face. As we follow his eyeline, we can see he is looking intently at Titan. Still image from *Celestial* (2014). (Timecode 04:52–04:55) Courtesy of the University of Central Florida Character Animation Specialization.

3. Light: Focus is given to areas of light that are surrounded by highly contrasted dark areas. This is particularly noticeable when looking at a still image, whether it be a painting or a screen, as our eyes scan to find the focal point. The study of Rembrandt's work helps you understand lighting used in this way. Rembrandt, a Dutch painter known for his dramatic use of three-point lighting, creates his paintings using light as focal point.

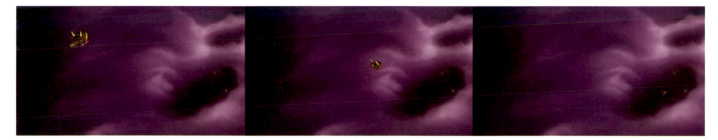

**Figure 7.23**
Titan is a small character, therefore he moves quite a bit in every shot throughout the story so that the audience's attention is drawn towards him. Still images from *Celestial* (2014). (Timecode 02:05–02:08) Courtesy of the University of Central Florida Character Animation Specialization.

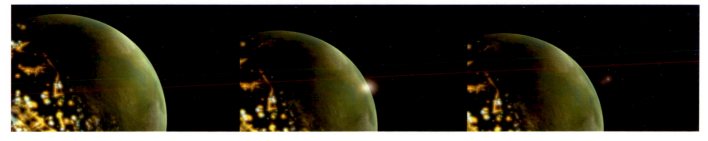

**Figure 7.24**
As the planet passes, our attention is on the lights of the cities. Because of this, light is used to shift our focus as shown in the second image, in order to see Titan launch from the planet. Still images from *Celestial* (2014). (Timecode 01:34–01:36) Courtesy of the University of Central Florida Character Animation Specialization.

## Continuity

Continuity is consistency in story and visuals.[10] In cinematic composition, visual continuity is the art of editing shots together while considering their relationship to each other in time and space. Each shot is connected to the next while making the action of the story seem smooth and uninterrupted, consequently making visual and logical sense. Continuity errors can often be noticed by the audience, resulting in confusion or distraction. While mistakes occur in every film made,[11] storyboarding and planning helps minimize the amount.

There are several different types of continuity problems that occur in both filming and digital creation, whether you are animating in stop motion, traditional, or computer generated. All visuals must remain consistent from shot to shot. For example, lighting from one shot to another in a scene should be the same. Shadows should fall in the same direction and key lights should illuminate the same side of the face. The colors of objects should also remain consistent. Objects and props should be present and in the same location from shot to shot. For example, if a character places a wine glass on a table in one shot, then the wine glass should be in the same location in the next. Clocks and calendars should be changed appropriately for calculated time changes throughout the film.

Anything moving in one shot should continue moving in the next to create a smooth continuance of motion. The direction the characters are moving in the environment, both on and off screen, should make sense. If a character exits screen left in one shot, then the character should re-enter screen right (unless exiting and re-entering through a door). If a plane is flying from New York to Paris, then the shot of the plane in the sky should be going from screen left to screen right, since on the world map New York is located on the left side of the map and Paris is on the right. All objects in motion should be carried through from one shot to the next.

Continuity editing is achieved by conscientiously following the rules of cinematography, camera motion, and position as discussed in Chapter 5, as well as editing rules covered in Chapter 8.

**Figure 7.25**

A visual continuity problem can be observed in this sequence of shots. Notice in shot 1, 2, and 4 there are crystals floating in the mid-ground, but in shot 3 the crystals are absent. Still images from *Celestial* (2014). (Timecode 04:08–04:24) Courtesy of the University of Central Florida Character Animation Specialization.

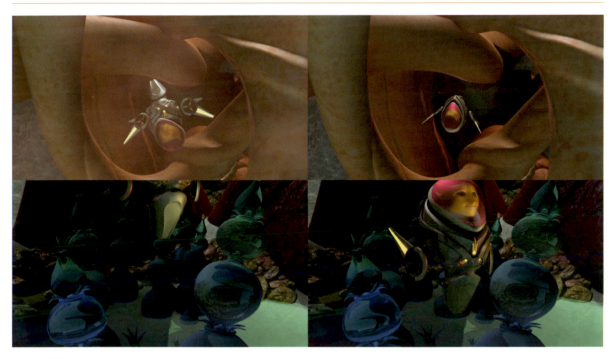

**Figure 7.26**
Continuity editing: In these two shots, Titan is landing on the planet. In the first shot we see Titan falling from top to center screen (top two images) which continues in the second shot as he lands from top to center screen (bottom two images). Still images from *Celestial* (2014). (Timecode 02:59–03:07) Courtesy of the University of Central Florida Character Animation Specialization.

## 2D, 3D, and 4D design
### (Vertical – Horizontal + Depth + Time)

The direction objects or subjects move on a screen can impact the emotions of the viewer. The two dimensions of the horizontal (x-axis) and vertical (y-axis) space have associated preconceived meanings, dependent upon the culture of the target audience. For example, because we read English from left to right, objects moving in screen direction from left to right feels comfortable to the viewer, while objects moving from right to left feels awkward and unsettling. Because of this, the hero always enters and travels from screen left to right and the villain enters and travels from right to left. Objects moving downward have an automatic association of gravity and the movement feels effortless, while objects moving upward can create the feeling of struggle.

The movement in direction from the foreground to the background (z-axis) pulls the audience into the created world, while movement from background to foreground forces the audience to focus intently on the object or subject. Objects in the foreground are larger, while objects in the background are smaller and less significant.

Time can be also used to influence emotion and affect composition. By implication or by actual manipulation of time, speeding up time can build tension while slowing down the action on the screen can create anticipation and anxiety.

**Figure 7.27**
Titan travels from screen left to screen right and from the foreground to the background, drawing the audience into the nebula. Still images from *Celestial* (2014). (Timecode 02:20–02:27) Courtesy of the University of Central Florida Character Animation Specialization.

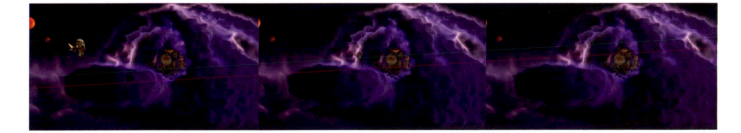

## Stereoscopic Composition: Negative and Positive Parallax

Visually, the third dimension is used to bring the audience further into the action on the screen. Stereoscopic composition engages the audience even further by increasing the experience of immersion through increased depth which is enhanced by the occasional use of first person point of view. While there are differing opinions of where the "zone of comfort" lies, a good goal of stereoscopic projection is to create an illusion of depth with about 80% of the image appearing inside and behind the screen frame (film space), while about 20% of the image appears to be in front of the screen (audience space).

Stereoscopic composition[12] is most memorable and widely used in adventure, science fiction, and fantasy, while taking the audience on breathtaking journeys and incredible flights, such as in Dreamworks' *How to Train*

**Figure 7.28**
Negative and positive parallax.

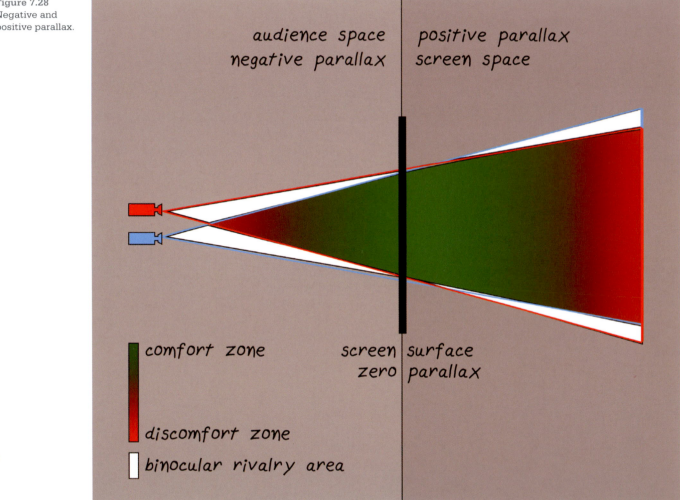

*Your Dragon*. There must be a balance, however, between using both film space (positive parallax) and audience space (negative parallax). Visual gimmicks that overuse audience space, such as objects flying out of the screen, tend to bore the audience and have the opposite of the intended immersion effect, taking them out of the story.

Objects that are supposed to be between the viewer and the screen (negative parallax) are sometimes occluded by the edge of the frame, and the viewer's eye becomes confused by the contradiction. The object should be in front, but because the frame behind the object obscures the field of view, the visual confusion undermines the stereoscopic effect.

This problem can be avoided by using negative parallax effects only within the center of the screen. However, another way to minimize confusion is to dynamically crop the edges of the top and bottom or the left and right of the screen depending on the position of the objects at the edge of screen. This use of the *floating window*, also known as *floating crops*, enhances the 3D experience of the negative parallax. A black frame, much like a letter box, is added to the shot, and can then float in front of this screen boundary, appearing to pop out of the frame.[13] These frames appear and disappear between camera cuts or are animated slowly, contracting and expanding as needed.

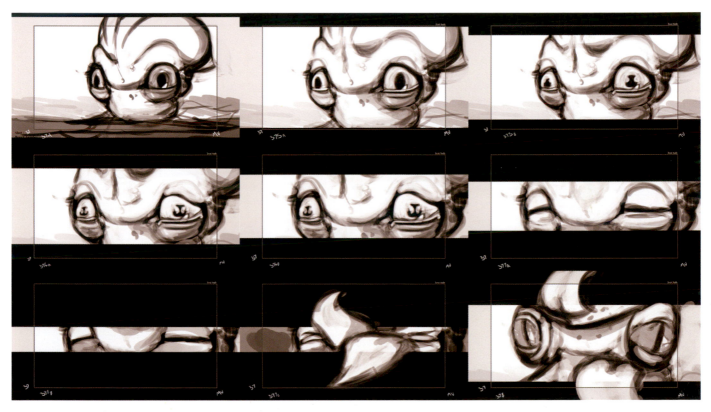

**Figure 7.29**
Storyboard panels for a storyreel which indicates floating crops, drawn by Marchand Venter for *Cuddle Fish* (2016). Timecode (04:11–04:21). Courtesy of the University of Central Florida Character Animation Specialization.

## Using the Elements of Art and Design to Create Composition on the Screen

In any work of art, an artist uses the elements of art and design to effectively communicate ideas visually. These same elements can be used for screen composition in the same way. Everything seen within the frame can be used to evoke emotion from your audience. What follows is a description of each element and an example of how it can be used in screen composition.

**Figure 7.30**
**Points are used to represent stars in the background, as well as stars on Gan Vogh's wings and body texture.** Still image from *Celestial* (2014). (Timecode 04:19–04:22) Courtesy of the University of Central Florida Character Animation Specialization.

**Figure 7.31**
**Lines are added as texture to the projected objects which imply analog scan lines.** Still image from *Celestial* (2014). (Timecode 04:50–04:55) Courtesy of the University of Central Florida Character Animation Specialization.

### Point

A point is the simplest design element. In the plainest understanding, a point is represented by a dot and is most commonly understood in design as the focus or focal point. Points can be created at the intersection of two or more lines, whether they are drawn or implied, such as in the rule of thirds, discussed earlier in this chapter.

### Line

A line is defined as a path created by a point that is moving through space. On screen, lines can be created vertically, horizontally, diagonally, or curved. Lines can be drawn, such as a painted line on the road, or implied, as when a wall meets the floor. When several points are created in combination, they create an implied line that can represent something more complicated, such as a constellation. Lines can be used in the environment to create a path that our eyes should follow.

### Color

Of all the elements, color is probably the most important since it has psychological effects on humans that are very real. Because of this, color can be used to manipulate the emotions of the audience.[14] In addition, color can also have a physiological effect on us. The color red, for example, actually raises blood pressure and heart rate, which is why it is associated with both love and danger.

We consider half of the color wheel to be "warm" and the other half to be "cool." Psychologically, we associate warmer colors with the heat of the day and cooler colors with coolness of the night. Magentas, reds, yellows, and oranges can actually physically "feel" warmer, whereas cyans, blues, greens, and purples "feel" cooler. Studies have actually proven that by painting a room "warm" or "cool" can affect the occupants inside that room accordingly. Warm colors advance, and cool colors recede. High-contrast bright colors advance, and darker colors recede as well.[15]

The meanings of color differ from culture to culture. All colors have both positive and negative meanings attached to them. Below are some common color associations:

Yellow: cowardly, sunny, cheerful, eye-catching

Orange: hot, playful, happy, childlike

Red: passionate, dangerous, exciting

Purple: contemplative, sensual, spiritual, regal, mystical, mourning, death

Blue: honest, dependable, sad, calm, tranquil

Green: new, earth-friendly, little experience, associations with money and prestige, nature, fresh

White: pure, clean, sterile, innocent

Grey: depressing, timeless, sophisticated, classic

Black: elegant, magical, mysterious

Brown: earthy, secure, rich[16]

From this, we can see how Pixar used these associations when creating their characters for *Inside Out*. Joy is yellow, Sadness is blue, Disgust is green, Fear is purple, and Anger is red. Don't forget Bing Bong, the pink elephant that represents seeing something that isn't there (from the idiom singing pink elephants).

## Shape

A shape, both defined or implied, is created when a line surrounds an area. Shapes suggest a range of associated meanings which elicit emotions from the viewer on a conscious or subconscious level. There are only two fundamental shapes: organic and inorganic. Organic shapes tend to be curved, while inorganic shapes tend to be angular. Organic shapes suggest sentiments of nature, softness, flexibility, romanticism, and childlike qualities. Inorganic shapes are associated with industrial, unnatural, rigid, man-made, and adult-like characteristics.

The meaning of any shape is dependent upon how it is used in the framework of your story. Below are the most common shapes and some of the meanings associated with them.

- Circles suggest infinity (without beginning or end), inclusion (the inner circle), repetition, cycles (circle of life), karma (what goes around comes around), protection (sacred circle of protection), confusion (I'm just running around in circles), celestial (planetary, sun, or the element of spirit), mobility (the shape of the wheel).

**Figure 7.32**
**The chosen colors for Gan Vogh and his environment were not accidental.** These colors imply that Gan Vogh is inexperienced yet honest in his attempts at being a celestial creator. His environment supports his contemplative and spiritual qualities. Still image from *Celestial* (2014). (Timecode 02:31) Courtesy of the University of Central Florida Character Animation Specialization.

**Figure 7.33**
**Circles and curved shapes fill the characters and environments of this short film to augment the planetary other-worldliness of the story.** Still image from *Celestial* (2014). (Timecode 04:59) Courtesy of the University of Central Florida Character Animation Specialization.

- Triangles have been used throughout history by artists to denote a sub-consciously pleasing composition. Creating triangles of color and value will create visual harmony in a composition. Emotionally, triangles can indicate stability and strength when the base is down and the point is facing upward. The opposite feeling of instability occurs when the triangle appears upside down. Other meanings include harmony, proportion, creativity (creation, preservation, destruction), trinity (spirit, mind, body; Father, Son, Holy Ghost; past, present, future), family (mother, father, child), as well as disharmony (love triangle; third wheel).

- Rectangle and square shapes represent balance (three square meals a day), order and stability (as in a brick wall), logic (mathematical and geometrical), civilization (buildings), honesty (fare and square), thresholds (the shape of a window or doorway), and old-fashioned (don't be a square).

In the Pixar movie *Up*, a circular shape is used to reflect the personality of Ellie by suggesting her youthfulness, spontaneity, and outgoing nature. If you notice, her belongings have an organic, circular shape. All of the frames around her pictures have a circular shape. Even her chair is organically shaped. Contrasted with Carl, who is represented with an inorganic, angular, rectangular shape representing the measured, controlled, and reserved nature of his personality. By giving them contrasting shapes, the suggestion is that Ellie is the perfect complement to Carl.

### Texture

Texture is the tactile quality of a surface. In a two-dimensional composition, such as a screen frame, visual texture draws on our experiences and becomes an optical illusion of how we assume an object's surface would feel. As with all of the elements of art and design, texture can influence the audience's perception of what is happening on screen. Texture adds detail to animation, drawing the viewer's focus by creating visual interest.

### Space

Space is defined as an area in which all things exist and move. As covered earlier in this chapter, film space refers to the dimensions within the frame. As noted, since we view a film as a sequence of frames, the motion and direction of objects within the frame become influential elements in a film by impacting the emotions of the viewer. In addition to the influence of horizontal, vertical, and depth movement covered earlier in the section on 2D, 3D, and 4D design, as well as the different camera positions, angles, and movements in Chapter 5, the following movements through space can add emotional impact to your film.

**Figure 7.34**
**Titan's design includes several subtle triangular shapes with triangles of color which indicate his stability and underscore his creation.** Still image from *Celestial* (2014). (Timecode 02:33) Courtesy of the University of Central Florida Character Animation Specialization.

**Figure 7.35**
**Titan's projection serves as a window into the world that Gan Vogh has created and destroyed.** Still image from *Celestial* (2014). (Timecode 05:22–05:25) Courtesy of the University of Central Florida Character Animation Specialization.

- Diagonal Movement: Like the motion implied by vertical (y-axis) and horizontal (x-axis) movement, diagonal movement combines the two, creating greater emotional momentum and impact. Since our eye moves effortlessly from screen left to screen right, and gravity aids in the feeling of natural descent from top to bottom, diagonal movement from top-left to bottom-right gives the highest level of momentum and emotional ease, while movement from top-right to bottom-left is not as comfortable. In contrast, movement at a diagonal from bottom-right to top-left presents the highest level of difficulty and emotional struggle, while movement from bottom-left to top-right is not quite as hard.

- Planes of Action: The z-axis depth can be divided into three areas often referred to as *planes of action*: foreground, middleground, and background. Objects in the foreground appear larger and more dominant, while objects in the background appear smaller and less significant. The middleground is often used for secondary action when the audience's focus is on the foreground. Emphasis on all three planes creates deep focus requiring a wide-angle lens. A specific focal area can be identified using depth-of-field techniques discussed in Chapter 5. Shallow focus is then created when only one plane, usually the foreground or the background, is in focus. When the focus plane changes during a shot from foreground to background or vice versa, the audience's attention is forcibly shifted from one subject to another. This technique is called a rack focus.

- Perspective: Aside from the different views created from camera angles, as discussed in Chapter 5, linear perspective can be used to further increase the sense of depth in a shot as well as add a sense of unease to the audience. By framing your environment in a way that all visual parallel lines appear to converge on a single point directly in front and usually at eye level, you give the illusion of depth and distance. Forced perspective can also be used to create emphasis by changing the scale of objects to make them appear closer or farther from the camera.

**Figure 7.36**
**Varied textures create visual interest.** Still image from *Celestial* (2014). (Timecode 03:17) Courtesy of the University of Central Florida Character Animation Specialization.

**Figure 7.37**
**Diagonal movement accentuates the momentum of Titan as he enters the atmosphere of the planet he will explore.** Still image from *Celestial* (2014). (Timecode 02:54–02:57) Courtesy of the University of Central Florida Character Animation Specialization.

**Figure 7.38**
**Deep focus.** Background: stars; middleground: clouds and crystals; and foreground: character. Still image from *Celestial* (2014). (Timecode 00:26–00:34) Courtesy of the University of Central Florida Character Animation Specialization.

**Figure 7.39**
**Shallow focus.**
Background:
laboratory;
foreground:
character. Still
image from *Of
Mice and Mustard*
(2018). (Timecode
00:40) Short film
created by Oneida
Loo, University of
Central Florida.
All rights owned
and used with
permission by
Oneida Loo.

**Figure 7.40**
**Rack focus.** The image on the left shows Marcy clear and Gus blurred. The image on right is after the rack focus, leaving Marcy blurry
and Gus now clear. Still images from *Yours, Mime and Ours* (2014). (Timecode 01:06–01:08) Courtesy of the University of Central Florida
Character Animation Specialization.

**Figure 7.41**
The composition on the left is a forced perspective of Titan, making him seem larger than he actually is, which draws focus to
what he is doing. (Timecode 05:08) The composition on the right occurs in the next shot, returning the perspective to normal. (Timecode
05:07) Still images from *Celestial* (2014). Courtesy of the University of Central Florida Character Animation Specialization.

## Form, Value, and Lighting

As elements of art, form and value are listed separately. Combining them here with the addition of lighting seemed most appropriate since a form cannot be seen without light creating values on a surface. A form without value is simply reduced to a shape.

When light hits an object, we can see the form as it reacts with the surface. The area that the light hits directly is called the highlight. As the light drops off over the distance we can see the midtone, which is the local color of the object, followed by a core shadow which is a darker value of the object's color. The ground surface where that object is sitting receives the cast shadow created by the object. This surface also reflects some light back onto the object (reflected highlight) as well as a reflection of the cast shadow itself. If the surface is shiny, then the reflected light and shadow are clearer. The surface material also affects how light interacts with the object—if the surface is smooth (such as metal or polished stone) the light will act differently than if the surface has a texture (such as fabric or carpet).

Lighting controls not only how we see objects but also how we feel about what we see. Directors use many artificial lights to create the best possible lighting scenario, setting the proper mood and making sure the characters will be lit to reflect that mood choice. This often involves cheating reality, such as flooding characters with bright blue light for a night scene when in reality the scene would be much darker. There are three aspects of lighting that need to be considered for setting the right mood:

1. Placement of lights (three-point lighting)
2. Contrast created by the intensity of lights on the subject(s) and environment (high-key/low-key and high-contrast/low-contrast)
3. Color of the lights[17]

The standard of any lighting setup is three-point lighting, composed usually of spotlights and made up of a key light, fill light, and back light. The key light is the main light hitting the subject and is usually placed at an angle to bring out the contours of the subject, about 45 degrees from the camera/subject axis. This lighting angle illuminates one-half of the face and creates a triangularly lit area under the eye of the subject on the dark side of the face, as can be seen in many of Rembrandt's paintings.[18] The background environment is barely lit. Known as Rembrandt lighting, this is a low-key lighting scheme (also known as *chiaroscuro*) and has a high contrast. Brightly lit areas of hard light are juxtaposed with the remainder of the scene disappearing into unlit and very dark shadows, creating a moody, atmospheric, and dramatic scene. The value range is wide, showing very bright whites and very dark blacks with a wide range of values in between.

Low-key lighting is used to create the following moods:

- Film noir–style drama
- Scary or suspenseful
- Spooky and mysterious
- Romantic
- Warm and cozy

In high-key lighting, most of the subject is illuminated with the key light. The background is also brightly lit. The level of contrast is dependent on the fill lighting, and can have some areas that are washed-out and white (also known as *overexposure*).

**Figure 7.42**
**Low-key lighting is used in this shot to indicate danger and build suspense.** Still image from *Gaiaspora* (2013). (Timecode 03:11) Courtesy of the University of Central Florida Character Animation Specialization.

High-key lighting is used to create the following moods:

- Upbeat
- Cheerful
- Energetic
- Expansive
- Ethereal

The second light in a three-point lighting setup is the fill light, which is placed to shine on the dark side of the subject, usually 45 degrees

**Figure 7.43**
**High-key lighting is used in this shot to indicate Jake's cheerful energy.** Still image from *Box Forts* (2012). (Timecode 01:17) Courtesy of the University of Central Florida Character Animation Specialization.

**Figure 7.44**
**A back light is used in this shot to highlight Bob's body.** Still image from *Gaiaspora* (2013). (Timecode 02:29) Courtesy of the University of Central Florida Character Animation Specialization.

on the opposite side of the camera and lower in intensity than the key, softly illuminating the dark shadowy parts of the subject. The general rule is that if the key light color is warm, the fill light color should be cool, and vice versa. Depending on the intensity of the color, a magical or dramatic effect is created because the shadows then take on a subtle complementary color. All light has color, even if it is barely noticeable. The intensity of this light can vary greatly, from very little and barely noticeable in a low-key lighting scenario to very bright in a high-key lighting scenario removing almost all shadows.

The back light is the third light and is usually placed at the back of the subject and shining down from above, creating a highlighted outline of the head and shoulders. Its intensity can vary from soft to very intense, the latter creating a glow and separating the foreground character from the background. For eeriness or mysterious moods, such as in film noir, create a shadowy silhouette when the character is in a low-light setting and lit brightly from behind. The audience can see their side profiles or the shapes of their bodies. This light can be warm or cool.

Showing the silhouettes of shadows alone on the screen can help tell the story while even reducing some of the work needed for that shot, particularly if creating 2D or 3D animation, since drawn shadows do not need the amount of detail and time necessary to fully render.

Gobos or cucoloris (cookies) can be used to control the shapes of the light and shadow as it is cast across the space and onto the objects in the environment. Gobos create a projected, sharp-edged pattern by placing a stencil (cut out in metal or painted on glass) at the focal point of the light. Gobos can also mimic the look of light going through a stained glass window if a glass gobo is painted with colored translucent paints. Cookies create a softer pattern of shadows by holding larger stencils further away from the light source. Both gobos ad cookies can also be simulated in computer graphics by using an alpha texture file mapped onto the intensity or color of a spotlight or directional light. An example of this would be the shadows of leaves projected as if the sunlight was filtering through the trees, or, as if the sunlight or streetlight were beaming through the frame of a window pane or mini-blinds and casting shadows in a room.

Stylistically, shadows alone can create a mood and atmosphere of mystery. The animation created by shadows alone must have a strong silhouette so that the audience can understand what is happening from the actions playing out on screen.

If lighting an environment for 3D animation, the software does not automatically generate the bounce lights from these three lights unless you are using the render heavy process of global illumination. You may want to add a fourth light to mimic a low intensity, reflected light onto the subject.

It is also a point to mention that lighting changes can be made in postproduction by adding more contrast, fixing white balance, and adding color. However, direction of light sources is not something that can be changed. So, it is best to have a plan before you begin creating your shots, if you are working in stop motion, 2D, or 3D animation.

There are two categories of lighting: *motivated lighting* and *unmotivated lighting*.

Motivated lighting is any light source that can be seen by the audience appearing directly on-screen as part of the environment, such as lamps, candlelight, television screens, windows, etc. Unmotivated lighting is any light source that cannot be seen by the audience but is necessary to illuminate the scene, such as the sun (if not onscreen) or lights that are positioned off-camera. Unmotivated lighting can also be used to create an effect, such as God rays illuminating a character to imply a sense of holiness.

A cross between both motivated and unmotivated lighting is divine radiance, an inexplicable light source being emitted from an object or a character. In this scenario, the audience knows where the light source is located but the light appears to be radiating from the object or character as if they were divine.

While three-point lighting is considered the standard, other lighting schemes can be used to create mood, elicit emotion, and direct the viewer's attention. All of the following schemes can be created in the real world, drawn as two-dimensional effects, as well as in 3D software.

**Figure 7.45**
A shadow of the main character, Oscar, is used in this shot to show the arrival and the actions of raising the garage door, before entrance. Still image from *Expend* (2018). (Timecode 00:59 – 01:05) Used with kind permission from Bismark Fernandes, Savannah College of Art and Design.

**Figure 7.46**
Divine radiance illuminating Turtle once he finally grows his mustache. Still image from *Mustache Mayhem* (2011). (Timecode 02:34–02:38) Courtesy of the University of Central Florida Character Animation Specialization.

- Sunlight: There are several different lighting scenarios that can be created with sunlight (or the virtual creation of the sun and sky in the computer). Whether the light is full contrast and hot during high noon, or soft and cool during dusk, sunlight can be used to create a look that enhances the meaning of your film. The colors of the sunlight change due to how it is perceived through the earth's atmosphere. Some feelings and emotions associated with common lighting scenarios using sunlight are:
  - Sunrise/Early Morning: warmth, fresh, joy, beginning, solitude (the start of a new day), but can also be associated with dread and exhaustion (not getting enough sleep, having to go to work or school)
  - High Noon: upbeat, cheerful, or hot, fear (most duels occurred at high noon)

  - Sunset: romance, hope, satisfaction, warmth (as they ride off into the sunset)
  - Dusk: cool, anxiety, depression, somber, mysterious, shadowy
  - Night (lit by moonlight): cool, romance, passion, mystery, evil (lurking in the shadows)

**Figure 7.49**
**Sunset lighting scheme.** Still image from *Mustache Mayhem* (2011). (Timecode 06:24–06:34) Courtesy of the University of Central Florida Character Animation Specialization.

**Figure 7.47**
**Sunrise/early morning lighting scheme.** Still image from *Flower Story* (2012). (Timecode 05:17–05:20) Courtesy of the University of Central Florida Character Animation Specialization.

**Figure 7.50**
**Dusk lighting scheme.** Still image from *Flower Story* (2012). (Timecode 02:25) Courtesy of the University of Central Florida Character Animation Specialization.

**Figure 7.48**
**High noon lighting scheme.** Still image from *Box Forts* (2012). (Timecode 00:51–01:00) Courtesy of the University of Central Florida Character Animation Specialization.

**Figure 7.51**
**Night (lit by moonlight) lighting scheme.** Still image from *Of Mice and Mustard* (2018). (Timecode 00:48) Short film created by Oneida Loo, University of Central Florida. All rights owned and used with permission by Oneida Loo.

- Atmospheric: While technically some of atmospheric lighting is created by the sun, the main difference is the inclusion of particles in the air to create a scattering of the light rays. If you look into the distance, you will notice that faraway objects have muted and tinted bluish-white color tones, dependent on the time of day and the amount of mist or haze in the air. In art, this phenomenon is called atmospheric perspective. A small amount of atmosphere can add depth and volume to the scene as well as add a hint of mystery and intrigue. Additional variations are as follows:
  - Crepuscular rays (pointed down towards earth) or anticrepuscular rays (point upward towards the sky), also known as sunbeams, sun rays, or God rays, are rays that are created as sunlight streams through clouds. They can also be created when sun breaks through the leaves of trees, windows, or architecture. When coming through a window, dust particles can be seen floating in the air. A similar effect is created with a spotlight in a smoky nightclub.
  - Fog has different densities but is generally understood as visibility less than 200 meters. Fog during daytime is a low contrast ambient lighting scheme giving an even, gray illumination over everything that can be seen. Variations include "smog," which is pollution, and "vog," which is the result of volcanic activity. All of these vary in density and value, and can even appear to be a tint of purple, blue, green, or pink depending on the time of day.
  - Smoke is used to add depth and volume to an interior, or create eerie feeling to an outside scene. Practical means of creating these include the use of fog or smoke machines or dry ice in water.

**Figure 7.52**
**Crepuscular rays illuminate the piles of treasure.** Still image from *Snacktime* (2015). (Timecode 01:51–01:55) Courtesy of the University of Central Florida Character Animation Specialization.

**Figure 7.53**
**Fog heightens Mo's struggle to walk through the storm.** Still image from *Ember* (2013). (Timecode 04:56 - 05:12) Courtesy of the University of Central Florida Character Animation Specialization.

**Figure 7.54**
**Smoke hides the magical appearance of Winston as he returns to life after being a statue.** Still images from *Snacktime* (2015). (Timecode 00:47–00:50) Courtesy of the University of Central Florida Character Animation Specialization.

- Candlelight and Fire: Candlelight is a subtle low-key lighting scheme that is very intimate. Using candlelight as the key light creates the ambiance of romance (candlelight dinner) or celebration (birthday cake), while softening facial features and adding warmth to a scene. Torches, gas lamps, oil lamps, campfires, fireplaces, and other sources of fire can be used as key lights to create mood. Like candlelight, fireplaces can create the cozy feeling of romance, while kerosene lamps and torches work very well in creating historical settings. Campfires can be used to enhance the feeling of adventure and being out in the elements. In the 2016 release of the *Jungle Book*, a forest fire was used as the main light source and set the scene for danger.

- Artificial Light: Electric light sources historically replaced firelight in the late 1800s when Thomas Edison created the first commercially available light bulb. Incandescent light bulbs, neon lights, fluorescent lights, halogen lights, and LEDs are all types of light that can be utilized when creating your animation.

  - Lamps, flashlights, headlights, and other light fixtures can be placed within the scene to illuminate the action, environment and characters.

  - Screens: Television, movie, and computer screens (or the implication thereof) can be used as key lights to create a low-key lighting scheme to set the mood and location of the scene. In the beginning of Pixar's *Up*, Young Carl's face is lit from the light of the movie screen showing his interest and excitement, while 20 minutes later, Old Carl's face is lit from the light of the television screen in his living room, showing him shutdown and dissociated.

**Figure 7.55**
The character Ember embodies the element of fire and acts as the light source in this shot. Still image from *Ember* (2013). (Timecode 01:54–02:07) Courtesy of the University of Central Florida Character Animation Specialization.

**Figure 7.57**
The television glow serves as a backlight for illuminating Turt's face in this shot. Still image from *Mustache Mayhem* (2011). (Timecode 01:35–01:37) Courtesy of the University of Central Florida Character Animation Specialization.

**Figure 7.56**
Oscar's face is illuminated from the glow coming from his new energy source. Still image from *Extend* (2018). (Timecode 01:52–01:57) Used with kind permission of Bismark Fernandes.

**Figure 7.58**
Chip and Flint have luminescent markings, while the seed pod itself is completely bioluminescent. Still image from *Flower Story* (2012). (Timecode 01:19–01:25) Courtesy of the University of Central Florida Character Animation Specialization.

- Luminescence: By definition, luminescence is light emitted by something that has not been heated. Technically, fluorescent lights are part of this category, as well as fluorescent paint. Other examples include phosphorescence (such as glow in the dark paint), bioluminescence (made by living creatures like glowworms, including fictional ones, such as the Na'vi and all of the glowing plant life in *Avatar*).Using luminescence in your scenes gives a sense of magic and wonder to whatever is glowing.
- Moving Light Source: Moving lights can be created by a character holding the light source (a candle or a flashlight) or by something else moving the light (hanging from a wire, a strong wind, headlights on a moving vehicle). Unpredictable movement can be used to build tension. Chaotic movement evokes fear. In *Finding Nemo* (timecode 00:32:39), Marlin is trying to catch a falling diver's mask as it plummets into the depths and into pure darkness. In the blackness, Marlin and Dory see a small light and swim over to investigate. When the source of the light is revealed as an anglerfish, a nerve-racking chase sequence ensues. The chaotic movement of the light evokes anxiety and fear in the audience. Eventually the location of the mask is revealed and results in Marlin pushing past his fear to achieve his goal. The audience's emotional climax results in feelings of victory as we applaud our hero's achievement.

**Figure 7.59**
**Joey's flashlight is a moving light source which adds to the eeriness of the scene.** Still image from *Shadow Play* (2010). (Timecode 01:38–01:43) Courtesy of the University of Central Florida Character Animation Specialization Archives.

## Time

In the animated storytelling process, our imagination is our only boundary. We have the opportunity to do whatever we have only dreamt of doing in our own lives. One of these dreams is the ability to control time. Instead of unfolding our stories chronologically at a normal pace, we can present things in an order that makes the story more intriguing. We can speed time up or slow it down. Time can be reversed and it can even stand still. We can even jump into the future or go back into the past.

Manipulating time can be used to influence emotion and affect composition. Speeding up time can build tension, while slowing down the action on the screen can create anticipation and anxiety. Time travel can be used as a storytelling device to explain events that have occurred or those that are going to happen.

- Pacing: This is the rhythm and tempo created when placing the shots together into a finished film from beginning to end. Each shot is created as a certain length of time, but the director and editor can adjust these shots to further craft the emotional impact of a scene or sequence. Pacing take practice to get it right. The only rule for pacing is that the audience feels the intended emotion. A good story becomes a great film when it is presented in a way that is understandable, interesting, and entertaining.

  In animation, much of the pacing decision making happens during the storyboarding and storyreel process. Unlike live action filming, every frame of animation must be created by hand, even if it is in the computer, therefore pacing must begin early in the preproduction process of story creation to avoid unnecessary work. Pacing of the edit is an iterative process that is fluid, ongoing and fluctuating until the film is finished. The editor, therefore, is an important part of the entire process in animation, since even a wonderfully written story will flop if the pacing does not feel right to the audience.
- Expanding Time: There are times when the director or editor may intentionally use uncomfortable pacing to create an uncomfortable or anxious feeling within the audience. A great example of this is in

*Zootopia*, when Officer Judy Hopps and Nick go into the Department of Motor Vehicles to speak to Flash. The pacing of the shots between those of Flash, the sloth, and then those of Judy, the rabbit, create contrast between their personalities, making time seem uncomfortably expanded when we see Flash. The shots that focus on Flash also frame Judy so that the audience can compare Judy's quick eagerness alongside Flash's sloth-like movements.

- Ellipsis: An ellipsis is an editing technique that removes periods of time from the visual story.[19] Showing everything to an audience can be very boring, therefore, using an ellipsis indicates a passage of time.
- Slow Motion: Also known as time warp or slo mo, this effect is used to create drama, suspense, and emphasis by making time appear to slow down. It is achieved with film or digitally by capturing or creating action at a higher frame rate (more than 24fps)

**Figure 7.60**
The short walk from the house to the trash can is expanded with the use of multiple camera angles and shots. Still images from *Shadow Play* (2010). (Timecode 01:34–02:18) Courtesy of the University of Central Florida Character Animation Specialization Archives.

**Figure 7.61**
Multiple shots are cross dissolved to illustrate a faster sequence of Judy building a box fort. Still images from *Box Forts* (2012). (Timecode 02:15–02:17) Courtesy of the University of Central Florida Character Animation Specialization.

and then playing back that action in real time. The faster the action that needs to be slowed down, then the higher the frame rate needs to be when capturing the action. Slow motion can also be created by slowing down playback of real time frame rate, but this is not visually the best solution as the shot then plays back with a stutter and is jerky. In the archery scene from the Pixar movie *Brave*, Merida shoots her last arrow and in slow motion we see it split the arrow already in the target.

- Fast motion: Also known as fast mo, this effect is the opposite of slow motion and is used to create emphasis, as it appears to make time speed up. It is achieved with film or digitally when capturing or creating action at a lower frame rate (less than 24fps) and then playing back that action in real time. Time-lapse photography also creates this effect. Fast motion can also be created by speeding up playback of real-time frame rates.

**Figure 7.62**
In these two shots, slow motion is used to show Marcy's fixation with the box that her father flung across the room as it flies **through the air.** Still images from *Yours, Mime, and Ours* (2014). (Timecode 02:23–02:35) Courtesy of the University of Central Florida Character Animation Specialization.

**Figure 7.63**
Fast motion is used in this shot to show Judy building a pyramid shaped box fort. Still images from *Box Forts* (2012). (Timecode 02:41–02:45) Courtesy of the University of Central Florida Character Animation Specialization.

- Flashback: A flashback is a scene, or a sequence of scenes, that occurred in the past, but is inserted into the present time of the film to explain part of the backstory. When used effectively, they contribute an emotional tug to the heartstrings of the audience. A successful flashback is used in Pixar's *Ratatouille*, when the food critic Anton Ego takes one bite and is brought back to when he was a child and his mother prepared the same food, explaining in one quick scene the comfort he felt when consuming the presented dish at the restaurant.

- Flashforward: A flashforward is a scene used to move the story forward from the current point in time to a new point, interrupting the story with an expected or imaginary future event. In Pixar's *Up*, Carl is dangling Russell out of the house with a series of tied together sheets. When Russell slips out of the knot and begins to fall, we are jolted back into present time, realizing that Carl was imagining a plan of action he wished to take, but didn't occur.

- Freeze-Frame: Stopping time is achieved using a freeze-frame. A freeze-frame is when a single frame stops and is held, much like a photograph, which makes the audience notice the importance of the moment. It is usually accompanied by a voice-over narrative. An example in Pixar's *Ratatouille* is when Remy is chased through the window, which becomes a freeze-frame as he says, "This is me. I think it's apparent I need to rethink my life a little bit."

**Figure 7.64**
In this shot, a different artistic style indicates a flashback memory. Still image from *Gaiaspora* (2013). (Timecode 00:50–01:32) Courtesy of the University of Central Florida Character Animation Specialization.

**Figure 7.65**
Here, the passage of time is indicated through the use of lighting changes that cycle through the day and move the story forward, giving the foundation that Chip and Flint are only alive during nighttime. Still images from *Flower Story* (2012). (Timecode 02:18–02:28) Courtesy of the University of Central Florida Character Animation Specialization.

**Figure 7.66**
Gator finally gains his 'stache after the credits roll. The film ends with a freeze-frame to immortalize the moment. Still image from *Mustache Mayhem* (2011). (Timecode 07:40–07:44) Courtesy of the University of Central Florida Character Animation Specialization.

## Using the Principles of Design

A director uses the elements described in the previous section to visually communicate the action and the story to the audience. How the director uses these elements to create a composition is by using the principles of art and design. In the previous section, the examples given were also all examples of the different principles. What follows is a description of each principle and an example of how they are used to arrange the visual elements in screen composition. Most of this section will seem like a repeat of information, but it is important to recap this information, as these principles are the guidelines of creating great compositions.

### Emphasis/Dominance/Center of Interest

The center of interest is the part of the composition that our eye is drawn towards. We can control the audience's focal point by using the elements of art and design along with the principle of contrast, as covered earlier in this chapter. The positioning of the audience's eyes should continue into the subsequent shot, from shot to shot. Wherever the point of attention is on the screen at the end of one shot should be the same point of attention into the next shot as it is put together in edit, creating a comfortable visual sequencing. This is referred to as continuum of movement. On the other hand, purposely creating an uncomfortable, jumping eye movement around the screen can build tension.

**Figure 7.67**
This composition emphasizes the star indicating its elusive importance for Gan Vogh. Still image from *Celestial* (2014). (Timecode 00:36–00:39) Courtesy of the University of Central Florida Character Animation Specialization.

## Contrast/Similarity

Visual contrast is the juxtaposition of opposites and the reason our attention is drawn to something. The greater the contrast between objects that are juxtaposed, the more interesting and noticeable something becomes and the more our eyes will be drawn to it. Examples include:

- Something light surrounded by darkness
- Something moving surrounded by stillness
- Something that is a bright, saturated color surrounded by muted tones
- Larger objects placed next to smaller objects

The less contrast and the more similar[20] the visuals appear, the more the audience will take in the entire image as a whole. With affinity, the audience will have visual rest.

**Figure 7.68**
In this image, contrast creates the focus on the opening of the pyramid, where we see our conquistador enter. Still image from *Snacktime* (2015). (Timecode 02:37–02:49) Courtesy of the University of Central Florida Character Animation Specialization.

## Hierarchy

The order of visual hierarchy directs the audience to the most important information first. It is important to remember that what works for a still image is similar, but different, from moving images on a screen. In addition, our eyes continuously shift around the screen. The visual hierarchy of importance is:

1. Faces
2. Movement
3. Light values

**Figure 7.69**
The focus of this shot is on the projection, which is the brightest as it moves and encircles Gan Vogh, whose face is purposely kept in the dark. Still image from *Celestial* (2014). (Timecode 04:42–04:45) Courtesy of the University of Central Florida Character Animation Specialization.

**Figure 7.70**
In the first shot on the left, Titan is launched from the planet to show his small scale. In the next shot his scale is significantly larger so that he dominates the screen and the audience has an opportunity to really see him. Still images from *Celestial* (2014). (Timecode 01:32–01:45) Courtesy of the University of Central Florida Character Animation Specialization.

## Scale/Proportion

Larger objects also dominate the screen and draw focus. The closer an object is to the foreground, the larger and more important it will appear. The farther an object is from the camera, the smaller and less significant it appears to the audience. Having a contrast of foreground elements with background elements brings depth to the screen.

Proportion is relative to the size of other objects in the scene. In general, large objects are perceived more significant than smaller ones.

## Balance and Imbalance

Balance is an equal distribution of the elements throughout the composition to create equal visual weight on each side of a central axis. Balanced compositions are symmetrical, while imbalanced compositions are asymmetrical. Imbalanced compositions are visually more interesting and appealing, so even balanced compositions should be slightly asymmetrical for visual appeal.

## Harmony

Harmony is when elements of the composition are integrated to create a pleasing visual combination, such as in color harmony. Visual harmony can be achieved through the use of repetition and rhythm. Visual discord can be created when a contrasting element is introduced.

**Figure 7.71**
Even balanced compositions should remain slightly imbalanced to create visual appeal. Still image from *Celestial* (2014). (Timecode 05:12–15:18) Courtesy of the University of Central Florida Character Animation Specialization.

**Figure 7.72**
Visual discord. The large flower is clearly the focal point in this shot. Having the flower be darker and the complementary color of the environment helps bring focus to the larger petals. Still image from *Celestial* (2014). (Timecode 03:22–03:28) Courtesy of the University of Central Florida Character Animation Specialization.

**Figure 7.73**
**Repetition of objects.** Still image from *Celestial* (2014). (Timecode 03:02–03:07) Courtesy of the University of Central Florida Character Animation Specialization.

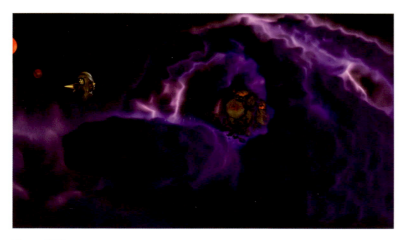

**Figure 7.74**
**Unity of composition.** Still image from *Celestial* (2014). (Timecode 02:21–02:28) Courtesy of the University of Central Florida Character Animation Specialization.

## Repetition/Pattern/Rhythm

In the previous section, the principle of rhythm was defined using the element of time to describe the pacing of the film. Additionally, rhythm can be used as part of the visual composition when placing elements inside of the frame. A repeated stationary object can create rhythm, as well as movement that is repeated in a pattern. Rhythm can be regular or irregular.

## Unity

A composition has achieved unity when similar elements are combined to create a completed, whole, and harmonious image. The image looks and feels right because everything is working together. To avoid monotony, variety is achieved when different elements are added to the composition to create visual interest.

Now that you have an understanding of screen design and composition, it is time once again to update the shot list with any additional changes or notes. After this is completed, you can begin storyboarding your idea. Initially, start working with simple stick figure thumbnails. You can find template documents on the companion website for this book that can be printed and penciled in quickly as a first pass. You may be able to reuse some of the beat boards you created earlier in the process. Think about each panel as a key moment or snapshot of the story. Those are the beats. Then add several panels for each shot to clarify the action. You may want to read the next chapter before beginning this process. As you will see, understanding the creation of animatics and the consideration of editing transitions can also be helpful when creating your storyboard panels.

## Bibliography and Further Reading

Bellantoni, P. (2013). *If it's purple, someone's gonna die: The power of color in visual storytelling*. Burlington, MA: Focal Press, an imprint of the Taylor & Francis Group.

Block, B. A. (2008). The visual story: Creating the visual structure of film, TV and digital media. Amsterdam: Focal Press/Elsevier.

Block, B. A. (2017). *3D storytelling: How stereoscopic 3D works and how to use it*. Burlington, MA: CRC Press.

Bordwell, D. (2011, February 14). *Watching you watch There Will Be Blood*. Retrieved from http://www.david bordwell.net/blog/2011/02/14/watching-you-watch -there-will-be-blood/.

Cabrera, C. (2013). Reel success: Creating demo reels and animation portfolios. Burlington: Taylor & Francis.

Catmull, E. E., & Wallace, A. (2014). Creativity, Inc.: Overcoming the unseen forces that stand in the way of true inspiration. New York: Random House.

Pennington, A. (2017). *Exploring 3D: The new grammar of stereoscopic filmmaking*. Burlington, MA: CRC Press.

## Notes

1. Catmull, E. E., & Wallace, A. (2014). Creativity, Inc.: Overcoming the unseen forces that stand in the way of true inspiration. New York: Random House.
2. I am always asked about resolution. Resolution is a topic that seems confusing but really isn't. 72PPI is standard for display screens and 300DPI is standard for print. It really is that simple. The important factor for display is total pixel dimensions, W × H, even if the screen is retina display, which has a higher PPI. I always say, design at the correct aspect ratio with the highest possible pixel dimensions that your computer and storage can handle. 16:9 (HD 1080) is what we use currently.
3. Within this protected area also lie the action safe and title safe areas, which are discussed in the next section about composition.
4. Interestingly enough, the display aspect ratio of 16:10 translates remarkably close to the Golden Ratio.
5. Cabrera, C. (2013). Reel success: Creating demo reels and animation portfolios. Burlington: Taylor & Francis.
6. Screen resolution is 72 pixels/inch. This is standard among all displays. Not to be confused with print resolution, which should be 300 pixels/inch when designing work to be printed. Photoshop has a Film & Video Document Type where you can choose HDTV 1080p from the Size drop-down menu.
7. Cabrera, C. (2013). Reel success: Creating demo reels and animation portfolios. Burlington: Taylor & Francis.
8. Most software (such as Premiere, Photoshop, Maya, etc.) has the option to turn on the action safe and title safe guides.
9. The technology finally exists to show research on this; a small study can be found at Bordwell, D. (2011, February 14). *Watching you watch There Will Be Blood*. Retrieved from http://www.david bordwell.net/blog/2011/02/14/watching-you -watch-there-will-be-blood/.
10. Story continuity is consistency in character relationships or event sequencing and should be considered and monitored during the writing process.
11. There is even an entire website dedicated to reporting and finding continuity problems: www.moviemistakes.com.
12. There are some great books that cover all of the technical aspects of stereoscopic filmmaking. Suggested reading includes Block, B. A. (2017). *3D storytelling: How stereoscopic 3D works and how to use it*. Burlington, MA: CRC Press and Pennington, A. (2017). *Exploring 3D: The new grammar of stereoscopic filmmaking*. Burlington, MA: CRC Press.
13. Examples of this can be seen in *Tangled*, *Oz*, and *Life of Pi*.
14. Suggested reading includes Bellantoni, P. (2013). *If it's purple, someone's gonna die: The power of color in visual storytelling*. Burlington, MA: Focal Press, an imprint of the Taylor & Francis Group.
15. Cabrera, Cheryl (2013). Reel success: Creating demo reels and animation portfolios. Burlington: Taylor & Francis.
16. Cabrera, Cheryl (2013). Reel success: Creating demo reels and animation portfolios. Burlington: Taylor & Francis.
17. Refer to the section about color earlier in this chapter to consider the emotional impact in the shot.
18. Rembrandt lighting generally uses only two lights: key and fill.
19. These editing techniques will be discussed further in Chapter 8.
20. In *The visual story*, by Bruce Block, he refers to this as contrast and affinity. Block, B. A. (2008). *The visual story: Creating the visual structure of film, TV and digital media*. Amsterdam: Focal Press/Elsevier.

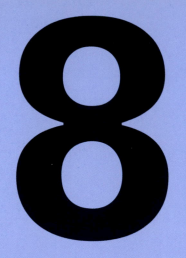

# Animatics and Editing

Once you have an initial pass at drawing your storyboards, putting them together in an animatic helps you visualize the story even better, to see what is working and what is not working, and get a feel for timing. Any adjustments that need to be made can happen before production begins. A traditional animatic, also known as a story reel in animation, is a timed-out succession of the storyboards with added rough sound and can be played as a movie. The frame numbers, timecodes, and shot numbers are displayed at the bottom of the animatic so that they can be referenced when someone gives any notes. The modern animatic has evolved to include video reference reels and 3D.[1] The purpose of the animatic is to be able to preview the scenes and the story before it is created in animation.

# Story Reel

A story reel is synonymous with an animatic. The best way to create a story reel is to use a non-linear editing program, such as Adobe Premiere Pro or Avid. If the storyboards were created traditionally by drawing on paper, each one will need to be digitized by scanning or photographing.[2] A great animatic will read as a simplified 2D animation with a few key movements to get the action across.

The use of simple pans and zooms can simulate most of the camera movement, and the use of the editing techniques described in this chapter will give the initial pacing and meaning of the film. In addition, a scratch track will be added for a preliminary suggestion of sound effects, Foley, and music. The final section of this chapter covers more information about sound.

**Figure 8.1**
**Four storyboard panels from the *Celestial* (2014) story reel.** Courtesy of the University of Central Florida Character Animation Specialization.

# Live Action Reference Reel

Finding the pacing of the film can be a very difficult task, especially for a first time filmmaker. Exactly how many frames does it take to get from point A to point B? For this reason, creating a live action reference reel first can be a valuable help when setting storyboards in a timeline. Creating video of each shot will allow you to edit together basic timing of each action with rough camera position and movement. Using this edit will help lay your storyboards out in proper pacing and timing for your story reel.

Alternatively, you can create this live action reference reel before you even begin the storyboarding process. In my experience, first time filmmakers have a difficult time framing their subject when storyboarding. Creating a live action reference reel provides a starting point for the drawings. When creating the video, you are forced to look through the viewfinder to frame your subjects. While the camera position and angle may not be completely accurate, this practice really helps provide a foundation for your drawings.

**Figure 8.2**
Four still frames from the live action animatic that match the storyboard panels from the *Celestial* (2014) story reel. The storyboard panels were actually created after the live action reel was made. Courtesy of the University of Central Florida Character Animation Specialization.

# Acting Reference Reel

Similar to the live action reference reel, the acting reference reel focuses mainly on performing the characters' actions with the intent of studying the motion, frame by frame, to use as reference while animating. This reel is usually put together on a shot or sequence basis as opposed to the entire film, and usually by the animator. Whereas the live action reference reel is more about overall shot timing and pacing of the edit, the acting reference reel serves as a tool for the animator. Various angles and takes should be made to capture body motion in multiple dimensions, especially if working in 3D animation.

**Figure 8.3**
The corresponding final rendered frames that match the four still frames from the live action animatic and the storyboard panels from the *Celestial* (2014) story reel. Courtesy of the University of Central Florida Character Animation Specialization.

# Scene Transitions and Editing

In a nutshell, editing is putting together everything with the right pacing and transitions into a continuous whole: the shots into scenes, the scenes into sequences, and the sequences into a final film. The goal of the editor is continuity editing, which is to connect the shots understandably without any jarring visual inconsistencies—unless there is a reason to deliberately jolt the audience. In other words, transitions and cuts should feel natural and should not be noticed unless they are meant to be noticed.

## Assembly Editing

One can begin editing an animated short by using a non-linear editor and placing all of the shots in the order that follows the shot list, otherwise known as assembly editing. Due to the cost of animation (nothing is free and everything must be made), editing starts early in the preproduction process and the film continues to be revised throughout the entire production process. Usually the first assembly is created with a sequence of storyboards and revised several times before going into production.

**Figure 8.4**
Assembly editing: Using a non-linear editor such as Adobe Premiere to edit the film together.

The average shot length (ASL) of an animated movie is approximately 3–3.5 seconds.[3] This equates into approximately 85–100 shots for a 5-minute short film. The faster the action, the shorter the shot length. A longer shot length gives the audience more time to see more of the details in the composition and characters, as in a mise-en-scène.

In traditional film editing, a master shot is a stationary long shot of the entire scene that keeps all of the characters in view. It is filmed as a whole take first, allowing the editor to use this take as a foundation for splicing in the remaining shots of the scene involving close-ups or insert shots. A moving master shot places the camera on a track or dolly and moves the camera around the actors and through the scene. A Steadicam can also be employed to create a moving master shot. In 3D animation, a master shot is also sometimes used, but only the necessary frames are rendered and brought through to the final edit. Animation also provides the opportunity to have highly choreographed and technical camera movement that would be difficult to do in live action without a complex motion rig (therefore, it is also difficult for stop motion).

In Pixar's *Inside Out*, the moving master shot is used throughout the film. One example is "Joy's Plan," when Joy is planning Riley's first day at her new school as one long, continuous, 48-second shot (timecode 20:16–21:03).

> It is a very high energy scene, but instead of using cuts, we used moving master shots with very complicated staging to create that energy. But, if you take all the complicated movements away, the cameras are extremely simple. There are only two cameras on tracks, the pan and tilt, and the boom.[4]
>
> Patrick Lin

Before there were digital, non-destructive, non-linear editors, the actual film had to be cut and spliced together. The terminology from linear editing has carried forward into digital editing. A cut[5] refers to a single shot following another, creating a rapid visual change from one shot to the next, and is the simplest and most common transition used in editing. How the cut occurs will impact the meaning of the story and the emotional response from the audience. All transitions can be combined in various ways to achieve different results. It is also important to note that transitions other than the cut are used sparingly as they are stylistic.

A continuity cut is when the action in a story occurs in a logical visual progression from one shot to the next. Using mostly continuity cuts creates an understandable and seamless visual story for the audience.

## Visual Match-Cut

A visual match-cut, also known as cutting on action, is created when the spatial-visual logic makes sense between two shots with different camera angles, positions, or moves. In a match-cut, the end of one shot visually matches the beginning of the next. There are several different scenarios where this usually occurs:

1. Match action is when an action from the first shot continues into the next. This usually happens during an action, such as when a character exits the frame and then re-enters in the next shot or in the middle of a fight scene, and can include changing the camera position (from medium shot to long shot). The key to this is making sure the subject is still in motion. Actions such as punches, kicks, turning or throwing something, or going through a doorway are prime examples of when an edit needs to "match on action" if the movement continues from one shot to the next.

**Figure 8.5**
In the first shot (left image), Marcy is reaching to make the top of her box. This action is carried through to the next shot. Still images from *Yours, Mime, and Ours* (2014). (Timecode 00:33–00:56) Courtesy of the University of Central Florida Character Animation Specialization.

2. Match-cut, also called a graphic match, is when two shots are cut matched in action or composition, creating a transition between two shots using the same or similar camera movements, colors, motions, and/or shapes of objects.

3. Eyeline match shows in one shot a character looking at someone or something in off-screen space; in the next shot, the camera angle logically lines up the position of the object or person they are looking at. An imaginary line created from the aim of the character's eyes towards the visual target should match the angle of the object in the next shot. This can even work to show what a character is thinking if the character looks at an object, then shifts the direction of his gaze in the first shot to indicate that the object has triggered a thought; in the next shot we see what is in their mind, usually a flashback or a flashforward.

4. The eyeline match is particularly important where a shot reverse shot is used. A shot reverse shot is a camera angle and editing technique where in the first shot of a character interaction scene (such as dialogue), one character is looking towards a second character who is either off screen or shown at an over-the-shoulder angle. The next shot is at the same camera position but of the second character looking back at the first. The composition should have some visual space in front of each character's face. The angle of the camera is dependent on the eye level of each character. A seated character looking up in the first shot should switch to an angle looking up at the second character in the next shot.

**Figure 8.6**
**These two shots are matched in similar shapes and movements.** Still images from *Atlas' Revenge* (2009). (Timecode 02:58–03:01) Courtesy of the University of Central Florida Character Animation Specialization.

**Figure 8.7**
**The eyeline match of Gus is followed by a shot that shows why his mouth is gaping open: a large air bubble is about to burst the inflatable cake.** Still images from *Yours, Mime, and Ours* (2014). (Timecode 04:38–04:44) Courtesy of the University of Central Florida Character Animation Specialization.

## Jump Cut

A jump cut is when two sequential shots of the same character or subject are cut together without a visual match, continuity is lost, and the abrupt transition is jarring and causes the audience to feel disoriented. Jump cuts can successfully be used as an ellipsis to create a sense of urgency and also give the effect of speeding up time and action while jumping from one spot of screen space to another or moving characters around within a static shot and therefore jumping forward in time.[6] Jump cuts have also been used as a visual effect to transport the character to another location or make something or someone disappear. Jump cuts are used to show repetitive actions to bring attention to that action, such as in stories about sports. If not used properly and effectively, a jump cut is simply bad editing. To avoid an unintentional jump cut, follow the 30° rule that is discussed in Chapter 5.

## Smash Cut

A smash cut is an abrupt change at a crucial point in a shot where a cut would not be likely to occur. A change in shot when it is unexpected jolts the audience. Waking up from a dream or a nightmare is a typical smash cut. A smash cut can effectively be created when a fast-moving camera is spliced with a stationary shot.

## Intercutting

Intercutting has several different meanings but is generally used to build a dramatic effect, create contrast, quicken the pace, or heighten the suspense of a scene. The following three definitions can also refer to intercutting:

1.  The process of cutting back and forth between separate shots occurring simultaneously in the same location, but focusing on different subjects

**Figure 8.8**
In these three shots, Judy's reaction is magnified using a jump cut. In reality, these shots have an animated camera which successfully has the same effect. Still images from *Box Forts* (2012). (Timecode 02:05–02:08) Courtesy of the University of Central Florida Character Animation Specialization.

**Figure 8.9**
The last bit of air that causes the cake to burst is cut to an exterior of the house and how it moves from the pressure of the released air. Still images from *Yours, Mime, and Ours* (2014). (Timecode 04:42–04:48) Courtesy of the University of Central Florida Character Animation Specialization.

2.  Inserting a flashback or flashforward between clips of a scene into current time
3.  Cutting from one camera position to another (such as a close-up to a long shot)

What follows are types of intercutting.

• Parallel editing is the process of cutting back and forth between two or more simultaneous actions of different characters who are not aware of each other; it can also be used for settings or objects. There is no interaction between the characters, but the shots are used to show the relationships between their parallel lives in order to heighten interest or to escalate tension. The Pixar short *BURN-E* is a perfect example of using this technique to build an entire short film as it parallels the story and actions of one robot named BURN-E during the time frame of the entire length of the movie *WALL-E*.

• Cross cutting is the process of cutting back and forth between two or more actions of different characters, settings, or objects that are occurring simultaneously and directly affect each other in order to heighten interest or to escalate tension. The shots are intertwined because the characters are aware of each other and their actions are dependent on each other to advance the story. It can also be used to show what the character is thinking. Cross cutting can be seen in Pixar's *One Man Band*. Shots of the little girl are cross cut with the performances of both Treble and Bass as they compete with each other to get her golden coin.

**Figure 8.10** Cross cutting is used in these shots to show Marcy's reactions to her father's actions. Still images from *Yours, Mime, and Ours* (2014). (Timecode 03:35–04:01) Courtesy of the University of Central Florida Character Animation Specialization.

**Figure 8.11**
A cut away is used in these shots to show what Gan Vogh is looking at and also prevents a jump cut. Still images from *Celestial* (2014). (Timecode 00:43–00:54) Courtesy of the University of Central Florida Character Animation Specialization.

- Cut away: A disruption of a shot with a quick inserted shot of something else and usually, not always, returns to the continuance of the original shot. Some reasons that cut aways are used:
  - To indicate what a character is thinking, aided by a change in the character's eyeline prior to the cut away using an eyeline match
  - To insert a flashback or flashforward
  - As a disrupted match-cut (a cut away inserted into a match-cut)
  - To prevent a jump cut
- Overlapping action[7] in film editing means that part of an action is repeated in the beginning of multiple shots and possibly repeated from different camera angles or positions, in order to slow time and create emphasis.

**Figure 8.12**
Overlapping action is used in these shots to build intensity and suspense as Sputnik orbits right into the box tower, ultimately causing Jake and his boxes to tumble back to Earth. Still image from *Box Forts* (2012). (Timecode 03:34–03:47) Courtesy of the University of Central Florida Character Animation Specialization.

## Split Screen

A split screen is an equal and visible division of the screen in order to run two or more shots simultaneously to suggest concurrent actions. The split screen is often used in the following scenarios:

1. To show phone conversations
2. To compare the actions of two people (victim/prowler, boyfriend/girlfriend, etc.)
3. For surveillance footage
4. To show a sporting event and crowd reactions
5. To compare two opponents

## Montage

Montage is a French word that simply means editing. A montage is an assembly of several short shots that relate to each other and are combined to emphasize an idea, which helps inform the audience and move the narrative forward more quickly. A montage is not accompanied by much dialogue, if any, and is commonly edited together with a song.

In Pixar's *Toy Story 2*, we learn of Jesse's story of love and heartache through the montage created with the Randy Newman song sung by Sarah McLachlan, "When She Loved Me."

A bridging shot is a short montage made of quick successional match-cuts or jump cuts used to move the story forward from the current point in time to a new point, in a very short amount of screen time. It can also be a single shot of movement, such as rotating car tires, falling calendar pages, or quick lighting changes to indicate the day has passed.

**Figure 8.13**
**A split screen is used in this shot to show the last two players of a poker game.** Still image from *Mustache Mayhem* (2011). (Timecode 03:51–03:55) Courtesy of the University of Central Florida Character Animation Specialization.

**Figure 8.14**
Calendar pages fall to show how many days go by since the mustache cream was applied to the faces of Turt and Gator. Still images from *Mustache Mayhem* (2011). (Timecode 02:13–02:17) Courtesy of the University of Central Florida Character Animation Specialization.

The montage created with Michael Giacchino's song "Married Life" in Pixar's *Up* moves the story forward many decades. Within this montage are additional flashes forward and examples of bridging shots, for example filling the coin jug and when several days or months go by, indicated by lighting changes. Another bridging shot is when Ellie is tightening Carl's ties, bringing the audience through many decades as his ties and shirt change from shot to shot.

## Dissolve

A dissolve is a soft transition between two shots, usually placed between scene changes to indicate a lengthier passage of time than that of a cut. The first shot is blended with the next as it gradually fades out, while the second shot gradually fades in.

A match dissolve links two similar visuals similar to a match-cut, but in this case, the first shot dissolves into the next, which indicates a longer passage of time than the match-cut. A character in one shot that dies, changes, appears, or disappears is often depicted dissolving into the next shot with the same composition. Types of dissolves include:

- Fade-in is a dissolve from a solid, usually black or white, to an image, and is used at the beginning of a scene.
- Fade-out is a dissolve from an image to a solid, usually black or white, and is used at the end of a scene.

**Figure 8.15**
A match dissolve is used to transition from the shot of the commercial to the shot of Turt picking up the actual jar of cream. Still images from *Mustache Mayhem* (2011). (Timecode 02:00–02:05) Courtesy of the University of Central Florida Character Animation Specialization.

## Focus

A transition using focus changes the clarity and blurriness of the image in between two shots. Types of focus include:

- Focus-in is when an image gradually comes into focus at the beginning of a shot.
- Focus-out is when an image gradually goes out of focus at the end of a shot.
- Whip pans[8] are a quick pan of the camera left, right, up, or down at the end of a shot that stops suddenly at the framing of the next shot.

## Wipe

A wipe is a screen transition where the next shot pushes the first shot off-screen, giving the effect of a page turning, indicating time has passed. Most wipes are about 1 second in length but can be faster, and slower wipes are used to show longer periods of time. If a character moves off screen, the wipe should follow in the same direction as the character. Wipes can move in the following directions:

- Left or right (horizontal).
- Up or down (vertical).
- Diagonally.
- Iris: This was originally an in-camera technique that created a transition to/from black by manually changing the size of the iris, a diaphragm in front of lens. To begin a scene, the iris is opened (iris-in), which creates a central circle shape that opens, going from all black to full image. When the iris is closed (iris-out), blackness encloses around a central circular shape

that eventually turns the whole image into black. Today, this effect is created digitally in editing software using a circular wipe going to or coming from black. The iris can also be used to create a focus on detail within a scene, such as a first-person perspective of what a pirate sees through a monocular.
- Circular wipe: This is similar to the iris but uses the beginning of another shot instead of going to black. Similarly, other shapes can be used to create this wipe, such as stars and hearts.
- Invisible wipe: If timed correctly, this is when moving objects or characters in the foreground of the first shot can appear to reveal the next shot while pushing the first shot off the screen. The camera can also move into darkness and then reveal the next shot as it continues to move back into the light.
- Radial wipe follows the motion of a clock's movement.
- Whip pans can also be used as a wipe.

An ideal cut is the one that satisfies all the following six criteria at once:

1. It is true to the emotion of the moment.
2. It advances the story.
3. It occurs at a moment that is rhythmically interesting and "right."
4. It acknowledges what you might call "eye-trace"—the concern with the location and movement of the audience's focus of interest within the frame.
5. It respects "planarity"—the grammar of three dimensions transposed by photography to two (the questions of stage-line, etc.).

**Figure 8.16**
A focus-in is used in this shot to show the wooziness of Bob as he comes in and out of consciousness. Still image from *Gaiaspora* (2013). (Timecode 05:27–05:30) Courtesy of the University of Central Florida Character Animation Specialization.

Figure 8.17 A vertical wipe is used to transition from Judy building her box fort to her standing proudly on top. Still image from *Box Forts* (2012). (Timecode 02:17–02:19) Courtesy of the University of Central Florida Character Animation Specialization.

6.  It respects the three-dimensional continuity of the actual space (where people are in the room and in relation to one another.

Each criteria should ideally make up a certain percentage of the cut:

Emotion: 51%
Story: 23%
Rhythm: 10%
Eye-trace: 7%
Two-dimensional plane of screen: 5%
Three-dimensional space of action: 4%

Emotion, at the top of the list, is the thing that you should try to preserve at all costs. If you find you have to sacrifice certain of those six things to make a cut, sacrifice your way up, item by item, from the bottom.[9]

In addition to visual editing transitions, there are also a few audio transitions.

## Audio Match-Cut

An audio match-cut is when we hear part of the audio in the first shot, and the next shot continues with the same or similar audio. Sentences can be begun by one character in the first shot and completed by another character in the next. Whistles can become screams.

## Audio Smash Cut

An audio smash cut is when we go from something loud in the first shot to quiet in the next, or reversed with something quiet in the first shot and loud in the next.

## Audio Bridge

An audio bridge is when two shots are connected with audio, usually dialogue, Foley, or a sound effect. Types of audio bridges include:

*   L cut is when audio in the first shot carries through to the next shot. This is commonly used with dialogue to help create a natural progression to the subsequent shot.
*   J cut is when audio in the next shot begins while the first shot is still being seen. The audience hears what is happening before they can see it. The J cut, like the L cut, is used to help create a smooth transition to the following shot as well as reveal a new element to the audience within the environment, since they hear it first.
*   Voice-over is when a narrative description of information is heard by a narrator who is not seen by the audience.

# Sound

"A truth whispered among animators is that 70% of a show's impact comes from the soundtrack."

Michel Dougherty

A film is not only a visual experience. An animated film is just as much an audio experience, if not more, yet the audio is frequently overlooked. By engaging the audience's sense of hearing, emotions are further manipulated in connection with their visual experience. However, the audience will not directly notice sound that is done well. Sound is so integral to success of a film that it should be considered and shaped from the beginning of the storytelling process—it should not be an afterthought.

Any sound should be recorded at the best quality possible. Recording voice has never been easier and more accessible. A computer, decent mic, and a pop-shield is all you really need, but if you can afford a professional recorder, something like the Zoom H4N Handy Portable Digital Recorder gives you the flexibility to record sound anywhere. An animation soundtrack will be composed of dialogue (if any), sound effects, and Foley.

An important note is that silence in the right places can be just as important and impactful as sound. Also, if the sound is too loud, too overpowering, or just not right, then it becomes distracting, and will take your audience out of the story.

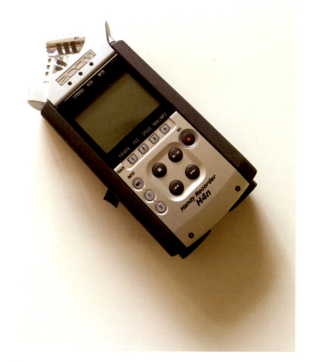

**Figure 8.18**
A Zoom H4n Handy Portable Digital Recorder.

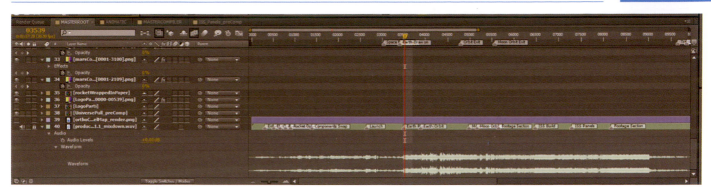

**Figure 8.19**
**A scratch track.** Image used with permission of Ninjaneer Studios, 2016.

## Scratch Track

A scratch track is a rough idea of what the sound should be like, and includes dialogue (if any), music, and sound effects. The scratch track is created when the first cut of the story reel animatic is created. Music and sound effects can be taken from any existing source and can be copyrighted, since this music is just used to give an idea of what the sound might be and will not be used in the final cut of the film. Recording your own voice to make all of the sound effects is a quick way of adding them to the reel.

## Dialogue

"Storytelling without dialogue. It's the purest form of cinematic storytelling. It's the most inclusive approach you can take."

Andrew Stanton

Dialogue should be used sparingly. Good dialogue can reveal who a character really is in only one line. Bad dialogue can kill a story.

If dialogue is being used in the story, it should be recorded before any animation is done, since the body animation of the character is what makes lip sync convincing. Once the dialogue recording is completed, it is used during the animation process for accurate lip sync. Taking video during the recording sessions of the voice talent is also done because this footage can be used as acting reference for the animators.

## Sound Effects

"There's no excuse for having a mental or creative block in sound. You can just go out and collect things in the real world—they make the sound, not you. It's very restricting to always use a library for sound effects. It's much more interesting and freeing to go out and record new sounds because you never know what you're going to get."

Gary Rydstrom

Recording sound effects takes plenty of creativity and patience. Nothing in animation is free, and this includes every sound heard. Every sound must be created or found in a sound library. Trying to find the right sounds is a long and tedious process, much like all of animation production. Usually, to get the right sound, it takes the combination of several different unrelated sounds. Sound effects should be cut into the story reel animatic and revised with every updated animatic to follow, evolving over time to the final soundtrack. This is the job of the sound designer.[10] Be sure that whatever found sound effects used are royalty free, otherwise written permission must be granted from the owner.

## Foley Sound

"It's all about the emotional associations of sounds. It's not about whether they're really technically correct or not. It's about whether they're scary or relaxing or threatening or whatever helps tell the story."

Dane A. Davis

Foley sound is different from sound effects in that it is performed to the animation. A Foley artist not only makes sound effects, but performs the sound so that it perfectly matches to the action on the screen, helping the audience achieve and maintain their suspension of disbelief. While the Foley artist is performing the sound in real time along with the animation, it is recorded and then laid into the edit of the film.

## Music

"I, over the years, have always felt more comfortable if I could go into a projection room and look at a film and not really know what to expect. If you read the script first, you form all kinds of preconceptions about how things look, what the location's like, what the actors are like."

John Williams

The musical score used to enhance your story can make or break your project. Added music, whether it is vocal or instrumental, affects our emotions and creates rhythm, harmony, and form that sets the tone while it supports the story's theme. Each character could also have their own theme. Think about different movies you have seen and the soundtracks that have accompanied them. Consider the timeless characters that have a place in our memories because of the thematic music attached to them. A few that come to mind are Darth Vader, Princess Leia, Indiana Jones, and Jaws. It is difficult to choose the right piece; therefore, experimentation is necessary. The genre of music should also align with the genre of your story.

Music used must be royalty free, otherwise permission in writing must be granted from the owner. Credit should appear at the end of your film as well. A quick Google search of the keywords "free music for animation" brings up many royalty-free resources that can be used. There are also many emerging musicians who are willing to work with an emerging filmmaker, so do not be afraid to reach out and ask.

## Realistic Sound

Realistic sound is what we would expect to hear in the world as we know it. For animation, realistic sound is possibly a great place to start, however, with animation, recording the actual sound may not work or even be possible with the actions on screen. Sounds may need to be imagined and created specifically so that the audience buys into the fact that something would sound that way.

Ben Burtt, an American sound designer, is famous for creating sounds for films such as *Star Wars* Episodes IV and V as well as Pixar's *WALL-E*, particularly for characters and objects that do not exist in our reality. By recording appliance motors, animals, jets, aircraft carriers, and sounds from striking metal objects, he orchestrated fabricated sounds for R2D2, Chewbacca, aliens, WALL-E, Eva, lightsabers, blasters, weapons, explosions, and spaceships.

## Expressive Sound

Expressive sound begins as a realistic sound and is then exaggerated for dramatic effect. The sound may get louder or it may continue longer than expected. Expressive sounds will alert the audience to something that needs particular attention.

## Surreal Sound

Surreal sound can be used to depict what a character hears in their inner world, as in their thoughts, dreams, hallucinations, nightmares, or daydreams. Because of this, sounds can be drawn from any source, allowing full creative license. Emphasis can be given to atmospheric wonderment to communicate the surrealistic presence of the character's thoughts to the audience.

*Coraline* (timecode 16:03–16:26) follows a mouse into a door that was previously sealed with a brick wall. This time, however, a tunnel unravels before her eyes. A phantom sound emerges from the magical and dream-induced corridor, indicating the surrealistic phenomenon before her.

This chapter covered the creation of animatics and the consideration of editing transitions with sound and music. It is time again to update the shot list with any additional changes or notes. Once this is completed, you can begin storyboarding if you have not done so already. Otherwise, you may have to update your thumbnails before continuing the process of creating your story reel animatic. Once you have your animatic in hand, it's time to move on to the next chapter: feedback, more revisions, and production planning.

## Bibliography and Further Reading

Beauchamp, R. (2005). *Designing sound for animation*. Burlington, MA: Elsevier/Focal Press.

Bordwell, D. (2006). *The way Hollywood tells it: Story and style in modern movies*. Berkeley: University of California Press.

Murch, W. (2001). *In the blink of an eye: A perspective on film editing* (2nd ed.). West Hollywood, CA: Silman-James Press.

Walice, E. (2015, May 12). Behind the camera of Disney Pixar's *Inside Out*: Riley cam vs. mind cam. Retrieved from https://momontheside.com/behind-the-camera-of-disney-pixars-inside-out

## Notes

1. 3D animatics are also known as a layout reel, or in live action as a pre-visualization or pre-vis reel. See Chapter 9 for more information about the layout reel.

2. As stated in the Chapter 7, a good file naming convention is something like the following: shotNumber.boardNumber.ext. The shot number of the storyboard is taken from the shot list. Each shot may need several boards to visually describe the action taking place. Therefore, if there are 110 shots in the five-minute film being created and the first shot has five boards, these boards would be labeled as 001.00.tga, 001.20.tga, 001.40.tga, 001.60.tga, and 001.80.tga. The board numbers allow for adding new shots in between if more boards are added to the shot. Some studios use alphabet letters, such as 001a.tga, 001b.tga, 001c.tga, 001d.tga, and 001e.tga. Whichever you use is fine, as long as you are consistent.

3. Bordwell, D. (2006). *The way Hollywood tells it: Story and style in modern movies*. Berkeley: University of California Press (p. 123).

4. Walice, E. (2015, May 12). Behind the camera of Disney Pixar's *Inside Out*: Riley cam vs. mind cam. Retrieved from https://momontheside.com/behind-the-camera-of-disney-pixars-inside-out

5. Also known as a hard cut or standard cut.

6. As in a bridging shot, described later with the description of a montage.

7. Not to be confused with overlapping action in animation, one of the principles of animation also known as follow-through, which means that not all things in motion move at the same time or stop at the same time, which creates fluidity.

8. Also known as pan blur, whip swish, or swish pan; more information can be found in Chapter 6.

9. Murch, W. (2001). *In the blink of an eye: A perspective on film editing* (2nd ed.). West Hollywood, CA: Silman-James Press (pp. 18–19).

10. For all of the nitty gritty details about sound design, I recommend the following book written by my colleague: Beauchamp, R. (2005). *Designing sound for animation*. Burlington, MA: Elsevier/Focal Press.

# 9

# Getting Feedback, Making Revisions, and Production Planning

Every artist knows how important critiques of their work can be. Having someone else take a look at your work and let you know what their opinion is can be invaluable. This is where your network of fellow artists can be beneficial. The real reason people go to a brick and mortar university is to develop a network of peers. Fortunately, today, there are many virtual networking opportunities on forums where like-minded people congregate and are usually happy to give input to your work. In addition, show your animatic to friends, family, peers, and anyone willing to watch and give you feedback. Find out if they understand what is happening. With visual storytelling, it is sometimes difficult to know if your ideas are coming across and through to the audience. Hollywood often prescreens a

**Figure 9.1**
Director's notes, *Yours, Mime, and Ours* (2014). Courtesy of the University of Central Florida Character Animation Specialization.

film during the crucial editing process to get feedback prior to final release. Find out what makes sense and what is not clear and you can make adjustments. Repeat this process after every revision until you are either satisfied with the results or run out of time.

There is always risk involved when sharing your work for feedback. Someone may "steal" your idea and do something better than you. Do not let that stop you from seeking feedback. Ideas are fluid things that can be appropriated and evolved into something new. A professor once told me that there is an ether of common thought and that artists around the world have the same or similar ideas all of the time. This is how art movements occur. Think about all of the ideas you have had that were amazing and wonderfully fresh and groundbreaking, only to discover after a little research that the same idea has been already developed by one or more other people. Did you stop pursuing that idea or did you alter it and make it your own? As established earlier in this book, everything has been done before, so make an idea your own by changing or combining it with something else to make it original.

**Figure 9.2**
**Storyboard animatic dailies,** *Farmer Glorp* **(2016).** Courtesy of the University of Central Florida Character Animation Specialization.

## Yours, Mime, and Ours
Notes from 11/03/2013

### Shot Fixes
*If you have a POV, there needs to be some drift or movement in it to show personality.
*Please reference the animatic as well as the workbook.

### Shot
001: Start zoomed in entirely to match the outside shot. Angle camera so that picture frames are parallel.
002: Starts rotating too soon. Hold first.
005: Too far away.
006: Tip camera a bit so his head isn't at the top of the frame.
007: Holds for too long before pull back. Should be closer on her face.
008: Camera is in the wrong place. Angle up more and face the couch.
009: Too far away. Should be in same position as 5. Moves too fast.
011: Too far away. It's supposed to start closer and then pull back.
012: Closer.
013: Make her head shake back and forth.
014: Closer, higher angle.
015: Try to match storyboard better.
018: Tighter.
019: Tighter. Softer bounce.
021: Drift a bit at the end following the box.
022: Drift a bit following the last shot.
024: Change to direct zoom. More subtle. Put the box in it.
027: Box needs to be in it.
028: Work on arc and don't come to a complete stop.
030: Try wider angle lens or shorter focal length. She should be closer to foreground.
031: Not close enough for pie in the face and faster zoom.
032: Move more because it's a POV, tighten in on her, higher angle.
033: We should see more of the box, may have to physically move box for composition. Weird arc when it zooms in.
034: Make her bigger and pull back a little.
035: Bring camera down and tilt up a little.
036: Hold longer on Marcy before it flips because she needs to laugh and point. Cake box will be more to the left so unhide it and aim camera at it. Camera move at the end should be more subtle.
037: Tighter.
039: Move camera so box isn't so high up.
040: Make Marcy bigger. Farther back from box.
044: Don't start pulling back yet. Pull back should be faster (see animatic).
045: Don't follow bubble. Simplify the camera. Truck in instead of camera swinging back and forth.
051: Try zooming in a bit.
054: Static camera and watch air bubble go in (same for 56).
056: Make longer and see above.
060: Boxes could be lower in frame. Zoom should be slower an start when he turns around.
062: Wider angle lens.
069: Wider lens for these shots and closer.
077: Pause before zooming so she has time to open flaps.
078: Needs to pull back.

### Notes
I love the idea of a "clown family" with their own clown set of rules. There are lots of possibilities for gags with this idea. I love that the mime baby has made her first mime box and that the kid just wants to play in the box. Isn't that what all babies do? (See *Tin Toy* for reference.) The balloon animal gags and little car, big clown bit is wonderful. We need to at least see mom as harlequin somehow (photo . . . not just silhouette . . . something) in the film. What if the dad gets into a little box rather than a big one, the same way he is able to get into a little car? What about a "dad in the box" gag? You need a shot of the destruction made in the room after the cake explodes so that we get why the mom sighs at the end. Love the old timey music and call out to silent movies which were told entirely through pantomime. Love that we can define the objects a mime makes in animation. This is a very animated story.

What if the dad is a "jack-in-the-box"? This concept works with the idea of the connection between the dad and his daughter as they each have their own "box"—something to share. I still don't think the mom needs to be physically present. Perhaps she is out shopping and has left the dad in charge for the day. This will help keep the story to two characters.

# Revisions to the Story, Storyboards, and Animatics

Once feedback is obtained it is time to sit down and take a hard look at what you have and what feedback you are going to implement in the revision. Reworking something that you have spent so much time agonizing over is extremely difficult. Our work is like our children. We nurture it, feed it, clothe it, and put it out into the world for everyone to see. Any judgment that comes is hurtful and feels like a direct attack to our abilities as an artist, storyteller, and animator.

The first thing to consider is, what is the purpose of your film? Here are some questions that you should think about:

- Is this film an artistic expression of your vision?
- Do you care what other people think?
- Do you expect to get into film festivals?
- Do you want to win awards?
- Are you trying to get funding for a larger project?
- Are you trying to get hired as a story artist?

If the answer is no to most of these questions, then move forward with your vision. In fact, feedback is not really necessary if there is no intention to do anything with the information given.

If the answer is yes to most of these questions, then it is crucial to consider the feedback given and make revisions. There is no easy way to say this. Thick skin and a critical eye must be developed and become the dominant quality of your personality. One of the best quotes that I use to remind me to not take criticism personally is from Mario Puzo's *The Godfather*, when Michael Corleone says, "It is not personal, Sonny, it's strictly business."

Just because someone thinks you should change or add something does not mean that you should. It does mean, however, for you to consider what they have said. Think about why they have suggested what they have said and whether or not it should be something implemented or changed in your idea, then make appropriate changes.

Good practice is to archive everything you do before and during changes so that you can go back if necessary. This does take up space, either physically or digitally, so this fact needs to be considered in your budget and organization is the key to finding something later down the line if needed. How often you save is a personal preference and can change at different stages of production. Fortunately for those working digitally, data storage is less expensive, but it does add costs to production. For those working in paper or clay, storage must also be humidity controlled and pest free.

# Revising the Shot List, Adding Characters, Effects, and Animation Details

Chapters 4 and 6 suggested that you create and edit a shot list. Now that notes have been given it is time to revisit the shot list once again and make some changes.

First and foremost, be sure to make changes and add additional shot descriptions, including anything new that will be adjusted in the next animatic. Once this is completed, an update of the shot numbers must be done in a way that does not change the current existing shot numbers. Adding an alphabet letter might be the easiest way to complete this task. Add the action description, update which characters are in each shot, and enter any changes or new camera direction as you progress through the shot list. Once the shot list is updated, then the script should also be updated.

If you have not begun production, the changes can be made and a new version of the document can be saved. However, if already in production, you must make the changes noticeable to the production crew. Traditionally, new script additions are printed on certain colored pages so that the cast and crew will notice the updates. Assuming you are working

digitally, turn on the ability to track changes of your word processing software and the software will automatically change the text color with every change. Otherwise, highlighting the changes can also be helpful using the same standard color order.

The standardized order of revision pages is:

1. Blue
2. Pink
3. Yellow
4. Green
5. Goldenrod
6. Buff
7. Salmon
8. Cherry
9. Tan
10. Gray
11. Ivory

After 12 revisions, the colors cycle back to white and begin again.

Stop motion animators want to ensure that the shot list is not in numerical order but in shooting order (grouping all of the same environment shots together for multiple locations)

# Creating the Workbook

In order to turn your story idea into an animated film, creating a workbook[1] is an important step of the preproduction process, especially if you plan to work with a team of people. The workbook is created after the shot list, script, storyboards, and animatics have been updated and before layout begins.

The workbook is a visual plan that has one or more pages for every shot in the film and shows the following:

- Storyboards of each shot
- The frame numbers for that shot
- A top and/or front orthographic view of the environment showing character and camera motion
- A description of the shot
- Dialogue (if any)
- Additional notes
  - Any special instructions or explanations for the shot
  - Lists of the people who are working on the shot
    - Layout artist
    - Animator
    - Effects artist
    - Lighting artist
    - Renderer
    - Compositor

Traditionally, the workbook is placed in a binder so that everyone in a studio can access it for questions and notes. Instead of a printed document, however, it is also perfectly fine to create a digital file such as a PDF that anyone on the project can access, as long as team members can add notes. By creating this document, a visual plan is created before production begins, mapping out the choreography of cameras and action before you start layout.

# YOURS, MIME, AND OURS

## Shot 007.00

### Key Storyboards

Shot Duration: 00:46.13 - 00:54.22 ; 0202 frames

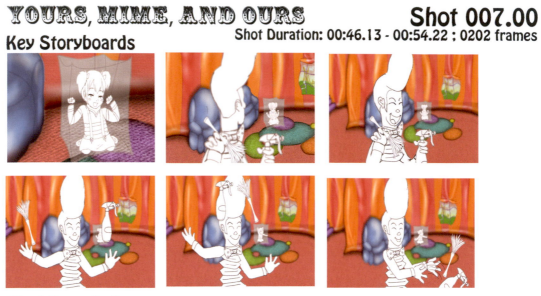

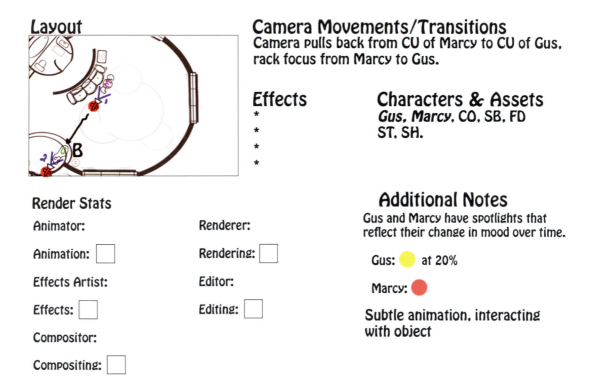

## Shot Description

Marcy is celebrating in her box. Gus notices and happily juggles his cleaning supplies and throws them down.

## Layout

## Camera Movements/Transitions

Camera pulls back from CU of Marcy to CU of Gus, rack focus from Marcy to Gus.

## Effects

*
*
*
*

## Characters & Assets

*Gus, Marcy*, CO, SB, FD
ST, SH.

## Render Stats

Animator:

Animation: ☐

Effects Artist:

Effects: ☐

Compositor:

Compositing: ☐

Renderer:

Rendering: ☐

Editor:

Editing: ☐

## Additional Notes

Gus and Marcy have spotlights that reflect their change in mood over time.

Gus: 🟡 at 20%

Marcy: 🔴

Subtle animation, interacting with object

Figure 9.3
Sample workbook page, *Yours, Mime, and Ours* (2014). Courtesy of the University of Central Florida Character Animation Specialization.

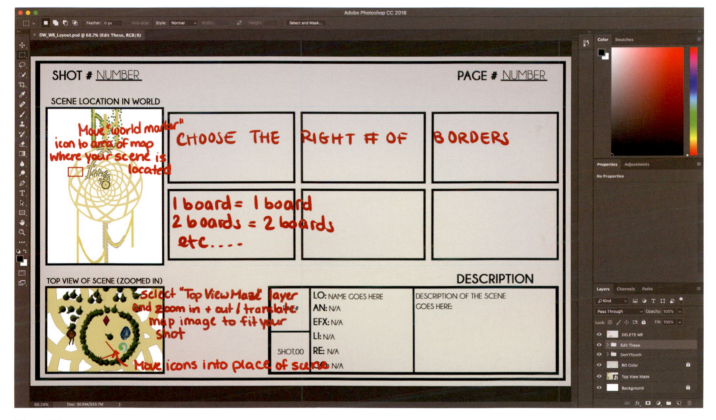

**Figure 9.4**
Sample workbook page template in Photoshop, *Dreamweaver* (2016). Courtesy of the University of Central Florida Character Animation Specialization.

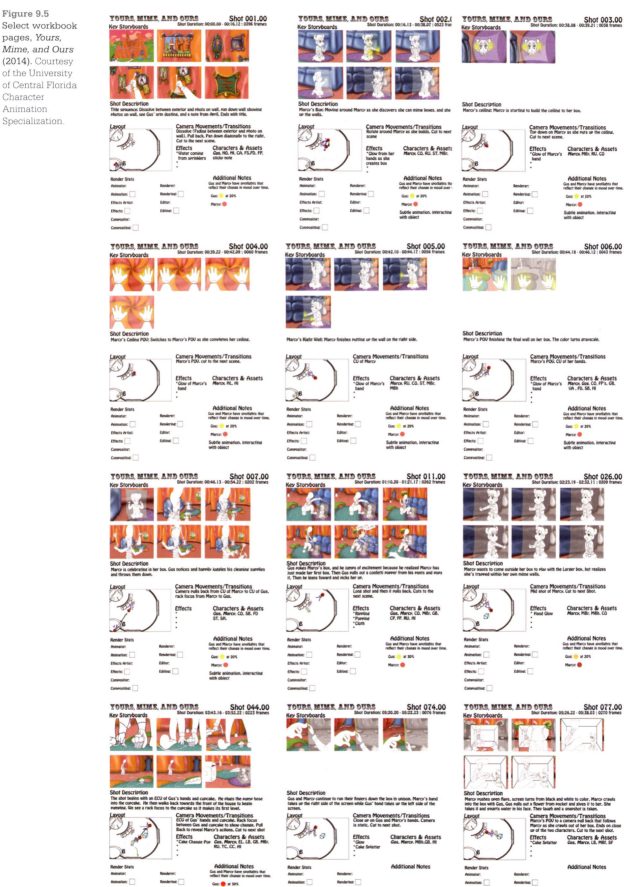

Figure 9.5 Select workbook pages, *Yours, Mime, and Ours* (2014). Courtesy of the University of Central Florida Character Animation Specialization.

## Choreography of Cameras and Action

Everything that has been decided in preproduction is brought together and prepared for animation during layout. Layout artists in animation are equivalent to cinematographers in live-action film and stop motion animation. The head of layout is considered the director of photography and works with the director to ensure the film is created in a way that supports the visual story being told.

If working in 2D, a layout artist will draw each of the detailed background planes while suggesting focal length, angles, and movement of the cameras based on the storyboards for each scene. The backgrounds then go to animation for keying, in-betweening, ink and paint, and cleanup.

In computer-generated animation, the camera focal length, angle, and motion is brought together with a temporary, low-resolution environment[2] and roughly animated characters to create a rough layout.[3] Rough layout will focus on an entire sequence before that sequence moves into final layout.

Final layout will then go through each shot and replace all temporary environment with the final environment.[4] Final layout will work with the set dresser to remove any models that are not in camera view for each shot, save out each shot from the sequence for animation, and then downstream through the production pipeline: layout > animation > lighting > effects > final layout > rendering > compositing. For continuity purposes, sometimes it's easier to leave all the shots together in one sequence for animation, lighting, and effects, then save each shot out for rendering and compositing.

When animation is finaled by the director, final layout will get the shot again for one last camera pass for finalling. Camera motions are adjusted if changes are needed to follow the character during animation. Camera shake is added if necessary at specific points in the animation during handheld shots and due to reactions caused by wind or heavy motions. Adjustments are also made to camera positions if necessary to ensure the focal point of the composition has continuity flow from shot to shot. Even after all of this work, a shot, scene, or sequence may still be scrapped or completely reworked if something is not working in the story.

**Figure 9.6** Layout frames interpreted from the storyboards in Chapter 7 from *Cuddle Fish* (2016). Courtesy of the University of Central Florida Character Animation Specialization.

# Creating the Color Script

As part of the preproduction process of art direction, a color script is created to show how the lighting and color palette will align with the emotions and moods of the characters and story. A color script is usually concept art of key moments of the story, all fitting on one board,[5] so that the entire movie can be seen at once. This shows the continuity of the art direction and demonstrates how every scene and sequence are related to each other and the story as a whole. The color script shows how the production designer and art director see the tone for the film as well as costume and setting ideas.

To create a color script, specific frames are taken from the storyboard and recreated as concept art.[6] Color scripts can be done in traditional materials, such as pastels, or digitally, using a graphics tablet and paint software, such as Photoshop.

**Figure 9.7**
Sample color key panel, *Yours, Mime, and Ours* (2014). Courtesy of the University of Central Florida Character Animation Specialization.

colorKey_01  colorKey_02  colorKey_03
colorKey_04  colorKey_05  colorKey_06
colorKey_06.01  colorKey_07  colorKey_08
colorKey_09  colorKey_09.01  colorKey_10
colorKey_11  colorKey_12
colorKey_14  colorKey_14.02
colorKey_15  colorKey_16  colorKey_17

**Figure 9.8**
Color script,
*Yours, Mime,
and Ours* (2014).
Courtesy of the
University of
Central Florida
Character
Animation
Specialization.

# Production Scheduling

The next big question is: how long does it take to make an animated film? The answer is: as long as it takes or however much time you have to finish. The best advice I can give someone is to start with the end in mind, just like you did when beginning to develop the idea for your story. When creating your production schedule, set a date for completion and work backwards from there. Whether there are 2 years dedicated to this project or 5 months, the schedule is the same but the time you have to complete each part of the schedule will change.

There are three phases of production: preproduction, production, and postproduction. While the three phases are similar in different mediums, there are some key differences. Preproduction, also known as development, is pretty much the same for any medium and is what this book covers:

- Concept development
- Brainstorming
- Outline
- Treatment 1st draft
- Character development
- Environment research
- Treatment 2nd draft
- Identifying premise
- Identifying theme
- Treatment 3rd draft

- Graphing story structure, character emotions, and visual structure
- Identifying story beats
- Creating the beat board
- Creating a shot list 1st pass
- Script 1st draft
- Revising the shot list 2nd pass
- Exploring art direction
- Creating a style guide
- Storyboarding 1st pass
- Editing: story reel and live action reference reel animatics
- Scratch track
- Revisions to treatment, script, shot list, storyboards, sound, and editing: animatics
- Get feedback
- Revisions to treatment, script, shot list, storyboards, sound, and editing: animatics
- Workbook
- Layout (2D) or rough layout (3D includes rough models, camera, and characters)
- Color script

If you schedule an average 1 or 2 weeks for each bullet point above, knowing that some of those points may overlap and take more or less time, approximately 28 weeks would be allotted for preproduction. A Gantt chart (also called a waterfall schedule) is commonly used as a visual overview of the production schedule.[7]

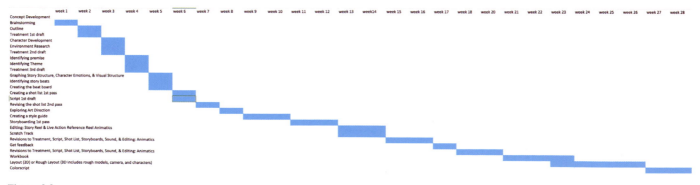

Figure 9.9
A Gantt chart waterfall preproduction schedule created in Excel.

Below is a chart of 2D animation, 3D animation, and stop motion animation for production and postproduction. There are obviously subdivisions of each category, such as in 2D animation, which can be done digitally using a Cintiq and software like Toon Boom and TVPaint or hand drawn on paper, but generally these can be used as guidelines at the starting point for production scheduling.

How long does each of these areas take to complete? The answer depends on the number and capabilities of the artists and the quality level desired. Laika completed *The Box Trolls* in 10 years.[8] In his article on the production process, Dan Sarto writes, "Each animator is responsible for producing four seconds, or 96 frames of animation, per week. They might take one day to block, two days to do a quick rehearsal and then a week and a half to shoot one shot."[9] That's 96 frames of animation per week with a team of 20–25 animators, for a total of 80–100 seconds of animation per week. The film was 87 minutes long, so there were 5,220 seconds or 125,280 frames of animation. Laika completed animation on *Boxtrolls* in 18 months.

Pixar has a schedule to release one new film every year and every two years, a sequel, meaning that they release a total of three films every two years. However, they have different teams working on each film at different times.

| | **2D animation, traditional hand drawn using a Cintiq and software like TVPaint** | **3D animation, computer-generated animation** | **Stop motion animation** |
|---|---|---|---|
| Production | Background and character design | Asset research, design, and building: models, UVs, shades and textures of all props, characters, and environments, lighting tests, effects tests | Maquetting research and design: models of all props, characters, and backgrounds |
| | Background layout | Rigging of all props and characters | Construction of all props, characters, and backgrounds, which includes armatures for any of the puppets |
| | Digital key rough animation | Final layout | Lighting |
| | In between and cleanup pencil keys | Animation | Animation |
| | Digital processing of clean pencil animation | Final layout | |
| | Test | Lighting | |
| | Paint | Effects | |
| Postproduction | Rendering | Rendering | Green screen removal |
| | Compositing | Compositing | Compositing |
| | Editing | Editing | Editing |
| | Final sound | Final sound | Final sound |
| | Output | Output | Output |

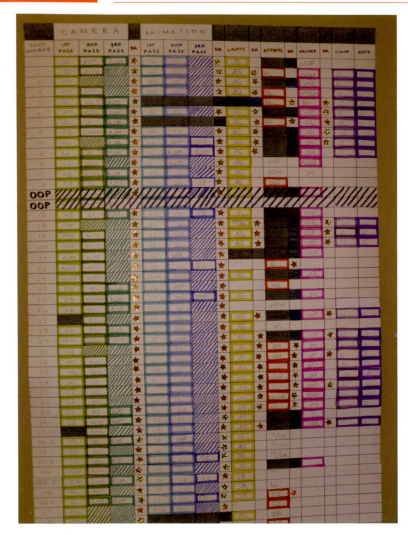

**Figure 9.10**
Sample shot progress, *Yours, Mime, and Ours* (2014). Courtesy of the University of Central Florida Character Animation Specialization.

**Figure 9.11**
A whiteboard can be helpful to keep up with shot progress, *Yours, Mime, and Ours* (2014). Courtesy of the University of Central Florida Character Animation Specialization.

Once a film gets started in production at Pixar, the film is completed in four years.[10] Each animator is responsible for approximately 3–4 seconds of animation per week. However, this goal is not written in stone. Not only does Pixar believe that "story is king," they also ensure that the quality of their projects is "king," spending 4–6 years on story development before the project moves into production.

*Sanjay's Super Team*, a 7-minute short that Pixar screened before *The Good Dinosaur*, was originally pitched in 2012. It took a team of about 27 professionals almost 3 years to create this short.

Every part of the pipeline of animation is an iterative process, no matter if you are working on a project for yourself, a class, a client, or a studio. Rarely, if ever, is anything done perfectly the first time. Because of this, one must build extra time into the schedule to account for adjustments and changes. A good recommendation is to double, if possible, the time initially allotted for each part of the pipeline, especially if you are working with clients. If you finish earlier, no one will complain.

As with any artwork, deciding when it is finished is subjective. Generally, it is when you run out of time or money.

## Animation Techniques

Generally, there are three main categories of animation techniques used for narrative storytelling. Any of these techniques can be combined to create a hybrid animation.

### 2D Animation

2D animation is considered animation that is hand drawn and working in a two-dimensional frame. Any illusion of depth, the third dimension, is done using artistic techniques that fool the eye, such as perspective and scale. Every frame is drawn over a background image. Variations include:

- Traditional animation is created with pencil and paper and transferred onto plastic cells, which are then hand painted. The cells are placed over the background painting, and one frame at a time, they are captured by a camera onto film or digitally into the computer for editing.
- Digital 2D animation is created by drawing directly into the computer using software and a tablet, such as an Intuos or a Cintiq. Digital

2D animation can also be created with two-dimensional puppets that are posed and animated, allowing the software to create the in-betweens.

- Sand animation involves drawing every frame by moving sand around on a sheet of glass that is placed on top of a light table. The animator then takes a photo of the image using a camera mounted on a down shooter and must destroy each drawing when making the next frame.
- Paint-on-glass animation is similar to sand animation in that it is also created frame by frame using a down shooter to capture the frames and destroying each frame when making the next. The animator paints every frame with slow-drying oil paints on glass and then manipulates the paint every frame, adding turpentine and more paint to create the images.

## Computer-Generated 3D animation

Computer-generated 3D animation is created using 3D software which allows the virtual three-dimensional space inside of the computer to be utilized for building virtual worlds and characters. The computer generates the final image renders using complex algorithms.

## Stop Motion Animation

Stop motion animation is created by taking a photo of physical static objects whose shape or positions have changed slightly from frame to frame. Stop motion usually uses puppet-like characters made with an articulating armature covered in latex, fur, paint, and other materials. Backgrounds are also created and painted, much like miniature theatrical sets. The characters are then posed frame by frame and photographed. Variations include:

- Object animation is made by using any pre-existing objects or assembled objects, such as a machine, computer parts, kitchen tools, toys, balls, etc. Objects with articulating pieces are especially interesting to work with.
- Clay animation is when the characters or objects are made with clay. The animator sculpts the clay in between each frame to give the illusion of movement.

**Figure 9.12**
Hybrid animation 2D/3D, *Enchanted Ink* (2015). (Timecode 00:20–00:35) Courtesy of the University of Central Florida Character Animation Specialization.

**Figure 9.13**
Hal Miles animating alien curator Draedel for *Dinosaur Zoo* (1993). All rights owned and used with kind permission by Hal Miles (1988).

- Cut-out animation is made using paper puppet-like characters and paper backgrounds. The cut outs are hinged and moved under the camera lens to be photographed frame by frame.

Deciding on what technique to use goes hand in hand with the stylistic decisions made by the art director, or simply based on the desired outcome of the film. Of course there are other techniques that are not covered here that can also be used, as well as experimentation and exploration into new techniques.

# The Pitch

Traditionally, the pitch was given to a studio in the hope that the idea would be picked up for production. There is still the possibility of finding an agent to represent you and your work. Unfortunately, most studios nowadays are not interested in any ideas coming from the outside. Studios such as PIXAR, Dreamworks, and Disney have an internal pitch process, so being an employee at the studio opens doors and opportunities not found elsewhere.

Today, however, there are many opportunities in the virtual world that simply did not exist several years ago. Perhaps at this point you are hoping to get financial support to create your film. Crowdfunding websites have opened the door for independent filmmakers to raise the funds to produce the work themselves. The internet has provided a venue for distribution. YouTube and Vimeo are platforms available for free and Amazon has a developed CreateSpace, where visual storytellers can reach millions of customers.

It is still great practice to pitch your idea to anyone who may listen. Practice speaking in front of a group of people until the nervousness is not noticeable. Be careful of the amount of "likes" and "ums" you use when speaking and pitching. You never know when you will find yourself in an elevator with a producer. Record your pitch for posting online to raise money for production.

Whether you want to try the traditional route with an agent, or a more current opportunity on a crowdfunding site, a pitch book is essential. This is a book that contains your idea, and can be given out to possible funders. It can be printed and spiral bound or combined into a single PDF document. In addition, a current animatic should also be available online (under password protection).

Assemble the information below into a pitch book. Descriptions of everything can be found in the previous chapter of this book.

- Working title, premise, theme, genre
  - Updated synopsis
- Synopsis
  - What is the premise?
  - What is the theme?
  - What is the genre?
- Who are the characters?
  - Character model sheets
  - Character analysis
- Where is the story set?
  - Reference imagery for environment, characters, time period, color scheme
  - The style guide
  - Concept art
- What is the inciting moment?
  - What are the conflicts?
  - What is the climax?
  - Does the character succeed or fail?
  - What is the ending?
- How does each character arc?
  - Story charts (emotion graph) and/or
  - Character charts (emotion graph)
- Story beats (8–12 illustrated)
  - Color script
- Treatment
  - Script
  - Shot list
- Story reel animatic
- Layout reel animatic

Well that is a wrap for concept and story development. It is time to celebrate. You have a fully formed idea that is ready for production. You even have a plan to make it happen. In the next chapter, you will find a case study of a student film to recap all that we have covered in the book.

**Figure 9.14**
Pitch book,
*Cuddle Fish*
(2015). Courtesy
of the University
of Central Florida
Character
Animation
Specialization.

**Figure 9.15**
The pitch, *Cuddle Fish* (2015). Courtesy of the University of Central Florida Character Animation Specialization.

## Bibliography and Further Reading

American Film Institute. (2014, September). *The Boxtrolls: Behind the world of stop-motion animation*. Retrieved from http://americanfilm.afi.com/issue/2014/9 /cover-story#.WtybfS_Gzap.

Catmull, E. & Wallace, A. (2014). Creativity, Inc.: Overcoming the unseen forces that stand in the way of true inspiration. Random House Publishing Group, Kindle Edition.

Sarto, D. (2014, July 10). *On the set of Laika's "The Boxtrolls."* Retrieved from https://www.awn.com /animationworld/on-set-laikas-boxtrolls.

## Resources

Gantt Chart Template. (2018). Retrieved from https://docs .google.com/spreadsheets/d/1JcX4sHAuBRGsbXIgktxj 5n72sMyFQutQyqJ7R_xQCCU/edit#gid=0.

## Notes

1. Also known as a director's workbook or layout workbook.
2. The environment is put together by the set dresser. The set dresser creates a low-res rough environment as a mock-up while the models are being created. Later, he or she creates a high-res final environment with all of the finished models in place.
3. Also known as a previsualization, pre-viz, or 3D animatic.
4. This is sometimes called "anim prep."
5. A board is 4' × 8' and framed, much like a bulletin board, where story panels can be pinned to hang and display in a room for pitching and dailies.
6. Also known as color keys. A good start is to take the beats from the story and use those for the starting point when adding color.
7. A Gantt chart template is included on the companion website for this book, and a template for Google sheets can be found here: https://docs .google.com/spreadsheets/d/1JcX4sHAuBRGsbXIg ktxj5n72sMyFQutQyqJ7R_xQCCU/edit#gid=0.
8. American Film Institute. (2014, September). *The Boxtrolls: Behind the world of stop-motion animation*. Retrieved from http://americanfilm .afi.com/issue/2014/9/cover-story#.WtybfS_Gzap.
9. Sarto, D. (2014, July 10). *On the set of Laika's "The Boxtrolls."* Retrieved from https://www.awn.com /animationworld/on-set-laikas-boxtrolls.
10. Catmull, E. & Wallace, A. (2014). Creativity, Inc.: Overcoming the unseen forces that stand in the way of true inspiration. Random House Publishing Group, Kindle Edition.

# The Making of an Animated Short Film: *Dreamweaver*

Throughout this book, examples of every part of the pre-production process have been shown to help illustrate the concepts, including examples from the film *Dreamweaver*. This final chapter is a case study of this short film, created by the students in the 2017 cohort of the Character Animation Specialization at the University of Central Florida in Orlando, Florida. While you will most certainly see imperfections in this film, their overall process was a success, as you can see below in its film festival screenings and awards:

### National Awards
- Winner Best Animation Film (Student) May 2017 at the Los Angeles Independent Film Festival Awards (Los Angeles, CA)
- 3rd Place Winner MYHERO International Film Festival (Santa Monica, CA)
- Finalist of the 42nd Annual American Indian Film Festival (San Francisco, CA)

### Regional Awards
- Best Inspirational Film of the 2017 15 Minutes of Fame (Palm Bay, FL)

## Local Awards

- Finalist of the 2017 Central Florida Film Festival
- Nominated for Best Animated Short of the 2017 Orlando Film Festival (Orlando, FL)

## International Screenings

- Official Selection of the 2018 Chennai International Short Film Festival (Chennai, India)
- Official Selection of the 2018 Animation Dingle (Killarney, Kerry, IE)

## National Screenings

- Official Selection of the 2018 Franklin County North Carolina International Film Festival
- Official Selection of the 2018 New Hope Film Festival (New Hope, CT)
- Official Selection of the 2017 California International Shorts Festival (Winter) (Hollywood, CA)
- Official Selection of the 2018 Green Bay Film Festival (Green Bay, WI)
- Official Selection of the 2017 Anchorage International Film Festival (Anchorage, AK)
- Official Selection of the 26th St. Louis International Film Festival (St. Louis, MO)
- Official Selection of the 2017 Red Nation Film Festival & Awards—The Authentic Voice of American Indian & Indigenous Cinema (Los Angeles, CA)
- Official Selection of the 2017 KIDS FIRST! Film Festival
- Official Selection of the 2017 SIGGRAPH Faculty Submitted Student Work Exhibit (Los Angeles, CA)

## Regional Screenings

- Official Selection of the 2017 Melbourne Independent Film Festival (Melbourne, FL)
- Official Selection of the 2017 Urban Film Festival (Miami, FL)

## Local Screenings

- Official Selection of the 2018 Love Your Shorts Film Festival (Sanford, FL)

**Figure 10.1**
Poster adorned with festival laurels by Kelvin Nguyen for *Dreamweaver* (2017).
Courtesy of the University of Central Florida Character Animation Specialization.

# Initial Treatment and Final Treatment for *Dreamweaver*

The first pitch was initially about a sandman character who is trying to teach his son the tricks of the trade. After research, the team changed the idea into one about a dreamcatcher, based on the ancient legend of the Ojibwe people, a native North American tribe. Their reasoning was because there are many interpretations of the sandman in animated films, such as Dreamworks' *Rise of the Guardian*, but very little exists about the legend of the dreamcatcher. This short was completed in May of 2017.

The Sandman tries to manage his young son's eccentric attempts at creating good dreams for the first time as he strives to teach his son how to be a Sandman.

The Sandman's two greatest joys come when the world is asleep and when his son shows an eagerness to learn how to create dreams. Overwhelmed with joy, the Sandman is eager to teach his son all he knows so one day, he will become the next sandman. Much like his father, young Sandman is eager to learn from his great and loving father. However, young Sandman is hasty and impatient. His elaborate attempts at designing wonderful dreams start to spiral out of control. The sheer amount of magic that young Sandman trifles with soon overwhelms his father. The magic dream sand takes on a life of its own, turning dark and transforming into a monstrous nightmare. In an attempt to save his son, the Sandman is captured by the nightmare. Fearing the worst for his father, young Sandman must use all that he has learned to free his father and learn a lesson in patience.

**Figure 10.2**
*Dreamweaver* was originally called *The Sandman*. This is the initial treatment, by Katherine Ryschkewitsch, 2015. The final treatment image has one. Courtesy of the University of Central Florida Character Animation Specialization.

Figure 10.3
*Dreamweaver*
final treatment,
Katherine
Ryschkewitsch,
2015. Courtesy
of the University
of Central Florida
Character
Animation
Specialization.

# The Dream Weaver

Once upon a time, there was a little girl named Namid who was afraid of the dark. Namid was running through the dark forest, away from the fast approaching darkness of the nightmare. As she is running, she sees streams of milky-white light moving through the forest. Namid, comforted by the light, follows them. The light streams (good dreams) lead her into a clearing. She turns around when she hears the hiss of the nightmare, and jumps back when she sees it quickly approaching her. But then the nightmare halts, stopped, seemingly, by an invisible wall. She looks up and sees the glowing white lights above her. Above her is a large hoop-like structure formed from the trees; their branches intertwining with each other to surround the clearing. From the eight largest trees, comes spider webs, the white light from the good dreams making the webs glow and the dew on the webs sparkle. Following the dreams along the webs, Namid's gaze is brought to the center of the clearing where the dreams are trickling down to. The bush is made of feathers, the dreams seemingly attracted to them like magnets. Namid approaches the bush and marvels at its beauty. She hears the sweet sound of bells behind her, and she turns to sees a beautiful long and slender woman standing behind her, dressed in white spider webs, glowing like the webs above. She wears a cloak of spider webs, with animals shaped out of webs, moving through the cloak. Namid, intrigued by the woman, approaches her. Kaashi greets her with a smile and holds out her hand. Just before Namid takes her hand, she hears the hiss of the nightmare once again and stops, looking towards the nightmare, spreading around the clearing. Kaashi, seeing that Namid is scared, tries to distract her. She captures Namid's attention, and shows her an animal in her cloak. She moves her hand in such a way that she seems to pull the animal out of her cloak and form it into a physical animal. Like a puppet, she guides the animal around the clearing, and Namid, finding comfort in the cute animal, chases it. She follows it up a tree and onto the hoop of the dream catcher above the clearing. As she is following the animal around the hoop, she trips on a splintered part of the hoop, creating a crack in the hoop. Namid, her attention still on the animal, continues the chase, not seeing the fatal crack. The nightmare notices the crack though, and starts to constrict the area, trying to break the hoop, and creates more cracks in the wood hoop. The unrelenting force of the nightmare's strength on the hoop, causes it to weaken, and with this pulling, the webs are being strained and pulled, the steady stream of good dreams becoming disrupted. In front of her, Namid sees the disruption and notices the strain being put on the webbing, and just as the webbing snaps, Namid catches it. But it is too late, the webbing being the final obstacle, the nightmare is now able to break through the barrier into the clearing. It goes straight towards Namid, intent on harming her; Namid is helpless and vulnerable. Kaashi makes it just in time to be ensnared in the nightmare's darkness. Namid watches in horror as Kaashi is repeatedly bombarded by the nightmare's attacks, weakening with every blow unable to fight back due to the tight grip of the nightmare. Namid looks around, desperate to find anything she can use to help her. She sees the disconnected/broken webbing and the dreams are trying to force their way through the ends but can't. She grabs one strand and stretches out to the other failing a couple times until she finally grasps it.  She fuses the ends together, but the dreams are halted and not moving. She looks around and sees the good dreams have stopped, looking for guidance to the center once again. She looks to the center of the clearing to see the feather bush and remembers how the good dreams were attracted to the feather bush like a magnet. She scrambles down the tree, making towards the feather bush at the center of the clearing. Namid, quickly picks some feathers from the bush and when she turns around, she sees the nightmare inflict a final blow to Kaashi, and Kaashi falls, unconscious to the to the floor. Determined to save her, she scrambles back up the tree and starts to place feathers into the cracks of the hoop. The good dreams dart to the feathers in the hoop, and, like magic, the good dreams begin to repair the hoop. The final crack is repaired and the magic of the dreamcatcher is restored, good dreams starting to flow to the center again, light returning to the area. The nightmare, being in the middle of the clearing is then sucked up and trapped in the dreamcatcher, unable to break free. Namid rushes to Kaashi, and helps her up. Kaashi thanks Namid just as the first rays of morning come over the horizon. Namid and Kaashi watch as the nightmare is vanquished with the morning light, and Namid squeezes her eyes shut from the brightness. When she opens them again, she is in her wigwam, the morning sun streaming in through a crack in the door. She hops out of bed, inspired by the flashes of her dream running through her head. She fashions a wood hoop and weaves a string through the hoop then holds her creation out in front of her: a dreamcatcher.

# Character Development

The hero character, Namid, is a young girl who has trouble with nightmares.

Figure 10.4
Concept drawing of Namid, Kelly Herbut, 2016. Courtesy of the University of Central Florida Character Animation Specialization.

**Figure 10.5**
Character T-pose model sheet for Namid, Kelly Herbut, 2016. Courtesy of the University of Central Florida Character Animation Specialization.

**Figure 10.6**
Character maquette for Namid, Sean Ademoye, 2016, photo credit Anthony Balinas. Courtesy of the University of Central Florida Character Animation Specialization.

**Figure 10.7**
Final render of Namid in *Dreamweaver* (2017). Courtesy of the University of Central Florida Character Animation Specialization.

The Dream Weaver
*Character Analysis*

**Figure 10.8**
Character analysis description for Namid, 2015. Courtesy of the University of Central Florida Character Animation Specialization.

**Namid**

Namid is a little girl who belongs to the Chippewa tribe located in Michigan. She knows no other lifestyle but the one passed down by her Chippewa native roots. Her tribe, which spreads through the region of the Great Lakes, is very dear to her. It's all she has ever known, yet she loves her culture, her lifestyle, her environment. Living in tents, gathering fruit and nuts, and beautiful handcrafting are but some of the many details of her life.

Namid, being an eight year old child, is very small in stature and petite in size. Being 4 feet tall and 57 pounds in weight, Namid is the smallest in her tribe. Her big round eyes, full spread of teeth, and radiant smile, along with her twin braids, makes for her beautiful yet fragile appearance.

She owns a doll named Keezheekoni, which means "Fire Briskly Burning." She named her such because of her warmer colored clothing. She is seen very rarely without it as it has become one of her closest friends since her mother passed away two years ago. Given to her on her 6th birthday by her mother, who wove it together for her. It is the reminder of her mother's sweetness and love.

One of Namid's favorite things to do before going to bed each night is to watch the small fire inside of her tent radiate and move. She loves fire, not only because of its warmth, but also because of its light, its shining radiance among the cold blackness of night. That's one thing she is frightfully scared of: the night. She despises the lack of ability to see, not to mention what the night brings: fears unseen, creatures that crawl into her head before bed, creating horrible nightmares each night for her to experience. Sitting by the fire seems to be the only thing that gives her comfort when the sun goes down. Her mother, who died when she was six, used to bundle her up close to her chest and tell her stories late each night. But she isn't so fortunate now.

Her father, who is the chief of the Chippewa tribe, remarried, and though she is a great wife, she doesn't have much connection to a daughter not of her own blood. It didn't help Namid's situation when the news that her father's new wife couldn't bear children emerged as a surprise for her stepmother. This just made things between Namid and her grow tense and cold. She couldn't have children, yet she felt taunted by another woman's child, an accomplishment for the Chippewa tribe's leader, a failure on her own end to meet the standard.

Namid's father, a strong leader who somehow holds the whole of the Chippewa tribe together, be it as large as it is, loved Namid's mother. When she died, it tore his heart to bits. His relationship with Namid became more distant, as looking at her just reminded him of his once Love now gone. He sought refuge, elsewhere and found it in the heart of his recently acquired wife. Being the chief of the tribe, he looked forward to the idea of having a son, and when the news was given about his new wife not being able to bear, he became angry and resentful, not only towards his wife, but towards Namid. He had wanted a son, and gotten a daughter instead, one that he couldn't share the joys of leading a tribe with. One he could give nothing of worth to as an inheritance.

Namid, battling with the internal struggle of a strange family dynamic and being the chief's only child, slowly became secluded from her environment. Fear growing more rampant at night, her dreams getting more and more frightening. She was left alone to fend for herself against her fears, without her mother and her warmth.

The mentor character, Kaashi (Asibikaashi), is the spider woman and part of the Ojibwa legend of the dreamcatcher.

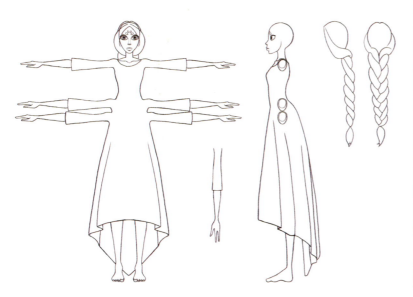

**Figure 10.9**
Character T-pose model sheet for Kaashi, Kelly Herbut, 2016. Courtesy of the University of Central Florida Character Animation Specialization.

**Figure 10.10**
Concept drawing of Kaashi, Kelly Herbut, 2016. Courtesy of the University of Central Florida Character Animation Specialization.

**Figure 10.11**
Kaashi maquette, Katherine Ryschkewitsch, 2016, photo credit Anthony Balinas. Courtesy of the University of Central Florida Character Animation Specialization.

**Figure 10.12**
Final render of Kaashi in *Dreamweaver* (2017). Courtesy of the University of Central Florida Character Animation Specialization.

**Figure 10.13**
Character analysis description for Kaashi, 2015. Courtesy of the University of Central Florida Character Animation Specialization.

## Asibikaashi

Asibikaashi, a spiritual guardian who is motherly in nature, cares for the Chippewa tribes by creating Dream Catchers to catch the bad dreams of the children who live there. Graced with the most beautiful, long, black flowing hair, as well as an unusually tall stature (6'6") and thin frame (172lbs). Her oval shaped face and wider eyes give her a mature nature about herself.

Gifted in storytelling and caring for children, she has a big heart. In nurturing the children of the Chippewa tribes, she meets them inside their good dreams, since that is her main way of communication. Living at the center of her dream world – a Dream Catcher, she creates Dream Catchers using magical threads and teaches other women how to make them for their children.

Being spider-like, she has four arms and four eyes. She has some very magical, yet spider-like powers, which she uses mainly for weaving her Dream Catchers.

# Environment Research

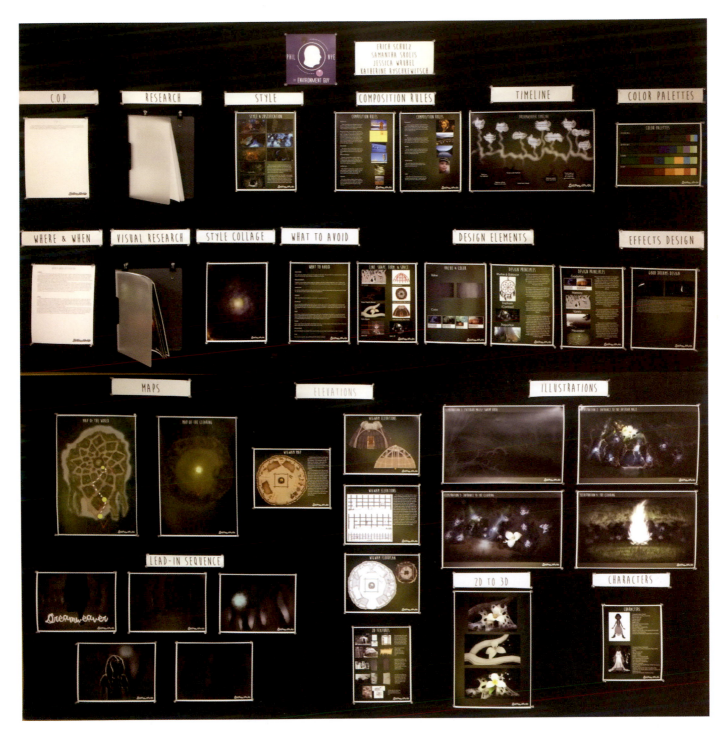

**Figure 10.14**
Environment pitch, Erich Schulz, Samantha Sokolis, Jessica Wrubel, Katherine Ryschkewitsch, 2016. Courtesy of the University of Central Florida Character Animation Specialization.

# Identifying Premise and Theme

Figure 10.15
*Dreamweaver*,
initial premise
and theme,
Katherine
Ryschkewitsch,
2015. Courtesy
of the University
of Central Florida
Character
Animation
Specialization.

## The Dream Weaver

### Premise

Conquering your fears leads to the inner freedom of peace acquired through truth. This knowledge and experience can be shared so the multiplication of freedom can happen in the lives of others.

### Log Line

A little Chippewa girl overcomes her deep psychological fear of spiders after she meets a supernatural being that teaches her how to use a Dream Catcher to vanquish nightmares.

### Theme

Conquering your fears can open up new pathways of creativity, knowledge, craft, and character that could have not been seen, discovered, or attained otherwise.

# Identifying Story Beats

Figure 10.16
*Dreamweaver*,
story beats,
2015. Courtesy
of the University
of Central Florida
Character
Animation
Specialization.

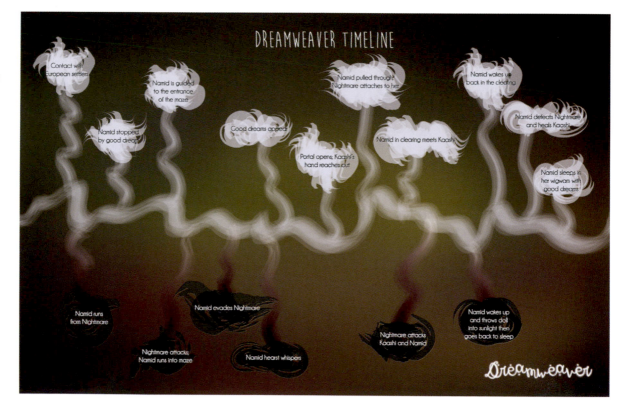

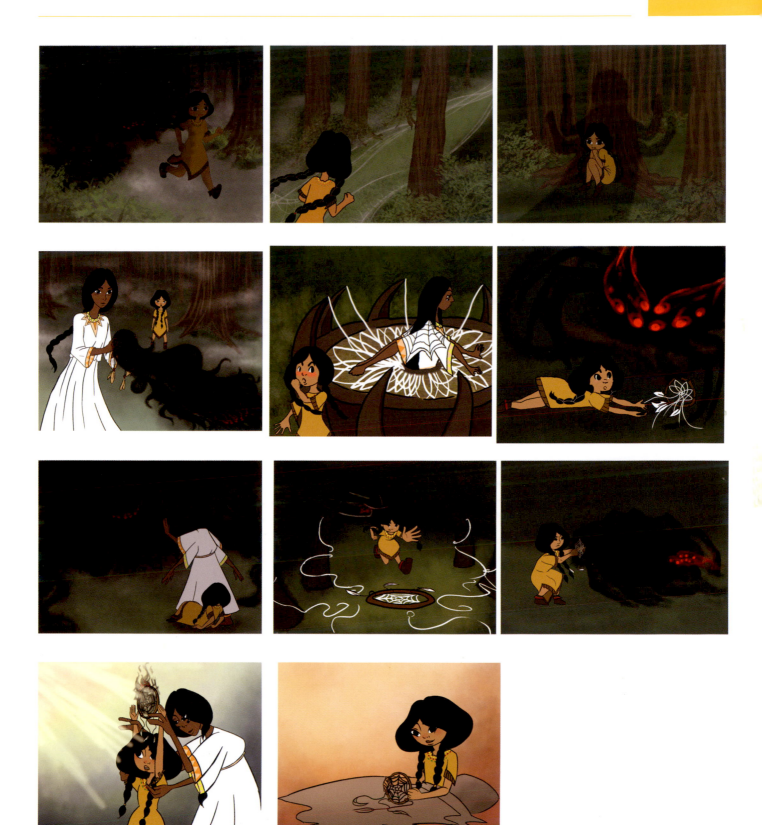

**Figure 10.17**
*Dreamweaver*, illustrated story beats, 2015. Courtesy of the University of Central Florida Character Animation Specialization.

# Script Final Draft

<u>BLACK SCREEN</u>

*FADE IN.*

*Words on the screen (or 2d animation) telling the legend of the Dreamcatcher.*

*On screen white text:*

"It is believed that with the night, come good and bad dreams. A spider woman named Asibikaashi, created the dreamcatcher to protect the Ojibwa people from the bad dreams that came with the night. Bad dreams get lost trying to navigate through the maze-like webbing but the good dreams easily find their way to the center, down the feathers, and into to the head of the sleeping individual bringing her good dreams. When the morning sun rises, the trapped bad dreams are vanquished by the sunlight. One never fears bad dreams while sleeping under a dreamcatcher."

*Namid runs across the screen, as a blur, in front of the text (or animation) and the text (or animation) fly away as if made of smoke.*

<u>EXT. DREAMCATCHER - DARK FOREST</u>

*Namid is running through the forest from the nightmare. Namid running, looking behind her frequently, a scared look on her face.*

*Nightmare following behind her at a distance.*

*Namid sees a bright white light to her right, and when she looks over, she sees a swarm of ethereal good dreams keeping pace with her.*

*The good dreams speed up slightly, move in front of Namid, and cause her to halt.*

*They spiral around her body, nuzzling her lightly, up her torso and down her arm, leading her field of vision in the direction they wanted her to go.*

*She turns a corner, and watches as the good dreams approach a maze like forest.*

*As she is following the good dreams towards the entrance of the thick forest, she hears a hiss behind her, and turns to see the nightmare has found her once again.*

*It lurches up above her, ready to strike.*

*She turns back to see where the good dreams are going, but she doesn't see them.*

*She's been left behind.*

*She darts into the thick forest maze, away from the nightmare as it launches itself at her, narrowly missing her.*

## EXT. DREAMCATCHER - MAZE

*Namid runs through the maze-like forest turning corner after corner, hitting dead end after dead end, getting more and more lost as she desperately looks for the good dreams.*

*She slows when she sees the nightmare is no longer following her.*

*She peaks around a corner, looking for the nightmare, then decides it's safe and walks around it.*

*She halts when she realizes she's hit a dead end and looks around scared and confused wondering if she was ever going to find her way through the maze.*

*She begins hearing a bombardment of harsh whispers in hear ears and clamps her hands over her ears to attempt to silence the sounds.*

*The sweet sound of bells is heard behind her (silencing the harsh whispers completely).*

*Namid turns to see an animal, glowing white and semi-transparent like the good dreams, watching her.*

*Namid smiles and takes a few steps towards the animal, comforted by the soft white light in the dark, and kneels down holding out her hand for it to come toward her.*

*It walks towards her, sniffs her hand, and pushes its head into her hand.*

*Namid smiles and scratches the animal behind the ear.*

*It looks content then runs around her and runs a small distance away.*

*It stops and looks back at Namid and motions for her to follow it.*

*Namid follows the animal through the maze. The animal leads Namid to a wall.*

*The nightmares are getting lost in the maze of webbing as they start to close in on Namid.*

*Loud hissing can be heard, and crescendos in volume.*

*Web-like hands emerge from the walls of the labyrinth.*

*The animal approaches the hands in the wall. The animal jumps through the wall.*

*The animal sticks its head back through the wall waiting for Namid as the hands gesture her to follow.*

*The whispering/hissing is louder as the nightmares come up right behind her.*

*The nightmare closes in on Namid and she looks over her shoulder in horror.*

*Namid takes hold of the hand.*

*Right before she is pulled through the web wall, the nightmare attaches itself to her and is pulled through with her.*

CUT TO BLACK

<u>EXT. DREAMCATCHER - CLEARING</u>

Center of the Maze.

*Namid falls into the clearing from the wall.*

*Namid stands up and sees the animal.*

*She watches it as it runs to the center.*

*Namid looks up to see Asibikaashi petting the animal and playing with it.*

*Asibikaashi pets the animal then lifts her arm.*

*The animal jumps into the cloak of Asibikaashi.*

*Namid recognizes Asibikaashi from the stories from her tribe.*

*She runs to Asibikaashi and embraces her. The nightmare emerges from behind Namid. It coils to strike her.*

*Right before it hits Namid, Asibikaashi pushes Namid and takes the blow.*

*Asibikaashi's skin begins to turn black at her hands.*

*The infection starts to slowly move its way up her hands to her wrists.*

*She looks at Namid, fear in her eyes. Namid is paralyzed with fear.*

*The nightmare makes a loud hissing howl bringing Asibikaashi's attention back to it.*

*Namid looks to Asibikaashi, scared.*

*Asibikaashi gives her a comforting look and turns to confront the nightmare.*

*She looks down at her arms.*

*The infection is spreading to her elbows.*

*Her shoulders slump slightly, feeling the effects of the infection on her body.*

*Asibikaashi continues to fight the nightmare.*

*She goes into one of the tunnel entrances on the ground to dodge the nightmare's first attack.*

*The nightmare sees.*

*Namid has a scared expression on her face.*

*Asibikaashi comes out of the tunnel behind the nightmare swinging a webbed tethered ball.*

*She throws it at the nightmare hitting it just as it took a step towards Namid.*

*The nightmare falls to the ground.*

*Namid looks relieved and smiles at Asibikaashi thankful.*

*Asibikaashi looks at her arms once again. The infection now spreads to her shoulders.*

*Asibikaashi looks more tired and weak as the infection spreads.*

*She looks to see Namid smiling and cheering her on.*

*The nightmare (still on the ground) turns its attention back to Asibikaashi.*

*It gets up and moves to strike her.*

*Asibikaashi jumps to the right, narrowly dodging the attack.*

*She stands, then slumps down onto one knee, weak and out of breath.*

*The infection now at the base of her neck.*

*Namid's smile fades as she watches Asibikaashi drop to one knee.*

*The nightmare towers over Asibikaashi.*

*Asibikaashi looks up at it, scared and breathing hard, and struggles to stand back up.*

*Asibikaashi slumps back to the ground, unable to gather the strength to stand and continue to fight.*

*The infection has spread over her entire body and is up to her cheeks moving to her eyes.*

*Asibikaashi looks at the infection on her body. Asibikaashi looks to Namid and reaches for her. Namid reaches for her.*

*Asibikaashi's right eye is in close up and the infection can be seen closing in on her eye.*

CUT FROM CLOSE UP OF ASIBIKAASHI'S EYE TO NAMID'S EYE

INT. NAMID'S WIGWAM

Sunrise.

Close on Namid's right eye.

NAMID

   NO!

            (screaming with arm stretched out in front of her as if
            reaching or Asibikaashi.)

At this point Namid realizes it was just a dream and the sun shines into her eyes through the window.

*She lays back down in bed and tries to go back to sleep.*

*Close on Namid.*

*She shuts her eyes tight.*

CUT FROM NAMID EYES IN WIGWAM TO NAMID IN DREAM

<u>EXT. DREAMCATCHER - CLEARING</u>

Sunrise.

This time when Namid returns to her dream it is sunrise and the sun is fighting to come through the trees.

>    *The infection has almost spread entirely across Asibikaashi's face.*

>    *The nightmare gets ready to deal the final blow to Asibikaashi.*

>    *Namid looks around frantically for anything she can use to help Asibikaashi.*

>    *She sees the sun is fighting to come through the trees.*

>    *Namid climbs a tree where she sees the sunlight is fighting to come through.*

>    *She parts the leaves allowing the light to destroy the nightmare.*

The sun rises higher.

>    *NIGHTMARES IN THE MAZE BEING VANQUISHED AS THE SUNLIGHT SPREADS OVER THE LANDSCAPE.*

>    *Namid climbs down from the tree.*

>    *She approaches Asibikaashi, the spread of the infection slowing considerably.*

>    *She helps Asibikaashi up.*

>    *Namid leads a weakened Asibikaashi back to the center of the clearing where the good dreams are flowing.*

>    *The good dreams revive her as they flow over her body.*

>    *Asibikaashi hugs Namid one last time as the sun rises and the dreams disappear.*

Crane above Asibikaashi/Namid.

We see the landscape as a dreamcatcher.

>                                                 FADE TO WIGWAM DREAMCATCHER

<u>INT. NAMID'S WIGWAM</u>

Morning.

We see the dreamcatcher in Namid's Wigwam

>    *Namid wakes up, stretches.*

>    *She looks at her dreamcatcher (above her head or hanging from her window) and smiles.*

>                                                                    CUT

<u>CREDITS</u>

# The Shot List

Dreamcatcher Shot List

| Shot # | Length | Shot Description | Camera Movement | Camera Angle | Camera Position | Action Description | Character Position | Characters in shot |
|---|---|---|---|---|---|---|---|---|
| | | Legend explanation | Static | | | | | |
| | | Title | Static | | | | | |
| 1 | | Namid runs into the shot | Static | low angle | Close up -> Full/VL | Namid is running | Enters foreground (left) and runs into background(right) | Namid |
| 2 | | Namid Running through the forest from the Nightmare and sees good dream when it floats in front of her | Hand held | Eye level | POV | Namid running and stops, Good dream interupts path | | Namid & Good Dreams |
| 3 | | Good dream wizzes around Namid revealing her and then exits | Static | Low angle - slight | Full, Front | Good dream circles around namid | Namid (center), good dream exits upper right | Namid & Good Dreams |
| 4 | | Namid spots good dreams flowing through the forest | | Low angle/eye level w/tilt | , 3/4 View | Multiple good dreams fly through the canopy | | Namid & Good Dreams |
| | | Namid Reaction Shot | | | | | | |
| 5 | | Namid follows the path that the good dreams are taking | | Eye level | Medium Long, Front of Namid | Namid changes direction | | Namid |
| 6 | | Namid stops at the edge of a line of trees and looks up in amazement | Crane | Eye level -> High angle | Medium close up, Front of Namid | Namid looks upward | | Namid |
| 8 | | Establishing shot of dreamcatcher maze | | High angle | Extreme long, behind Namid/ 3/4 View | | | Namid & Good dreams |
| 9 | | Namid turns around to the sound of the nightmare | | Eye level | Long, Behind Namid | Namid hears the nightmare behind her | | Namid |
| 10 | | Nightmare moves towards Namid | Dolly In | Point of View | Long shot, Behind Namid | | | Namid |
| 11 | | Nightmare fills right frame coming closer | | Low angle | Long, Behind Namid | Nightmare aproaches Namid | | Namid & Nightmare |
| 12 | | Namid follows the good dreams to the dreamcatcher labyrinth | | Low angle | Long, Behind Namid | Namid running and dreams flying | | Namid & Good Dreams |
| 13 | | Namid is frantically looking for the good dreams to follow but is unable to find any | | High angle | Medium Long | Namid Running and dreams flying | | Namid |
| 14 | | Namid peeks around the corner and sees a dead end | | eye level | Long, Front Namid | Namid peaks | | Shadow & Namid |
| 14A | | Sees Dead end. | | eye level | Over the shoulder | Sees dead end, walks away | | |
| 15 | | Namid peeks around a second corner, another dead end | | eye level | Long, Front Namid | Namid peaks | | Shadow & Namid |
| 16 | | Namid keeps running through the labyrinth lost and confused and we see her come up on an 3-way-intersection | Slow Tracking | Birds-Eye | Very Long, Front of Namid | Namid Running and dreams flying | | Namid |
| 17 | | Namid comes to an intersection and is hesitant, not knowing what to do. | | Eye Level | Long, Front of Namid | Namid looking left and right | | Namid |
| 18 | | She cringes in fear as the whispers and noises of the shadow get louder and louder, we zoom in and then do a quick zoom out at the sound of a bell. | Zoom in(or dolly) | Eye Level | Long into Close up | Namid covering her ears and quivering as she squats downward | | Namid |
| 19 | | The sound of bells ques the camera to pan over and show a little forest creature made of webs | Pan Left | High Angle or Eye level | Long, Front Namid | | Namid right of frame, animal left of frame | Namid, Web Animal |
| 20 | | The creature tilts its head sideways in a cute gesture. the creature looks right and notices something coming out of the wall Namid also turns her head to see | Static | High Angle, OTS | Long, Behind Namid | | Namid right of frame, animal left of frame, Animal Turns Head, Namid turns head | Namid, Web Animal |
| 21 | | a weblike hand reaches out of the wall in front of Namid and the animal | Static | Eye Level | Long, Side view of Namid and animal | Hand comes from the wall | Namid left third, Animal right third, hand center | Namid, Web Animal |
| 22 | | The animal and Namid are looking at the hands and the animal takes off towards the hands | Static | Low angle | Long, 3/4 view | The Animal exits right of frame | Namid right third, Animal left third | Namid, Web Animal |
| 23 | | The animal climbs up the arm and into the wall | Static | Eye Level? | | | | Web Animal |
| 24 | | The animal pokes its head out of the web wall as if it's wondering why Namid isn't following. | Static | Eye Level | Long, Front of animal | Animal pokes its head out of the webbing | | Web Animal |
| 25 | | Namid smiling seeing the animal waiting for her, (seperate shot:) a screeching sound forces Namid's attention as she turns her head to look behind her | Static | Eye Level | MCU, Front of Namid | Namid smiling, turns her head to look back | | Namid |
| 25b | | Namid turns around to see Nightmare | | | | | | |

Figure 10.18
*Dreamweaver*,
shot list, Erich
Schulz, 2015.
Courtesy of the
University of
Central Florida
Character
Animation
Specialization.

Figure 10.19
*Dreamweaver*,
shot list, Erich
Schulz, 2015.
Courtesy of the
University of
Central Florida
Character
Animation
Specialization.

Dreamcatcher Shot List

| Shot # | Length | Shot Description | Camera Movement | Camera Angle | Camera Position | Action Description | Character Position | Characters in shot |
|---|---|---|---|---|---|---|---|---|
| 26 | | Screeching, the nightmare breaks around the corner and heads straight for Namid | Static | Dutch Angle | Long | Shadow is coming towads her | | Shadow |
| 27 | | Namid looks horified as she catches sight of the nightmare headed toward her | Dolly, Zoom | Eye Level | Long -> CU | Namid Scared | | Namid & Nightmare |
| 28 | | She gathers her courage she takes the web-hand of Asibikaashi | | Eye Level | Medium | Namid takes the web hand | Namid Left third | Namid |
| 29 | | A nightmare attaches itself to Namid as she is being pulled through web wall. | Static | Eye Level | Medium Close Up (on namid's back) | Nightmare grips onto namid's back | Namid back fills most of the frame | Namid & Nightmare |
| 30 | | Namid is pulled into the webbing | | Low Angle - slight | Long, 3/4 view | Namid pulled into Web | Behind Namid | Namid |
| 31 | | Namid falls into the clearing from the wall | Static | Low Angle | Long, 3/4 view | Namid falls out of the wall onto the ground | Namid Right third, Animal Left third | Namid |
| 32 | | Namid stands up and sees the animal waiting for her | Static | High Angle | Long, OTS | Namid stands up | Namid Left third, Animal right third | Namid & Animal |
| 33 | | She watches it run into the center of the clearing and camera reveals Asibikaashi | Tumble | High Angle | Very Long | Animal running | Namid left third, Asibikaashi right third | Namid, Animal, & Asibikaashi |
| 34 | | The animal runs and jumps into the cloak of Asibkaashi | Static | High Angle | OTS | Asibikaashi is Kneeling down accepting the animal into her cloak | Asibikaashi left third, animal right third | |
| 35 | | Asibikaashi stands up and looks over towards namid | Pedestal | Eye level | Medium, side | Asibikaashi stands up, turns head | left third, Namid right third background | |
| 36 | | Namid recognizes Asibikaashi from the stories | Static | High Angle - Slight | Medium Close Up | Namid smiles | | 2: Namid & Asibikaashi |
| 37 | | Namid runs to embrace her, Nightmare emerges from behind her | Truck | High Angle- slight | Long | Nightmare grows on her back | | 2: Namid & Asibikaashi |
| 38 | | The Nightmare coils to strike her | Static | High Angle | OTS of Asibikaashi | Nightmare coils back | | 3: Shadow & Asibikaashi & Namid |
| 39 | | Asibikaashi notices the shadow and is scared | Static | Low Angle - Slight | Close Up | Asibikaashi worried | Fills frame | Asibikaashi |
| 40 | | Right before it hits Namid, Asibikaashi pushes Namid and takes the blow | Static | High Angle | Long | | | 3: Shadow & Asibikaashi & Namid |
| 41 | | | Circular | Eye Level | Long | Asibikaashi is struggling spinning in circles trying to force the nightmare off | | Asibikaashi & Nightmare |
| 42 | | Asibikaashi's skin darkens(nightmare spreads) as it is infected by the nightmare | Static | Eye Level | Close up (of arm?) | | | Asibikaashi & Nightmare |
| 43 | | Asibikaashi continues to fight nightmare with her spider abilities, she dodges a strike from the nightmare by going into a tunnel and pops out of another tunnel swinging a Weblike ball(like a teather ball) and hitting it forcing it to the ground | Static | Low Angle | Long | Asi jumps into burrow and jumps out swinging a weblike ball | | Asibikaashi & Nightmare |
| 44 | | Asibikaashi weakens as the infection spreads as she fights | Static | High Angle | Full | Asibikaashi is getting tired, panting, and the shadow spreads | Asi right frame, shadow left frame | Asibikaashi & Shadow |
| 45 | | strike at asibikaashi | Static | Eye Level | Full | Shadow spreads on asibikaashi | | 2: Asibikaashi & Shadow |
| 47 | | Namid wakes up | Static | Eye Level | Extreme Close up | | | 1: Namid |
| 48 | | Namid wakes up and screams "NO!" | Static | Eye level | Medium Close up | | | 1: Namid |
| 49 | | Namid realizes it was just a dream, feeling herself as if to check that she is in reality | Static | Eye Level | Medium | Namid feels herself double checking she's ok | | 1: Namid |
| 50 | | Sun starts to shine through her wigwam | Static | Low Angle - Slight | OTS | | Namid Right Third | 1: Namid |
| 51 | | Namid tries to force herself back into her dream | Static | Eye Level | Medium | Namid curls onto her side | | 1: Namid |

Dreamcatcher Shot List

| Shot # | Length | Shot Description | Camera Movement | Camera Angle | Camera Position | Action Description | Character Position | Characters in shot |
|---|---|---|---|---|---|---|---|---|
| 52 | | Namid shuts her eyes tight and goes back to sleep | Static | Eye Level | Extreme Close up | Namid Closes her eyes tight | | 1: Namid |
| 53 | | Namid returns to the dream in the center of the clearing | Static | Eye Level | Medium | | | 1: Namid |
| 46 | | Nightmare spreads to Asibikaashi's face | Static | High Angle, Dutch | Close up | Asibikaashi spreads | | 2: Asibikaashi & Shadow |
| 54 | | Namid sees Asibikaashi still struggling with the nightmare. The sun cannot shine through the trees onto Asibikaashi and it is fighting to get through the trees. | Static -> Slight Zoom | Low angle - Slight | OTS | | | 3: Asibikaashi & Namid & Shadow |
| 55 | | Namid swiftly climbs a tree | Static | High angle | Long | | Namid runs into frame from top | 1: Namid |
| 56 | | Namid parts the leaves allowing the light to shine through | Static | Low angle - Slight | Long | | | 1: Namid |
| 57 | | Light shines onto Asibikaashi and the Nightmare | Static | Low angle | Long | | Namid upper left, asibikashi and shadow lower right | 2: Asibikaashi & Shadow |
| 58 | | Nightmare is destroyed | | | | | | 2: Asibikaashi & Shadow |
| | | Nightmare is cleansed from asibikaashi | | | | | | |
| 59 | | The sun rises higher | Static | Eye Level | Extreme Long | | | 0 |
| 60 | | We see other nightmares within the maze | Static | Birds Eye | Extreme Long | | | Many |
| 61 | | Those nightmares are also vanquished within the light of the sun | Static | Eye Level / High Angle? | Medium | | | Many |
| 62 | | Namid approaches Asibikaashi and helps her up | Static | Low Angle | Medium-Long, OTS | Namid aproaches asibikaashi from right of screen | Asibikaashi left of frame, Namid right | 2: Asibikaashi & Namid |
| 63 | | Namid leads Asibikaashi to the center post of the clearing | | | | | | 2: Asibikaashi & Namid |
| 64 | | The good dreams flow through Asibikaashi again, revitalizing her | Static | Low angle | Long | | | 2: Asibikaashi & Good Dreams |
| 65 | | Asibikaashi hugs Namid one last time as sun is rising | Dolly out - slight | Eye Level | Very Long Shot | Namid and Asibikaashi hug | Asibikaashi and Namid are hugging center frame | 2: Asibikaashi & Namid |
| 66 | | See the landscape as a Dream Catcher | Crane? | Birds Eye | Establishing shot / estreme long | | | 0 |
| 67 | | Transition into a Dream Catcher hanging in Namid's Wigwam | Static-> Pedestal | Eye Level | Medium | | | 0 |
| 68 | | Namid wakes up, stretches, and looks at Dreamcatcher and smiles | Static | Eye Level??? | Full | Namid Looks at dreamcatcher and smiles | | 1: Namid |
| 69 | | The End - Credits Roll | | | | | | 0 |

Figure 10.20 *Dreamweaver*, shot list, Erich Schulz, 2015. Courtesy of the University of Central Florida Character Animation Specialization.

Figure 10.21
*Dreamweaver*,
character
emotion graph,
2015. Courtesy
of the University
of Central Florida
Character
Animation
Specialization.

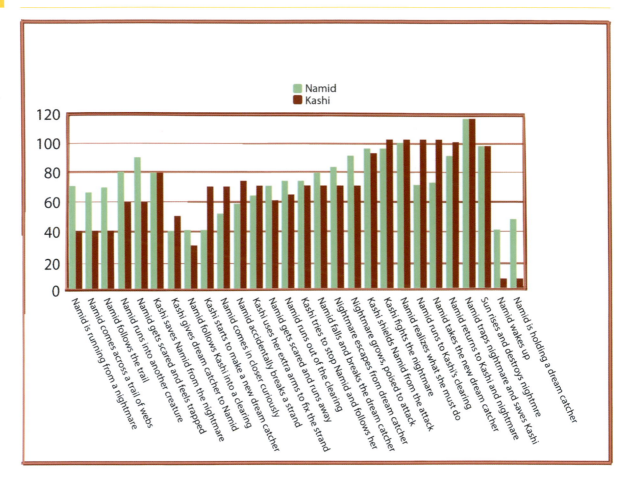

Figure 10.22
*Dreamweaver*,
emotional graph,
2015. Courtesy
of the University
of Central Florida
Character
Animation
Specialization.

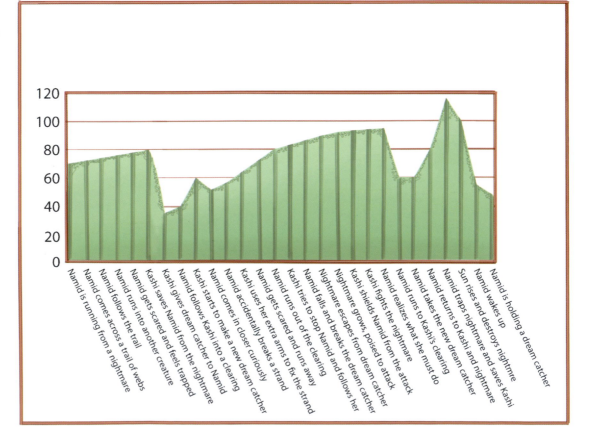

# Exploring Art Direction

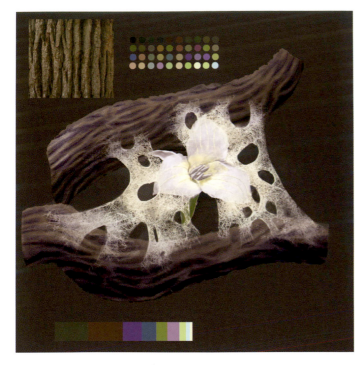

**Figure 10.23**
Concept art: the trillium and the webs, *Dreamweaver*, 2015. Courtesy of the University of Central Florida Character Animation Specialization.

**Figure 10.24**
Final render: the trillium and the webs, *Dreamweaver*, 2017. Courtesy of the University of Central Florida Character Animation Specialization.

**Figure 10.25**
Concept art: top-down view of the forest, *Dreamweaver*, 2015. Courtesy of the University of Central Florida Character Animation Specialization.

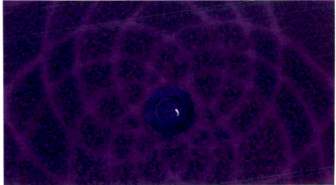

**Figure 10.26**
Final render: top-down view of the forest, *Dreamweaver*, 2017. Courtesy of the University of Central Florida Character Animation Specialization.

**Figure 10.27**
Final render: top-down view of the forest as it transitions, *Dreamweaver*, 2017. Courtesy of the University of Central Florida Character Animation Specialization.

**Figure 10.28**
Final render: view of the dreamcatcher after the forest transition, *Dreamweaver*, 2017. Courtesy of the University of Central Florida Character Animation Specialization.

**Figure 10.29**
Concept art: trees in the maze, *Dreamweaver*, 2015. Courtesy of the University of Central Florida Character Animation Specialization.

**Figure 10.30**
Final render: trees in the maze, *Dreamweaver*, 2017. Courtesy of the University of Central Florida Character Animation Specialization.

**Figure 10.31**
Concept art: the clearing, *Dreamweaver*, 2015. Courtesy of the University of Central Florida Character Animation Specialization.

**Figure 10.32**
Final render: the clearing, *Dreamweaver*, 2017. Courtesy of the University of Central Florida Character Animation Specialization.

# SETTING

There are three areas, or "zones", to the setting:

    Zone 1 — The Outer Forest
    Zone 2 — The Dreamcatcher Maze
    Zone 3 — The Clearing

As Namid moves through the environment, her surroundings become more and more surreal, twisted, and extreme. This is to represent her falling deeper and deeper into her nightmare the longer she sleeps.

The clearing (Zone 3), has a stark contrast to the forest environment. While the forest areas will be dimly lit and have sharp, jagged curves, the clearing will be brightly lit and have soft, shallow curves. The clearing and Asibikaashi are supposed to be the light in Namid's darkness.

Figure 10.33
Style guide
page from
*Dreamweaver*,
2016. Courtesy
of the University
of Central Florida
Character
Animation
Specialization.

# SETTING – continued
## LINE AND SHAPE

### Forest Areas (Zones 1 and 2)

The lines and shapes of the forest areas are sharp and jagged overall. In Zone 1, the lines and shapes, predominantly in the trees, have a stylized yet naturalistic look to them. Similar to how they would be seen in real life. But, when Namid enters Zone 2, the maze, the trees start to become more jagged and sharp, taking on nightmarish qualities. The further Namid goes into the maze, the more nightmarish the trees, flowers, and even the path she walks on, become.

In the maze (Zone 2), there are 3 "sub-zones". These sub-zones are designated to three different shapes of trees.

● – Zone 2-1

● – Zone 2-2

● – Zone 2-3

Figure 10.34
Style guide
page from
*Dreamweaver*,
2016. Courtesy
of the University
of Central Florida
Character
Animation
Specialization.

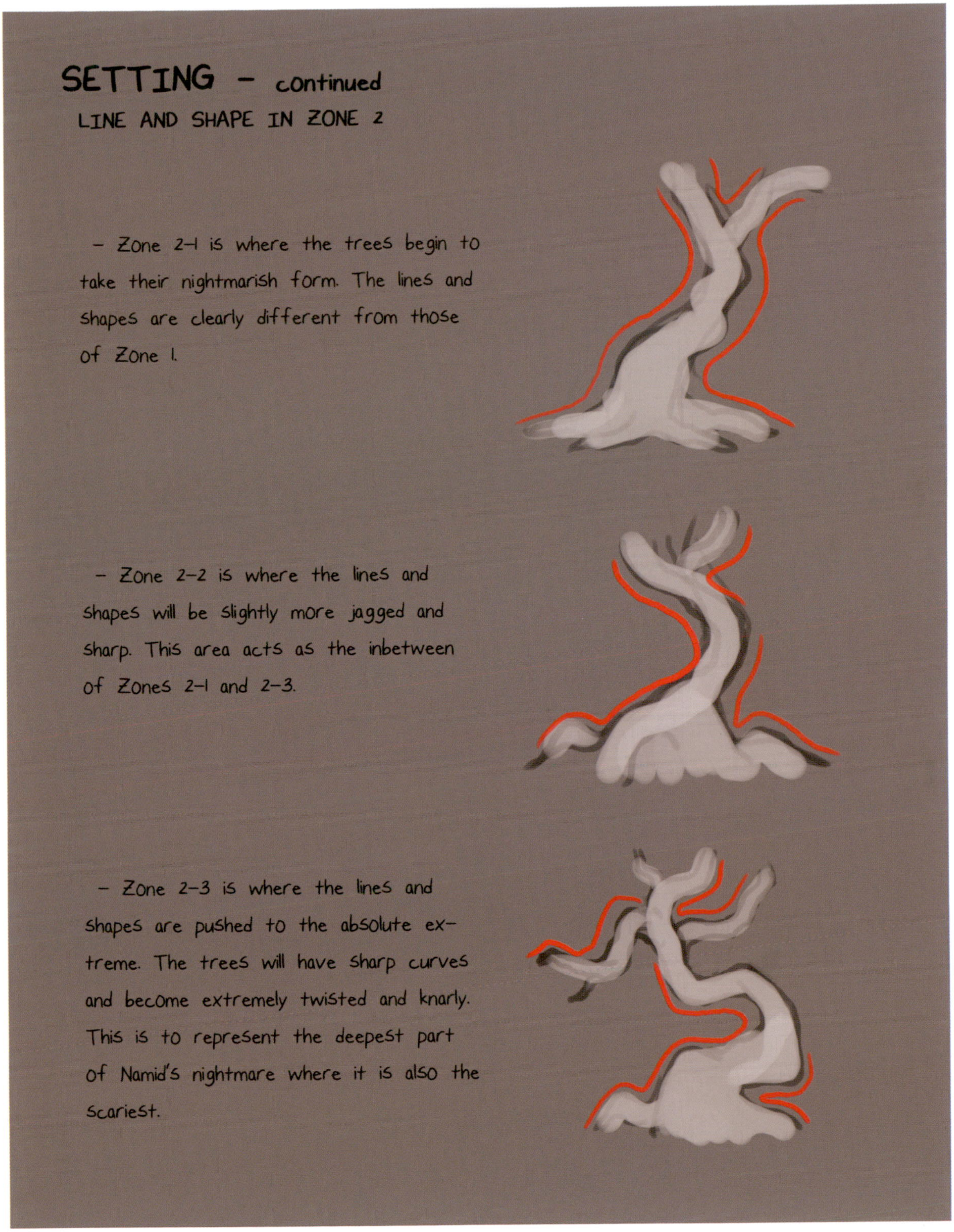

# SETTING – continued
## LINE AND SHAPE IN ZONE 2

– Zone 2–1 is where the trees begin to take their nightmarish form. The lines and shapes are clearly different from those of Zone 1.

– Zone 2–2 is where the lines and shapes will be slightly more jagged and sharp. This area acts as the inbetween of Zones 2–1 and 2–3.

– Zone 2–3 is where the lines and shapes are pushed to the absolute ex-treme. The trees will have sharp curves and become extremely twisted and knarly. This is to represent the deepest part of Namid's nightmare where it is also the scariest.

Figure 10.35 Style guide page from *Dreamweaver*, 2016. Courtesy of the University of Central Florida Character Animation Specialization.

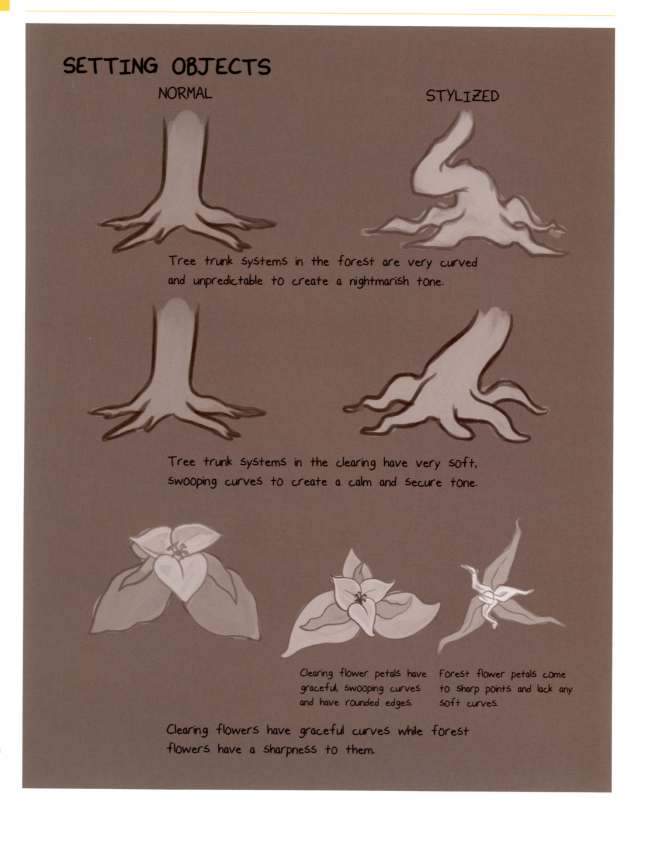

**SETTING OBJECTS**

NORMAL                    STYLIZED

Tree trunk systems in the forest are very curved
and unpredictable to create a nightmarish tone.

Tree trunk systems in the clearing have very soft,
swooping curves to create a calm and secure tone.

Clearing flower petals have        Forest flower petals come
graceful, swooping curves          to sharp points and lack any
and have rounded edges.            soft curves.

Clearing flowers have graceful curves while forest
flowers have a sharpness to them.

Figure 10.36
Style guide
page from
*Dreamweaver*,
2016. Courtesy
of the University
of Central Florida
Character
Animation
Specialization.

## LIGHTING — continued

Certain plants in certain Scene will emit a glow that will not have any effect on the lighting in the Scene.

The Trilium Flower will be the exception to this rule, it will emit a glow. A lighting aspect should be added to effect the area surrounding the glow.

Asibikaashi will also emit a colored glow which may effect her surrounding areas.

Figure 10.37 Style guide page from *Dreamweaver*, 2016. Courtesy of the University of Central Florida Character Animation Specialization.

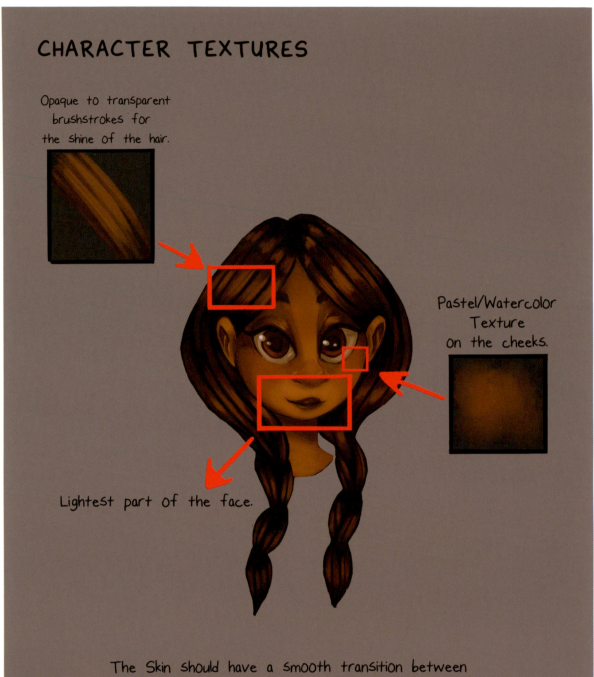

CHARACTER TEXTURES

Opaque to transparent brushstrokes for the shine of the hair.

Pastel/Watercolor Texture on the cheeks.

Lightest part of the face.

The Skin should have a smooth transition between light and dark shades of the the color palette.

Figure 10.38 Style guide page from *Dreamweaver*, 2016. Courtesy of the University of Central Florida Character Animation Specialization.

# ENVIRONMENT TEXTURES

## Tree Texture

## Flower Texture

Textures for the environment and props should have a more digital painting asthetic, semi-visible brushstrokes, and a smooth transition between the lightest and darkest areas.

**Figure 10.39** Style guide page from *Dreamweaver*, 2016. Courtesy of the University of Central Florida Character Animation Specialization.

# Storyboard

**Figure 10.40**
First pass storyboards, *Dreamweaver*, 2016. Courtesy of the University of Central Florida Character Animation Specialization.

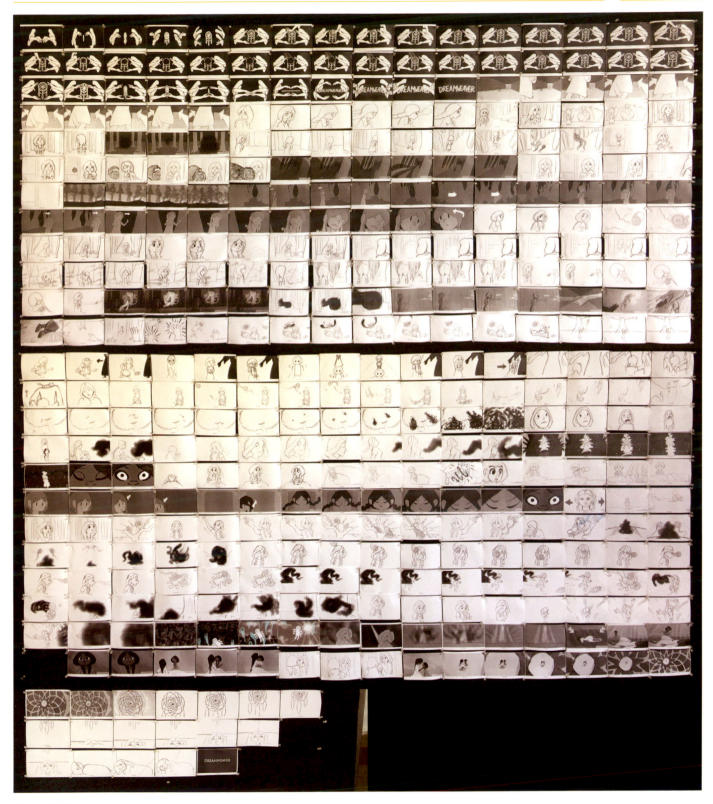

**Figure 10.41**
Final storyboards, *Dreamweaver*, 2016. Courtesy of the University of Central Florida Character Animation Specialization.

# Workbook

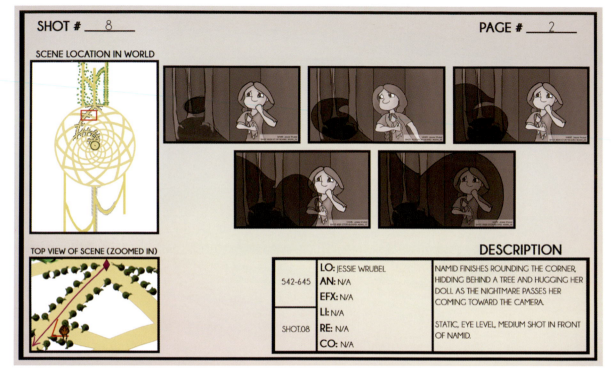

**Figure 10.42**
Sample workbook page for shot #8, *Dreamweaver*, 2016. Courtesy of the University of Central Florida Character Animation Specialization.

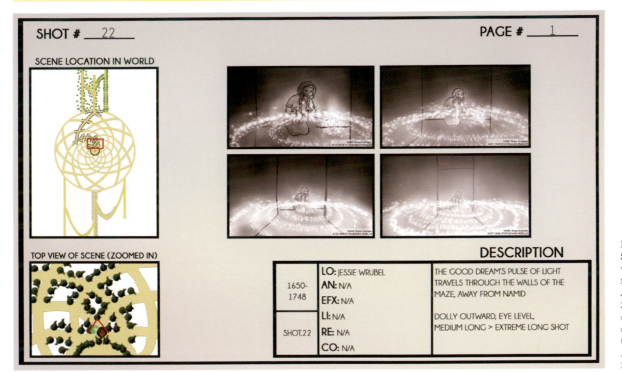

Figure 10.43 Sample workbook page for shot #22, *Dreamweaver*, 2016. Courtesy of the University of Central Florida Character Animation Specialization.

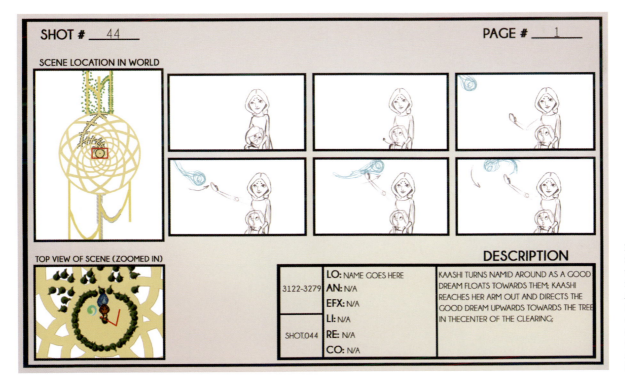

Figure 10.44 Sample workbook page for shot #44, *Dreamweaver*, 2016. Courtesy of the University of Central Florida Character Animation Specialization.

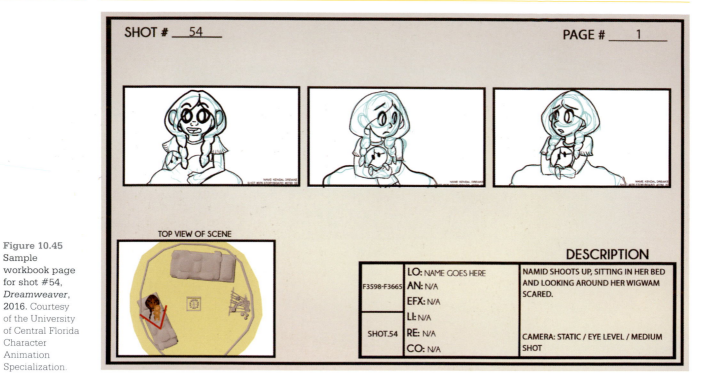

Figure 10.45
Sample
workbook page
for shot #54,
*Dreamweaver*,
2016. Courtesy
of the University
of Central Florida
Character
Animation
Specialization.

Figure 10.46
Sample
workbook page
for shot #88,
*Dreamweaver*,
2016. Courtesy
of the University
of Central Florida
Character
Animation
Specialization.

# Beat Board Color Script

**Figure 10.47**
Color script, *Dreamweaver*, 2017. Courtesy of the University of Central Florida Character Animation Specialization.

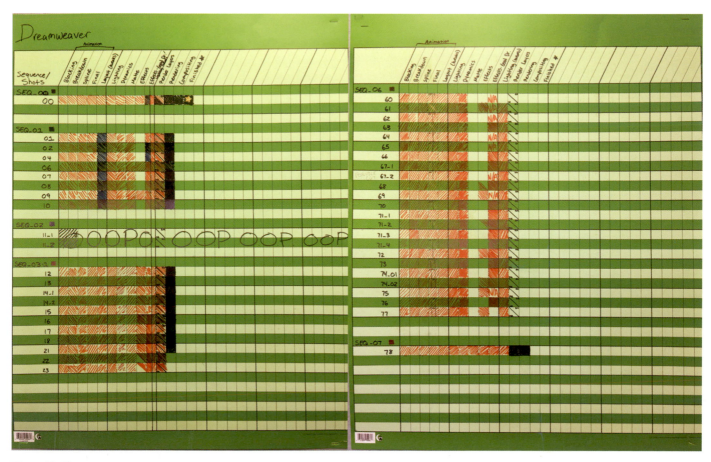

**Figure 10.48**
Shot production chart, *Dreamweaver*, 2016. Courtesy of the University of Central Florida Character Animation Specialization.

**Figure 10.50**
The pitch, *Dreamweaver* crew, 2015. Courtesy of the University of Central Florida Character Animation Specialization.

**Figure 10.51**
The pitch, *Dreamweaver* crew, 2015. Courtesy of the University of Central Florida Character Animation Specialization.

**Figure 10.52**
*Dreamweaver* crew, 2017. Courtesy of the University of Central Florida Character Animation Specialization.

**Figure 10.53**
Premiere night, *Dreamweaver* crew, 2017. Courtesy of the University of Central Florida Character Animation Specialization.

# Further Watching

## 2D

Draw with Me
  http://www.youtube.com/watch?v=DRkgH7Uu-hA
Fur by Gobelins
  http://www.youtube.com/watch?v=mUvk38Lu3l8
Shadow Puppets
  http://www.youtube.com/watch?v=WnltLPf8KcM
  &feature=youtu.be
The Reward by the Animation Workshop
  http://youtu.be/kkAYze6ae18
Death Buy Lemonade
  https://vimeo.com/15071571
The Reward
  https://vimeo.com/58179094
What's Opera Doc by Chuck Jones
  https://www.dailymotion.com/video/x2vbbh3
The Cat Came Back
  https://www.youtube.com/watch?v=Ck0jwS0CvKk
Le Building by Gobelins
  https://vimeo.com/14536540
Lavatory – Lovestory
  https://www.youtube.com/watch?v=ajLrFugsdMw
Prey, by Tom Kyzivat
  https://www.youtube.com/watch?v=ZaG9QXLX4dc
The Dover Boys
  https://www.youtube.com/watch?v=dpOPyjmB8SI
Peace on Earth by Harmon and Ising
  https://www.dailymotion.com/video/xuiou
Alexander Petrov's The Old man and the Sea
  https://www.youtube.com/watch?v=W5ih1IRIRxI

## Stop Motion

Lili
  https://www.youtube.com/watch?v=QzTQ4njlkgQ
The Maker
  https://www.youtube.com/watch?v=YDXOioU_OKM
Vincent
  https://www.youtube.com/watch?v=fxQcBKUPm8o
Fresh Guacamole
  https://www.youtube.com/watch?v=dNJdJIwCF_Y
Creature Comforts
  https://www.youtube.com/watch?v=PCOWE0EiCyo
  &t=1s
The Sea Is Blue
  https://www.youtube.com/watch?v=Dp2ZskwkhkA

Zero
  https://vimeo.com/24975340
Hedgehog in the Fog
  https://www.youtube.com/watch?v=oW0jvJC2rvM
Ode to G.I. Joe
  https://www.youtube.com/watch?v=pYI3MPVYyco
Neighbors by Norman McLaren
  https://www.youtube.com/watch?v=e_aSowDUUaY
The Potato Hunter
  https://www.youtube.com/watch?v=TbPAjyj1spQ
Balance
  https://www.youtube.com/watch?v=YQ_LjjBgOM4

## 3D

Kiwi!
  https://www.youtube.com/watch?v=sdUUx5FdySs
Get Out
  https://www.youtube.com/watch?v=-Ai2buD0i38
Mytho Logique
  https://vimeo.com/24258323
The Rose of Turaida
  https://www.youtube.com/watch?v=ZfFnb_12950
Oktapodi
  https://www.youtube.com/watch?v=badHUNl2HXU
Alma
  https://www.youtube.com/watch?v=U2k75zbchDA
ShapeShifter
  https://www.youtube.com/watch?v=3SDoHUKBlHw
One Rat
  https://www.youtube.com/watch?v=EZf8SDTMmls
The Legend of the Scarecrow
  https://www.youtube.com/watch?v=2CYUTILU0hk
Das Rad
  https://www.youtube.com/watch?v=HOPwXNFU7oU
Wanted Melody
  https://vimeo.com/25969993
French Roast
  https://www.youtube.com/watch?v=foQq32ZQyKc
The Lady and the Reaper
  https://vimeo.com/73118583
Ryan
  https://www.youtube.com/watch?v=nbkBjZKBLHQ
Doll Face
  http://www.youtube.com/watch?v=zl6hNj1uOkY

# Bibliography and Further Reading

## Chapter 1

Aristotle. (330 BC). Poetics. (Butcher, S.H., Trans.). Retrieved from http://classics.mit.edu/Aristotle/poetics.html.

Bellantoni, P. (2013). *If it's purple, someone's gonna die: The power of color in visual storytelling.* Burlington, MA: Focal Press, an imprint of the Taylor & Francis Group.

Block, B. A. (2008). The visual story: Creating the visual structure of film, TV and digital media. Amsterdam: Focal Press/Elsevier.

Budrys, A. (1994). Writing to the point: A complete guide to selling fiction. Evanston, IL: Unifont.

Campbell, J. (1972). *The hero with a thousand faces.* Princeton, NJ: Princeton University Press.

Cousineau, P., & Campbell, J. (1990). The hero's journey: The world of Joseph Campbell: Joseph Campbell on his life and work. San Francisco: Harper & Row.

Cron, L. (2012). Wired for story: The writer's guide to using brain science to hook readers from the very first sentence. New York: Ten Speed Press.

Field, S. (2005). *Screenplay: The foundations of screenwriting.* New York: Delta Trade Paperbacks.

Freytag, G. (1894). *Freytag's Technique of the drama: An exposition of dramatic composition and art.* An authorized translation from the 6th German ed. by Elias J. MacEwan. Retrieved from https://archive.org/details/freytagstechniqu00freyuoft.

Horace. (19 BC). *Ars Poetica.* (Kline, A.S., Trans.). Retrieved from https://www.poetryintranslation.com/PITBR/Latin/HoraceArsPoetica.php.

Poe, E.A. "Review of Twice-Told Tales" [Text-02], *Graham's Magazine*, May 1842, pp. 298–300. Retrieved from https://www.eapoe.org/works/criticsm/gm542hn1.htm.

Poe, E.A. "The Philosophy of Composition" [Text-02], *Graham's Magazine*, vol. XXVIII, no. 4, April 1846, 28:163–167. Retrieved from https://www.eapoe.org/works/essays/philcomp.htm.

Sohn, P. (Director). (2009). *Partly Cloudy* [Video file].

Stanton, A. (2012). The clues to a great story. Retrieved from https://www.ted.com/talks/andrew_stanton_the_clues_to_a_great_story?language= en.

Vogler, C., & Montez, M. (2007). *The writer's journey: Mythic structure for writers.* Studio City: Michael Wiese.

## Chapter 2
### Bibliography and Further Reading

Desowitz, B. (2004). *A Pixar vet gets directing shot with "Boundin'" short.* Retrieved from https://www.awn.com/vfxworld/pixar-vet-gets-directing-shot-boundin-short.

Forster, E. M. (1956). *Aspects of a novel.* New York: Mariner Books.

Vogler, C., & Montez, M. (2007). *The writer's journey: mythic structure for writers.* Studio City: Michael Wiese.

Wood, M. (2004). *The pocket muse: ideas & inspirations for writing.* Cincinnati, OH: Writers Digest.

Woodward, R. (2010). *Ryan Woodward: Art & animation.* Retrieved from http://ryanwoodwardart.com/my-works/thought-of-you/.

Young, J. W. (2012). *A technique for producing ideas: The simple five-step formula anyone can use to be more creative in business and in life!* Charleston, SC: CreateSpace Independent Publishing Platform.

### Resources

Brainstorm and mindmap online. (2018). Retrieved from https://bubbl.us/.

Heffner, J. (2018). *Story starters.* Retrieved from http://thestorystarter.com/.

Internet Archive: Wayback Machine. (2018). Retrieved from http://archive.org/web/.

XMind: The Most Popular Mind Mapping Software on the Planet. (2018). Retrieved from http://www.xmind.net/.

## Chapter 3
### Bibliography and Further Reading

Glei, J. K., Belsky, S., & Ariely, D. (2013). *Manage your day-to-day: Build your routine, find your focus, and sharpen your creative mind.* Las Vegas, NV: Amazon Publishing.

Keller, G., & Papasan, J. (2014). *The one thing: The surprisingly simple truth behind extraordinary results.* London: John Murray.

### Resources

Audible: Listening is the new reading. (2018). Retrieved from https://www.audible.com/.

Cirillo Consulting GmbH. (2018). The Pomodoro Technique®. Retrieved from https://francescocirillo.com/pages/pomodoro-technique.

Jung, E. (2018). Moosti. Retrieved from http://www.moosti.com/.

Nap26: Rest and rejuvenate in 26 minutes. (2018). Retrieved from http://www.nap26.com/.

TomatoTimer. (2018). Retrieved from https://tomato-timer.com/.

Trello. (2018). Retrieved from https://trello.com/.

## Chapter 4
### Bibliography and Further Reading

Catmull, E. & Wallace, A. (2014). *Creativity, Inc.: Overcoming the unseen forces that stand in the way of true inspiration.* Random House Publishing Group, Kindle Edition.

Coats, E. (2012, June 13). *22 #storybasics I've picked up in my time at Pixar.* Retrieved from http://storyshots.tumblr.com/post/25032057278/22-storybasics-ive-picked-up-in-my-time-at-pixar.

Stanton, A. (2012). *The clues to a great story.* Retrieved from https://www.ted.com/talks/andrew_stanton_the_clues_to_a_great_story?language=en.

Williams, P. & Denney, J. (2010). *How to be like Walt: Capturing the Disney magic every day of your life.* Health Communications, Kindle Edition.

### Resources

Korolov, M. (2016, July 13). *VR travel: 10 ways to see the world from your living room.* Retrieved from https://www.gearbrain.com/vr-travel-samsung-gear-vr-google-cardboard-1737536488.html.

## Chapter 5
### Bibliography and Further Reading

Alex, T. (2012). *Your CUT TO: is showing: The most complete spec screenplay formatting guide ever written.* Seattle, WA: CreateSpace Independent Publishing Platform.

Beauchamp, R. (2005). *Designing sound for animation.* Burlington, MA: Elsevier/Focal Press.

Brown, M. R. (2018). Screenplay format guide. Retrieved from http://www.storysense.com/format.htm.

Brown, M. R. (2018). Script format: dialogue. Retrieved from http://www.storysense.com/format/dialogue.htm.

Internet Movie Script Database (IMSDb). (2018). *WALL-E.* Retrieved from http://www.imsdb.com/scripts/Wall-E.html.

Riley, C. (2009). *The Hollywood standard: The complete and authoritative guide to script format and style* (2nd ed.). Studio City, CA: M. Wiese Productions.

### Resources

Amazon Storywriter. (2018). Retrieved from https://storywriter.amazon.com/.

BPC-Screenplay for Windows. (2018). Retrieved from http://www.bpc-screenplay.com/screenplay/installing.html.

Celtx. (2018). Retrieved from https://www.celtx.com/index.html.

DubScript Screenplay Writer | A screenplay app for Android that works with Fountain, Final Draft (FDX), and PDF. (2018). Retrieved from https://www.dubscript.com/.

Final Draft Screenwriting Software. (2018). Retrieved from https://www.finaldraft.com/.

Open Source. (2018). Trelby: A free, multiplatform, feature-rich screenwriting program. Retrieved from http://www.trelby.org/.

Page 2 Stage. (2018). Retrieved from http://www.page2stage.com/.

Plotbot: Write screenplays online with friends. (2018). Retrieved from http://www.plotbot.com/.

Screenwriting: Downloads related to <fade in>. (2018). Retrieved from http://www.rolandstroud.com/Screenwriting-1.html.

Storytouch: Scriptwriting at your fingertips. (2018). Retrieved from http://storytouch.com/.

## Chapter 6

Ebert, R. (2008, August 30). *How to read a movie.* Retrieved from https://www.rogerebert.com/rogers-journal/how-to-read-a-movie.

Mascelli, J.V. (1965). *The five Cs of cinematography: Motion picture filming techniques simplified.* Hollywood: Cine/Grafic Publications.

NoamKroll.com. (2018). *28mm lenses: The secret ingredient for achieving a film look.* Retrieved from http://noamkroll.com/28mm-lenses-the-secret-ingredient-for-achieving-a-film-look/.

Sijll, J.V. (2010). *Cinematic storytelling: The 100 most powerful film conventions every filmmaker must know.* Studio City, CA: Michael Wiese Productions.

## Chapter 7

Bellantoni, P. (2013). *If it's purple, someone's gonna die: The power of color in visual storytelling.* Burlington, MA: Focal Press, an imprint of the Taylor & Francis Group.

Block, B. A. (2008). *The visual story: Creating the visual structure of film, TV and digital media.* Amsterdam: Focal Press/Elsevier.

Block, B. A. (2017). *3D storytelling: How stereoscopic 3D works and how to use it.* Burlington, MA: CRC Press.

Bordwell, D. (2011, February 14). *Watching you watch There Will Be Blood.* Retrieved from http://www.davidbordwell.net/blog/2011/02/14/watching-you-watch-there-will-be-blood/.

Cabrera, C. (2013). *Reel success: Creating demo reels and animation portfolios.* Burlington: Taylor & Francis.

Catmull, E. E., & Wallace, A. (2014). *Creativity, Inc.: Overcoming the unseen forces that stand in the way of true inspiration.* New York: Random House.

Pennington, A. (2017). *Exploring 3D: The new grammar of stereoscopic filmmaking.* Burlington, MA: CRC Press.

## Chapter 8

Beauchamp, R. (2005). *Designing sound for animation.* Burlington, MA: Elsevier/Focal Press.

Bordwell, D. (2006). *The way Hollywood tells it: Story and style in modern movies.* Berkeley: University of California Press.

Murch, W. (2001). *In the blink of an eye: A perspective on film editing* (2nd ed.). West Hollywood, CA: Silman-James Press.

Walice, E. (2015, May 12). Behind the camera of Disney Pixar's *Inside Out*: Riley cam vs. mind cam. Retrieved from https://momontheside.com/behind-the-camera-of-disney-pixars-inside-out

## Chapter 9
### Bibliography and Further Reading

American Film Institute. (2014, September). *The Boxtrolls: Behind the world of stop-motion animation.* Retrieved from http://americanfilm.afi.com/issue/2014/9/cover-story#.WtybfS_Gzap.

Catmull, E. & Wallace, A. (2014). *Creativity, Inc.: Overcoming the unseen forces that stand in the way of true inspiration.* Random House Publishing Group, Kindle Edition.

Sarto, D. (2014, July 10). *On the set of Laika's "The Boxtrolls."* Retrieved from https://www.awn.com/animationworld/on-set-laikas-boxtrolls.

### Resources

Gantt Chart Template. (2018). Retrieved from https://docs.google.com/spreadsheets/d/1JcX4sHAuBRGsbXIgktxj5n72sMyFQutQyqJ7R_xQCCU/edit#gid=0.

# Index